CHARLES DICKENS

CHARLES DICKENS

Brian Murray

A Frederick Ungar Book
CONTINUUM • NEW YORK

1994

The Continuum Publishing Company
370 Lexington Avenue
New York, NY 10017

Copyright © 1994 by Brian Murray

Printed in the United States of America

Library of Congress Cataloging-in-Publication Data

Murray, Brian.
  Charles Dickens / Brian Murray.
    p.   cm.—(Literature and life. British writers)
  Includes bibliographical references and index.
  ISBN 0-8264-0565-7 (hardcover : acid-free)
  1. Dickens, Charles, 1812-1870. 2. Novelists, English—19th
century—Biography. I. Title. II. Series.
PR4581.M8 1994
823'.8—dc20
[B]   94-12092
                                                      CIP

For

Corinna Del Greco Lobner

Acknowledgements

I am grateful for the assistance of the Faculty Development Committee at Loyola College, and Dr. David Roswell, Dean of Arts and Sciences. I would like to thank David Marcus Green, Jody Bottum, and Evander Lomke.

"The man who reviews his own life, as I do mine, in going on here, from page to page, had need to have been a good man indeed, if he would be spared the sharp consciousness of many talents neglected, many opportunities wasted, many erratic and perverted feelings constantly at war within his breast, and defeating him. I do not hold one natural gift, I dare say, that I have not abused. My meaning simply is, that whatever I have tried to do in life, I have tried with all my heart to do well; that whatever I have devoted myself to, I have been thoroughly in earnest. I have never believed it possible that any natural or improved ability can claim immunity from the steady, plain, hard-working qualities, and hope to gain its end. There is no such thing as such fulfillment on this earth. Some happy talent, and some fortunate opportunity, may form the two sides of the ladder on which some men mount, but the rounds of that ladder must be made of stuff to stand wear and tear; and there is no substitute for thorough-going, ardent, and sincere earnestness. Never to put one hand to anything, on which I could throw my whole self; and never to affect depreciation of my work, whatever it was; I find, now, to have been my golden rules."

D. Copperfield

"The English are, so far as I know, the hardest worked people on whom the sun shines. Be content if in their wretched intervals of leisure they read for amusement and do no worse."

C. Dickens

Contents

Preface

This study aims to provide students and general readers with an introduction to Dickens's life and writings. Those seeking further discussion of issues related to Charles Dickens and his extensive, much-analyzed body of work are urged to consult the various biographical and critical studies mentioned in the text, and in the select bibliography at the back of the book.

—BJM

Chronology

1812   Charles Dickens is born February 7, in Portsmouth, England.

1814   Moves with family to London.

1817   Moves to Chatham, Kent, scene of happy childhood memories.

1822   Returns with family to Camden Town, London.

1824   Works for up to a year at Warren's Blacking Warehouse. Dickens's father, John, is arrested and spends several months in the Marshalsea, a debtor's jail.

1825   Enters the Wellington House Academy, London.

1827   Leaves school and works successively for two legal firms in Gray's Inn. Learns shorthand.

1828   Becomes freelance court reporter at Doctors' Commons.

1830   Becomes romantically involved with Maria Beadnell.

1831   Obtains a reader's ticket at the British Museum.

1832   Considers acting career. Works as a parliamentary reporter for the *Mirror of Parliament* and, later, the *True Sun*.

1833   Ends relationship with Maria Beadnell. Publishes his first sketch, "A Dinner at Poplar Walk," in the *Monthly Magazine*.

1834	Works as parliamentary and political reporter for the *Morning Chronicle*. Publishes additional "sketches." Meets Catherine Hogarth.
1835	Becomes engaged to Catherine Hogarth.
1836	*Sketches of Boz* appears. Begins publishing *Pickwick Papers*. Marries Catherine Hogarth. Becomes editor of *Bentley's Miscellany*.
1837	Death of Mary Hogarth. First child, Charles Culliford Boz Dickens, born. *Oliver Twist* begins serialization in *Bentley's Miscellany*.
1838	*Nicholas Nickleby* starts to appear. Mary Dickens born.
1839	Quits editorship of *Bentley's Miscellany*. Kate Dickens born.
1840	*The Old Curiosity Shop* starts publication in *Master Humphrey's Clock*. Pursues interest in mesmerism.
1841	*Barnaby Rudge* published. Walter Landor Dickens born.
1842	Visits America and Canada. *American Notes* published. Catherine's sister Georgina joins Dickens household.
1843	*Martin Chuzzlewit* is serialized. *A Christmas Carol*.
1844	Lives with his family in Italy. *The Chimes* published. Francis Jeffrey Dickens born. Leaves Chapman and Hall, his first publishers, for Bradbury and Evans.
1845	*The Cricket on the Hearth* published. Alfred Tennyson Dickens born. Tours Italy with Catherine.
1846	Serves briefly as editor of the *Daily News*. *Pictures from Italy* published. Moves with family (for seven months) to Lausanne, Switzerland, and then to France.
1847	Dickens and his family complete three-month stay in Paris. Sydney Smith Dickens born.

1848	*The Haunted Man*, the last of his "Christmas stories."
1849	Begins serialization of *David Copperfield*. Henry Fielding Dickens born.
1850	First number of *Household Words* appears. Dora Dickens born.
1851	Father, John Dickens dies. Charles buys Tavistock House. Dora Dickens dies. *A Child's History of England* starts to appear in *Household Words*.
1852	Serialization of *Bleak House* begins. Edward Plorn Dickens born.
1853	Gives first public reading, in Birmingham. Tours Italy with Wilkie Collins, a close friend of his later years.
1854	Serialization of *Hard Times* begins in *Household Words*.
1855	*Little Dorrit* begins serialization.
1856	Collaborates with Collins on a play, *The Frozen Deep*. Buys Gad's Hill, final English residence.
1857	Produces *The Frozen Deep*. Meets Ellen Ternan.
1858	Separates from Catherine. Begins series of public readings.
1859	*All the Year Round* begins to appear, featuring installments of *A Tale of Two Cities*.
1860	Begins serialization of *Great Expectations*.
1863	Walter Landor Dickens dies in India.
1864	*Our Mutual Friend* starts to appear.
1865	Sustains injuries in railway accident in Staplehurst, Kent.

1867   Undertakes American reading tour.

1868   Goes on "Farewell" reading tour.

1870   *The Mystery of Edwin Drood* begins serialization. Dickens dies of cerebral hemorrhage.

1

Performance Artist

Next to Shakespeare, Charles Dickens remains the best known of all English authors. Such works as *Oliver Twist* and *A Tale of Two Cities* still turn up regularly on high school syllabuses as well as in shopping mall bookstores and airport kiosks, stacked in racks alongside the latest products by Stephen King and Judith Krantz. Adaptations of Dickens's works remain common; David Edgar's version of *Nicholas Nickleby*, first staged by the Royal Shakespeare Company, was one of the most ambitious theatrical productions of the 1980s; Christine Edzard's similarly expansive—and brilliant—film version of *Little Dorrit* (1987) brought new attention to one of Dickens's best, but least-known, novels. For better or worse, film versions of *A Christmas Carol* continue to multiply; in *Scrooged* (1988) the eternal Ebenezer is transformed into a troublesome television executive; in *The Muppets' Christmas Carol* (1992), the roles of the Cratchits fall to Miss Piggy and Kermit the Frog. Given their many and varied reincarnations in plays, films, comic books, and cartoons, both Scrooge and Oliver Twist have become figures of modern myth, standing with Huck Finn and Count Dracula as, one suspects, the most widely recognized fictional characters of the past two centuries.

Dickens enjoyed wide and ardent appeal throughout his career; John Forster could thus begin his *Life of Charles Dickens* (1874) by noting simply that his subject was "the most popular novelist of the century, and one of the greatest humorists that England has produced." Today, Dickens is the subject of a steady stream of books and dissertations, and of articles not only in scholarly journals, but in popular publications that range from *MD* to *Modern Maturity*. Dickens's open admirers have included many of the leading literary figures of recent years, among them John Irving, Tom Wolfe, John Mortimer, Martin Amis, and—perhaps most notably—Vladimir Nabokov, who in the 1950s told his students at Cornell "if it were possible I would like to devote the fifty minutes of every class meeting to mute meditation, concentration, and admiration, of Dickens."

But Dickens has always had detractors too. In his lifetime, some critics called him verbose and morbid; some called his politics too radical or too simplistic or too opportunistic; some said he simply could not portray women convincingly, or put together a well-made plot. Indeed, as anyone teaching Dickens or writing about him can attest, the world is quite full of readers who, given almost any Dickens novel except maybe *Great Expectations* (1860-61), will be hard pressed to get far beyond the first few chapters. One suspects that the journalist and critic Gerald Kaufman wasn't speaking only for himself when recently—in the *Financial Times*—he called Dickens "vastly over-praised."

Certainly, Dickens's critical reputation did not climb ever steadily upward. In 1865, a young Henry James, for one, put Dickens in "an inferior rank in the department of letters," calling him a "superficial" novelist who "has created nothing but figure," and so "added nothing to our understanding of human character." By the start of the twentieth century this was a common view, at least among younger writers and critics seeking distance from attitudes and conventions that prevailed during the Victorian age. At a time of experimentation, skepticism, and far-reaching inquiry—of James Joyce, Friedrich Nietzsche, and Sigmund Freud—Dickens seemed obvious and superficial, too didactic and lax: in short, quite hopelessly passé.

Indeed, as late as 1938 Edmund Wilson could note that while Dickens's readership had remained huge, discussion of his work had fallen largely to "doddering Dickens-fanciers" bent on proving, for example, "that Mr. Pickwick stopped at a certain inn and slept in a certain bed." Wilson linked this critical neglect directly to Dickens's unmatched popularity. The man who made Tiny Tim and Sairey Gamp had become for the British middle class "so much one of the articles of their creed—a familiar joke, a favourite dish, a Christmas ritual—that," Wilson wrote, "it is difficult for British pundits to see in him the great artist and social critic that he was."

But there was also, Wilson implied, a question of upbringing—of class. Dickens's grandparents were, on his father's side, servants. His mother's father brought on a different sort of social embarrassment, being an accused embezzler who spent his last years in flight from British law. Dickens himself was largely self-educated, and thoroughly self-supporting. He wrote for newspapers. He dressed flamboyantly. He had a wild and fertile imagination—but in other ways behaved more like an entrepreneur than an artist, more like Henry Ford than Charles Baudelaire. The author of *Pickwick Papers* (1837)—and *Edwin Drood* (1870)—always kept close watch on his sales. For some, then, there has always been something hard to classify—something rather vulgar—about Charles Dickens. So it wasn't surprising, Wilson wrote, that "the literary men from Oxford and Cambridge, who have lately been sifting fastidiously so much of the English heritage, have rather snubbingly left him alone."

In fact, compared to the great modernist writers—Joyce, T.S. Eliot, Virginia Woolf, and Ezra Pound—Dickens had little interest in the discussion and analysis of abstract ideas. He was, as Bernard Shaw wrote, with only slight exaggeration, "quite in the dark as to the philosophy and art of his day." For Dickens, typically English in so many ways, "a philosopher, an intellectual, was a figure of fun." Still, despite the gaps in his formal education, Dickens knew a good deal about English literature. As his novels and letters make clear, he had read widely and avidly as a boy. At eighteen, he secured a reader's ticket at the British Museum, hoping to give himself—as David Paroissien puts it—"such knowledge that a conventionally-schooled middle-class youth might be anticipated to have." Moreover, Dickens managed throughout his career to stay current with the works of his contemporaries, and near contemporaries—including William Wordsworth, Alfred Tennyson (his favorite contemporary poet), Robert Browning, William Thackeray, George Eliot, and the Brontës. He was on particularly close terms with the works of Shakespeare, and with fiction published in the eighteenth century. He loved and admired the hugely prolific Walter Scott, who had similarly achieved international fame through the writing of fiction, and who—moreover—found time to involve himself in numerous charitable causes. Revealingly, Oliver Goldsmith's *The Vicar of Wakefield* (1766), much admired by Victorian readers, was also one of Dickens's favorite novels, for he believed it had "perhaps done more good in the world, and instructed more kinds of people in virtue, than any other fiction ever written." Dickens read and reread Daniel

Defoe, praising—again revealingly—his "wonderful genius for the minutest details in a narrative." Dickens's own voice is, of course, supremely recognizable: one of the most distinctive in all of English literature. But it was from his predecessors that Dickens derived his main assumptions about how novels are made, and what they are supposed to accomplish. Those who want to become Dickens scholars must then also become students of those novelists he most admired and learned from, including Laurence Sterne, Tobias Smollet, and Henry Fielding—as well as Scott, Goldsmith and Defoe.

But all who aim to understand Dickens's fiction more fully need to consider, first, its deep links to the popular journalism of the day. Dickens started his writing career as a shorthand reporter covering London courts. He then worked for various London publications, including the *Morning Chronicle*—a venerable daily whose previous contributors had included Lord Byron, William Hazlitt, and Charles Lamb. Dickens stopped filing daily copy when the vast success of *The Pickwick Papers* allowed him to focus more fully on his fiction. But he remained proud of his reportorial roots, attributing "my first successes" to "the wholesome training of severe newspaper work when I was a very young man." And he never cut his journalistic ties. At his highest fame as a novelist, Dickens actively edited two weekly magazines: *Household Words* and later *All the Year Round*. He was a consistent champion of the press, calling it "the great public safeguard," and "the axis on which the moral world turned." He even served, late in his career, as a vice president of the Newspaper Press Fund.

Dickens the journalist and Dickens the novelist are then very closely linked. His novels, published in regular installments, draw on topical issues, and aim to educate and persuade as well as entertain. They reveal a writer who, like the very best reporters, savors the role of the observer, and the fact that everything he sees and hears and smells is raw material for his prose. Dickens was one of the most astute *observers* of his century; much of the pleasure he provides in his fiction comes precisely from this ability to render— sometimes with exaggeration, and sometimes with a kind of stunning photographic clarity—the things he so brilliantly *sees*. He was unflinching too: drawn not only to the beautiful but to the grotesque and the grim. Thus in his *Pictures from Italy* (1846) Dickens describes not only Genoa's palaces and Parma's "cheerful, stirring streets," but the execution in Rome, by decapitation, of "a young man—six-and-twenty—vigorously made, and well-shaped." "There was a great deal of blood," Dickens notes, carefully detailing the look of the severed head—"it was dull, cold, livid, wax"—before adding: "It was an ugly, filthy, careless, sickening spectacle; meaning nothing but butchery beyond the momentary interest, to the one wretched actor."

Dickens was in many ways a private man: anyone who makes a living writing novels must be. But his need for solitude was more than balanced by a streak of extroversion rare in serious writers of any kind—by a continuing need for company and conviviality, for performance and play. Dickens was as comfortable on the stage as he was at his desk—perhaps the key factor in his decision, late in life, to carry on with the whirlwind reading tours that took such a great toll on his health. This passion for performance was so consistent—so intense—that one is tempted to argue that, in the end, Dickens was an actor who just happened to turn out books on the side. Thus, in 1842, during his first North American tour, one finds Dickens in Montreal rehearsing with other amateur actors for a farce, and telling a friend in a letter that he planned to wear "a comic wig—light flaxen, with a small whisker halfway down the cheek. Over this, I mean to wear two nightcaps; one with a tassel, and one of flannel. A Flannel wrapper, drab tights, and slippers, will complete the costume." One can hardly imagine, say, E. M. Forster doing the same.

Dickens's continuing love for—and involvement with—the popular theater must also be remembered by those who want to appreciate more fully the nature of his art. Peter Ackroyd, Dickens's most exhaustive (and exhausting) biographer, notes that "hardly a day" of Dickens's "life passed when he did not go to a play"; that he "preferred the theatre to practically any other form of activity"; that his eldest son thought him "'a born actor'" and that Dickens himself told friends that "he believed he had more talent for the drama than for literature, as he certainly had more delight in acting than in any work whatever." Ackroyd rightly suggests that if Dickens "had any image of the world in his head as he wrote, it was that narrowed and highly magnified one which he observed from the stalls or from the pit." The result, as many critics have noted, is that Dickens's novels are intensely theatrical in a host of ways. They feature strong scenes and "punch" lines: one thinks of Esther

Summerson, in *Bleak House* (1853), exclaiming: "For I cannot see you Charley—I am blind." And one recalls Miss Tox bringing down the curtain at the close of chapter 16 of *Dombey and Son* (1846-48): "Dear me, dear me! To think . . . that Dombey and Son should be a daughter after all!"

In Dickens's novels, one finds "elements of burlesque, of melodrama, of farce, of sentimental comedy," as Ackroyd notes. Dickens was "always concerned with his audience and with the effect he was having upon that audience, his preference was for writing which offered a direct and immediate appeal." And as Arnold Kettle points out, Dickens never forgot that his novels were frequently read aloud, a practice "which Victorian families went in for much more than their descendants of the television age." As a result, "The texture of Dickens's prose" is "whether through conscious effort or not, perfectly adapted for reading aloud." Moreover, "at this level his wit, which is apt, in the demanding silence of private reading, to seem a bit heavy-handed" turns out to be "just right," as Kettle notes. Dickens's "loud explicitness," writes Barbara Hardy, as well as his urge to leave "little to be subtly inferred," but to "put the case at the top of his voice" and then repeat it, "in capital letters," stems largely from the fact that his novels "were listened to by groups of illiterates as Thackeray's and George Eliot's never were." Ackroyd notes too that not only was Dickens drawn to "the more theatrical novelists"—Smollet over Jane Austen, say—but he "expressed a preference for what might be called middle-class drama"; he liked to quote from Robert Browning's *A Blot on the 'Scutcheon* and Edward Bulwer-Lytton's *Not So Bad as We Seem*, and he was openly fond of such plays as Douglas Jerrold's *Time Works Wonders*—a lavishly melodramatic piece.

Today the term *melodrama* is, as Robertson Davies puts it, "tinged with contempt." It suggests "a bygone vulgar form of theatre art in which violent appeals to the emotions and sensational incidents were used to body forth a simple-minded morality." One thinks of undoubted good at war with unrelenting evil. Of noble heroes and irredeemable villains. Of swooning maidens; of fulsome speeches endorsing sobriety, piety, chastity, thrift. Of coincidences, duels, and deathbed confessions. Of close calls and—always—happy endings. Of course the theater has changed much over the past century and a half. Today, an earnest revival of a Victorian

melodramatic favorite like *The Rent Day*—also written by Dickens's
friend Jerrold—would draw hoots, or be dismissed as nothing more
than an amusing curiosity.

But melodrama itself still thrives in a variety of contemporary
guises: in film, on television—especially on television—and in much
popular literature. It does so, one assumes, because the human desire
to watch the staging and the resolution of conflict runs so deep as
to be nearly instinctive; because "melodrama" however one defines
it, or finds it—whether in Hollywood or Bombay—invariably skirts
the brain and goes straight for the guts, playing to those hopes,
fears, and desires that involve power and sex and survival itself, and
that tend to turn up, blunt and unbidden, in our dreams. Davies
points to melodramatic strains in the most enduring of writers,
including Shakespeare and Fyodor Dostoyevsky, as well as George
Eliot, Dickens's contemporary, and very probably the most erudite
English novelist of her time. Davies calls melodrama "the prevailing
weather of art during the nineteenth century." He finds Eliot's *Mill
on the Floss* (1860) "highly melodramatic; if you agree with me that
melodrama may well mean a way of dealing with artistic material
that reveals the wonder and caprice of life, as well as its undeniable
tragedy." But he adds that, ultimately, melodrama differs from
classical tragedy in at least one crucial respect. Melodrama is "an art
in which not an implacable and malign fate dominates the life of
man, but art in which good and evil contend"—and in which good
almost always wins. For melodrama is optimistic, as Davies notes:
"The Villain is worsted. If he is not worsted, spiritually if not
physically, our melodrama draws very close to tragedy." This
underlying optimism surely accounts for melodrama's continuing
popularity—and for the particular popularity of Dickens's earlier
novels.

Few novelists have captured the wonder, caprice, and tragedy of
life as well as Charles Dickens. Few in more recent times have
sought so deliberately to portray the battle between evil and good.
"In all of Dickens," Davies writes, this battle is presented "vividly,
and for some readers, too vividly. Their taste is too refined for these
naked, hair-raising expositions of Nestorian dualism: or, to put it
another way, they lack the stomach for the gaudier aspects of the
Eternal Struggle." Or, to put it yet another way, they have simply
grown accustomed to the subtler, more elusive—and generally less
hopeful—ways of serious fiction written in the twentieth century. In

Dickens's fiction, writes Davies, "all of the Seven Deadly Sins are constantly on parade." ("Pride," for example, "is extensively dealt with," he writes; Mr. Dombey of *Dombey and Son* is Dickens's "masterpiece in this realm. Envy? Lots of it, with Uriah Heep at the head of the list. Wrath? . . . We think of Mr. Murdstone, whose cruelty to people for their own good is so impressively described in *David Copperfield*. Lechery? You'll find plenty of it in Uriah Heep and in Mr. Carker, in *Dombey*.") Modernist and postmodernist fiction tends, of course, to prize distance, ambiguity: questions are posed, but answers less frequently given. Evil is intractable, hard to define. Values have been systematically "transvaluated": the very notion of moral judgment and moral discrimination is—perhaps particularly in the wake of Nietzsche—often called into question; the meaning of life is anything but clear. Characters, then, are muddled and confused—less shapers of their fates than the victims of forces beyond their control. They aim not to triumph—but simply to survive.

Dickens's view of the world changed with the years. In many ways, his fiction does become richer and more interesting as it explores more fully the mysteries of human nature—and the roles that culture and environment play in the shaping of human character. Certainly, by the time he reaches *David Copperfield*, Dickens's main characters have become much more intricate; they are not "mere" melodramatic types. Indeed, these melodramatic elements—while never wholly absent—are increasingly subdued. And Dickens's sense of the comic also changes. It shows more frequently a more "modern" sense of pathos, futility, and absurdity. Moreover, and perhaps most interestingly, Dickens becomes more explicitly interested in showing the way in which the theater—or, more precisely, theatricality—informs everyday life. His best characters are not then simply heroes and villains. But they still play roles, donning costumes and masks in dramas of their own design. We are all of us actors, Dickens's novels repeatedly suggest—some in life, some on the stage.

Certainly, one should not think of any Dickens novel as if it were simply an elaborate tract—a blueprint for righteous living. Indeed, critics like John Carey have argued that any attempt to define and analyze the moral dimension of Dickens's art is doomed from the start. For that art, like the man who produced it, was rich in inconsistency. In *The Violent Effigy* (1973; second edition, 1991), an insightful and entertaining study of Dickens's imaginative tendencies, Carey notes that those who regard Dickens "primarily as a critic of society" must also underplay his frequent fondness for depicting social institutions as little more than great absurdities. And they must also write around his often wildly contradictory views. "As has often been remarked," writes Carey, Dickens at one point "warmly favoured the hanging of disaffected natives in Jamaica and the blowing of mutinous sepoys from the mouths of cannon. In America he regretted the 'melancholy absurdity' of giving blacks the vote, and objected besides that 'exhalations not the most agreeable arise from a number of colored people got together.'" Elsewhere Dickens

urges compassion for the occupants of prison cells, yet feels outraged when convicts are given better accommodation than impoverished working men. In the *History of England* he wrote for his children he includes a lecture on the wickedness of warfare which, he insists, can never be "otherwise than horrible." But when he recounts the havoc King Richard wrought among the Saracens "with twenty English pound of English steel," or celebrates the exploits of "bold Admiral Blake" who "brought the King of Portugal to his sense," it appears the horrible side of war has somehow slipped out of sight. "He was very much a man of one idea," affirmed his friend John Forster, "each having its turn of predominance." Almost any aberration, from drunkenness to wife-beating can be found eliciting at various times both Dickens's mournfulness and his amused toleration.

Often, Dickens does seem more interested in observing than in reforming. As a *comic* writer—and thus at his least political or ideological—Dickens shows unending delight in human diversity; he appears to accept quite serenely the inescapable fact that human beings are, in the final analysis, odd. Repeatedly he seeks to distance himself from those who appear smugly certain of what constitutes proper human behavior; in *Martin Chuzzlewit*, for example, as Steven Marcus notes, Dickens "almost never uses the words 'moral' or 'morality' in any but an ironic sense: being a true moralist in an era of middle-class piety, propriety, and prosperity, he regarded all claims made in the name of morality with skepticism." Indeed, in much of Dickens, such terms as "decent" and "respectable" are almost always suspect; they tend to suggest a soul frozen or poisoned with self-righteousness, a mind more dead than alive. The black-clad Mr. Vholes, a self-serving lawyer in *Bleak*

House is, for example, "a very respectable man." He "never misses a chance in his practice; which is a mark of respectability. He never takes any pleasure; which is another mark of respectability. He is reserved and serious; which is another mark of respectability. His digestion is impaired, which is highly respectable."

At times, Dickens does appear singularly, bitterly, unimpressed with human life: he sees selfishness and stupidity everywhere. And Carey is correct to point not only to Dickens's "inconsistencies" but to his consistent fascination with violence; with things morbid, grotesque. Carey notes that while such "inconsistencies" can be fatal in a social philosopher, they are no liability—are indeed an advantage—in an imaginative writer seeking to convey a wide variety of dramatic situations and comic types. Dickens was first and foremost a novelist—and not, thank God, as Carey puts it, "a social theorist." One could argue, moreover, that this flexibility translates into something like a Shakespearian scope: into an extensive, uneven canon that has long appealed in varying ways to an unusually wide range of readers. (D. W. Griffith admired Dickens, as did Federico Fellini.) But Steven Marcus also remains one of Dickens's best readers, and his calling the author of *Nicholas Nickleby* and *Bleak House* "a true moralist" is right on the mark. Dickens produced novels that, whatever their contradictions, are informed by a moral vision, by various moral ideals. Ignoring that vision, and those ideals, limits one's understanding of the nature of Dickens's art, which is perhaps as frequently sentimental as it is satiric.

Sentimentality is, of course, at the core of melodrama. Modern readers are likely to feel that sentimentality represents, by definition, a simplified view of the inherent complexities of human life. But again, as Fred Kaplan has also shown in his superb book *Sacred Tears* (1987), melodrama was a part of much nineteenth-century literature. Like many of his contemporaries, Dickens "believed there was an instinctive, irrepressible need for human beings to affirm both in private and in public that they possessed moral sentiments, that these sentiments were innate, that they best expressed themselves through spontaneous feelings, and that sentimentality in life and art had a moral basis." "People," writes Kaplan, "all people, except those who had been the victims of perverse conditioning or some misfortune of nature—instinctively felt, in Dickens' view, pleasure, *moral* pleasure, when those they thought of as good triumphed and those they thought of as bad were defeated. Most Victorians believed that the human community was one of shared moral feelings, and that sentimentality was a desirable way of feeling and or expressing ourselves morally."

Politically, Dickens is hard to define. He called himself a "radical"—a term loosely used in Britain during the nineteenth century. In his early, interesting, and sometimes wildly inaccurate study, *Charles Dickens: The Progress of a Radical* (1938), Thomas A. Jackson, a Marxist, argued that Dickens's "radicalism," instead of "mellowing in the sunshine of prosperity into a mere benevolent Liberalism . . . did the reverse." It "stiffened, hardened, and deepened [Jackson was not also a Freudian] into something that with a little outside aid might easily have emerged as positive Socialism or Communism." But Arnold Kettle, another Marxist, writing some two decades later, admitted that Dickens was neither "an unconscious Marxist or even a pre-Marxian socialist." Kettle finds, in one of Dickens's later speeches, "an extraordinary mixture of paternalism, radicalism, belief in self-help, religious idealism, anti-clericalism and straightforward practical business-sense."

In any event, Dickens was, or at least wanted to be, optimistic about human nature and human possibility. But like a growing number of social thinkers at work in the nineteenth century, he believed that the social changes taking shape in the wake of what became known as "the industrial revolution" were not likely to usher in an era of widespread fulfillment and joy. Dickens despaired when he considered the quality of most people's lives in the Britain of his day: people living in a society that, with its obsessive emphasis on work and competition and profit, was simply ignoring a wide range of other, but no less necessary, human needs—including, as he phrased it in his *American Notes* (1842), those "harmless fancies and the love of innocent delights and gaieties, which are a part of human nature: as much a part of it as any other love or hope that is our common portion." Dickens believed that modern industrial societies could be both prosperous and just; that an enlightened government should encourage social progress in appropriately earnest ways—should, then, do more than provide the climate in which the raw drive for profit would be allowed to thrive. As a novelist and journalist, Dickens tried to throw light on problems connected to education, health, poverty, and crime: he despised the kind of smug complacency he saw at work in Britain's most powerful political institutions. George Bernard Shaw called *Little Dorrit* "a more seditious book than *Das Kapital.*" "All over Europe," Shaw wrote, in the late 1930s, "men and women are in prison for pamphlets and speeches which are to *Little Dorrit* as red pepper to dynamite." But Shaw also knew that Dickens himself did not quite equate writing novels with lobbing bombs. In fact, in his political pronouncements, particularly those he published, Dickens tended to sound precisely like the Voice of Benevolent Liberalism—more like John Galsworthy, say, than Leon Trotsky. Dickens urged reform, not revolution. He wanted help for the helpless, hope and comfort for the suffering and the poor. Some "persons are in especial need of legislative protection and assistance," he wrote simply in a public letter in 1842. Still, Dickens never thrilled to the thought of the "People" actually having control. Shaw notes too that it seems never to have dawned on Dickens to "join one of the dozens of political reform societies that were about him." He "might have been a Comtist," Shaw writes, "perhaps ought to have been a Comtist, but was not. He was an independent Dickensian, a sort of unphilosophical Radical, with a complete disbelief in government by the people and an equally complete hostility to government in any interest but theirs."

Like many writers and intellectuals working in the wake of the French Revolution, Dickens was understandably worried when he wondered about how democracy in Europe might work itself out. Like Thomas Carlyle and Matthew Arnold, for example—like Alexis de Tocqueville—Dickens feared the spread of social anarchy at a time when, throughout much of Europe, movements of political protest were on the rise. (In Britain, during the 1830s, the Chartist Movement, for example, produced mass meetings and huge petitions in a drive for increased democratization; in Paris, a decade later, rioters filled the streets.) This fear is very plainly signaled in *A Tale of Two Cities* (1859), with its guillotines and infamous "death-carts" rumbling by. But again, as Shaw and others have noted, Dickens never really developed a compensating faith in democratic institutions. This is shown in *David Copperfield* (1850), by far Dickens's most autobiographical novel. David, like Dickens, comes to master "the noble art and mystery of stenography." He similarly lands a job reporting parliamentary debates, acquiring in the process a bleak view of politicians and the institutions they control. "Night after night," David recalls, "I record predictions that never come to pass, professions that are never fulfilled, explanations that are only meant to mystify." "I am sufficiently behind the scenes to know the worth of political life," he concludes, in words that could be Dickens's own. "I am an infidel about it, and shall never be converted."

But again, Dickens's art, as Barbara Hardy puts it, "is a highly moral art that depends on the creation of ideals of virtue." And a list of what Dickens loved—and what he loathed—is not hard to compile. Certain foibles and shortcomings seem at times simply to amuse him; in *The Pickwick Papers*, for example, he forgives Tupman his comical vanity, his continuing susceptibility to "the most interesting and pardonable of human weaknesses—love." But Dickens's writings do show a consistent loathing of self-righteousness and narrow thinking. They attack those who abuse power—and particularly those who exploit the poor and the young. In this regard, one must note his preoccupation with education. In novel after novel, Dickens deals in some way with this theme. His key characters are frequently students: they are taught in schools; they are taught by elders and mentors in the school of life. His novels are then also filled with teachers, some good, many bad. Betsey Trotwood in *David Copperfield*, is not a saint, but she is one of Dickens's good teachers, reminding David that success in life must include selflessness and compassion, and the avoidance, always, of meanness, cruelty, and gross deceit. Dickens's bad teachers are probably the most infamous in all of English literature: among these Murdstone in *Copperfield* takes his own prominent place. Murdstone would teach David virtue through intimidation and fear. So he humiliates the boy, and beats him—beating being an educational method much prized by Dickens's bad teachers.

Indeed, as Carey shows, Dickens's works do show a continuing fascination with violent characters and scenes. But in Dickens, violence is not glorified. Instead, he repeatedly makes clear his hatred for cruelty and brutality. Although he cannot deny the bleak fact of violence and envy and greed, Dickens as a novelist always evokes the hope that human beings are capable of something more. Of course it's a hope that seems hardly trite—that seems, indeed, hugely relevant—when, today, each morning brings news of some fresh slaughter, some staggering, full-color account of murder and mayhem in Europe or Africa or Asia or the United States.

Dickens hated hypocrisy as well as cruelty. He *detested* hypocrisy—a sin "very prevalent in the Victorian era," as Robertson Davies comments, "and a profuse growth in modern democracies." ("How well," Davies exults, "and in what a variety of tints he paints it! The full-length portraits, of course, are represented by Seth Pecksniff [in *Martin Chuzzlewit*] and Chadband [in *Bleak House*]. But how many hypocrites there are who are merely sketched, but sketched with a master-hand; like Mr. Spenlow, in *Copperfield*, who was all compliance himself, but dared not take action for fear of his invisible . . . partner, Mr. Jorkins.") Dickens also detested the belief—increasingly common in both England and America during the nineteenth century—that the pursuit of material gain was life's ultimate aim. One could fairly conclude that Dickens, or at least a large part of him, hated money itself. For money in Dickens's fiction is almost always associated with misery and ruin, with the warping of true feeling, and the thwarting of love.

Still, one hesitates to call Dickens a "religious" writer. For many, that term suggests strict adherence to the doctrines of an orthodox faith. Dickens rarely went to church. ("You will remember," he wrote to one of his grown sons, bound for Australia, "that you have never at home been wearied about religious observances or mere formalities.") Peter Ackroyd fairly suggests that, ultimately, Dickens's "religion" was "a religion of natural love and moral feeling," in spirit "not remarkably different from the rational 'cult of sensibility' which was part of his eighteenth century inheritance." Dickens was certainly hostile to those sects and creeds that—like Calvinism—stressed adherence to grim dogma before the daily display of compassion and goodwill; that centered obsessively on damnation and sin; that were more exclusive than welcoming; that condemned "worldly" pleasures however benign. Thus in the *American Notes*, we find Dickens ill at ease in stodgy New England, where he hears sermons that routinely condemn "all innocent and rational amusements." The women of Boston, he notes, have few opportunities for "excitement" beyond what is found in "the church, the chapel, and the lecture room"—and so to the church and the chapel they go, "in crowds." Writes Dickens:

Wherever religion is resorted to, as a strong drink, and as an escape from the dull monotonous round of home, those of its ministers who pepper the highest will be surest to please. They who strew the Eternal Path with the greatest amount of brimstone, and who most ruthlessly tread down the flowers and leaves that grow by the wayside, will be voted the most righteous; and they who enlarge with the greatest pertinacity on the difficulty of getting into heaven, will be considered by all true believers certain of going there: though it would be hard to say by what process of reasoning this conclusion is arrived at. It is so at home, and it is so abroad.

Elsewhere in his *American Notes* Dickens, in New York, visits a village where Shakers reside. They are, he concedes, good farmers, well-known for the high quality of their cattle, herbs, and seeds. But Dickens finds in Shaker codes a distillation of all that he loathed in certain forms of organized religion—and in much of Victorian society. Dickens comes to "a house where the Shaker manufactures are sold, and which is the headquarters of the elders." He finds "a grim room, where several grim hats were hanging on grim pegs, and the time was grimly told by a grim clock." He meets "a grim old Shaker" with "eyes as hard, and dull, and cold, as the great round metal buttons on his coat and waistcoat." The Shakers live a "Spartan" life: there is "no union of the sexes, and every Shaker, male and female, is devoted to a life of celibacy." The cult survives by taking "as proselytes, persons so young that they cannot know their own minds, and cannot possess much strength of resolution in this or any other respect." And this, for Dickens, is the last straw. From the start of his career until its end, from the *American Notes* to *Dombey and Son* to *Hard Times* (1854), Dickens issues many of his strongest attacks on those whose views stem from this belief that most pleasure is depraved and almost all amusement dangerous; that all human beings are born evil and inclined to stay that way; that, in the end, life comes down to an endless cycle of little more than work and boredom, work and fear; and who—worse—insist on shackling children with the same warped and neurotic worldview. He now lets loose a jet of invective that is so hot—and so frequently restated in various ways in his fiction—that it merits quoting in full. "I cannot, I confess," he begins, the voice slowly rising, "incline towards the Shakers; view them with much favor, or extend towards them any very lenient construction." For

I so abhor, and from my soul detest that bad spirit, no matter by what class or sect it may be entertained, which would strip life of its healthful graces, rob youth of its innocent pleasure, pluck from maturity and age their pleasant ornaments, and make existence but a narrow path towards the grave: that odious spirit which, if it could have had full scope and sway upon the earth, must have blasted and made barren the imaginations of the greatest men, and left them, in their power of raising up enduring images before their fellow creatures yet unborn, no better than the beasts; that, in these broad-brimmed hats and very sombre coats—in stiff-necked solemn-visaged piety, in short, no matter what its garb, . . . I recognise the worst among the enemies of Heaven and Earth, who turn the water at the marriage feasts of this poor world, not into wine, but gall.

Dickens was then suspicious of religious institutions, and of formal religious creeds. His works are particularly full of pious hypocrites—twisted believers who behave brutally. Not surprisingly, then, critics writing well before John Carey have been eager to downplay or simply discount the religious elements in Dickens's novels; to find in his writings an expression of their own, more skeptical, post-Victorian views. Sir Arthur Quiller-Couch, for example, once advised in an essay on Dickens's work that "to begin with, one must jettison religion." In *The Progress of a Radical*, T. A. Jackson complained of Dickens's "sentimental Jesusism"—his tendency to talk "with what, nowadays, we should call downright unctuousness about 'Our Saviour.'" Jackson added hopefully that it was John Forster, perhaps, who furtively tucked "these passages" into Dickens's works. This is a great example of wishful thinking.

Angus Wilson, no Baptist, knew better. Dickens, Wilson writes, "was always a simple New Testament Christian." He was "personal and modest" in his faith, explains Dennis Walder in *Dickens and Religion* (1981)—the best single work on the subject; he was "undemonstrative and reticent about his religion" and in this and other ways "Protestant to the core." Unlike many other artists and intellectuals of his time, including George Eliot, Dickens never abjured the faith; he never worried aloud about the need for artists and intellectuals to build an all-embracing, order-preserving system of secular belief in the face of Christianity's impending collapse. For Dickens, Christianity had not collapsed. But it was, he believed, too widely ignored. As the quote above suggests, Dickens's writings are tissued with Biblical allusions, but they also consistently show his liberal, broad-minded view of theological issues. Again: Dickens's novels do not contend that most men and women are innately evil. But they do appear to recognize that most people require a good bit of prodding—and frequent appeals to their more decent side. "One of my most constant and most earnest endeavours," he once wrote, "has been to exhibit in all my good people some faint reflections of the teachings of our great Master. . . All my strongest illustrations are derived from the New Testament; all my social abuses are shown to be departures from its spirit." Late in life, Dickens reminded his Australia-bound son that the Bible—or more particularly the New Testament—was "the best book that ever was or will be known in the world"; that there was "truth and beauty" in "the Christian religion, as it came from Christ Himself"; that, moreover, one should "never abandon the wholesome practice" of praying, privately, "night and morning"—noting too that "I have never abandoned it myself, and I know the comfort of it." In one of his last significant compositions—his will—Dickens wrote: "I commit my soul to the mercy of God through our Lord and Saviour Jesus Christ, and I exhort my dear children humbly to try to guide themselves by the teaching of the New Testament in its broad spirit, and to put no faith in any man's narrow construction of its letter here or there."

Often, Dickens's most appealing characters are the simplest, the least ambitious and complex. Often they are poor, struggling. Dickens particularly celebrates the poor, celebrates—in the tradition of much Romantic literature—their innate dignity and strength, their simple virtues. "Let me linger in this place," he writes in *The Old Curiosity Shop* (1840-41), referring to the home of Kit Nubbles and his mother, "to remark that if ever household affections and loves are graceful things, they are graceful in the poor." He continues:

The ties that bind the wealthy and the proud to home may be forged on earth, but those which link the poor man to his humble hearth are of the truer metal and bear the stamp of Heaven. The man of high descent may love the halls and lands of his inheritance as a part of himself: as trophies of his birth and power; his associations with them are associations of pride and wealth and triumph; the poor man's attachment to the tenements he holds, which strangers have held before, and may to-morrow occupy again, has a worthier root, stuck deep into a purer soil. His household gods are of flesh and blood, with no alloy of silver, gold, or precious stone; he has no property but in the affections of his own heart; and when they endear bare floors and walls, despite of rags and toil and scanty fare, that man has his love of home from God, and his rude hut becomes a solemn place.

Many of Dickens's most sympathetic figures—one thinks of Joe Gargery, Clara Peggotty, or Amy Dorrit—are completely indifferent to the allure of power and wealth; others—Vincent Crummles, for example, or John Wemmick—find their chief pleasures in the imagination, in the same spirit of play that sparked Dickens's own love of the theater. Against characters who are greedy and selfish, Dickens tends to set men and women marked by sympathy, charity, generosity: characters willing to help the helpless and the poor. In short, Dickens stands up for the underdog in his fictions, and always uses those books as a blunt means of airing his views. Dickens's close friend, the novelist Wilkie Collins, once described the reading of fiction as a "springboard to better things." Dickens shared this view. He believed throughout his career that it was a large part of the novelist's job to instruct and to clarify, to define anew what is virtuous, and so distance virtue from vice. Ackroyd points to a speech that Dickens delivered at a banquet in his honor, in Birmingham, in 1853. Here, as elsewhere, Dickens insisted that "'literature' was a serious enterprise with serious ends." "Literature cannot be too faithful to the people," Dickens told his audience. It "cannot too ardently advocate the cause of their advancement, happiness, and prosperity." It should not then be exclusive or recondite: "I believe no true man," Dickens proclaimed, "with anything to tell, need have the slightest misgiving, either for himself or for his message, before a large number of hearers." Ackroyd puts it well:

Dickens was no modernist . . . and in fact it was precisely the broader or more apparently "populist" elements of Dickens's art which prompted the negative reaction first of Oscar Wilde, then of the fin-de-siècle poets, then of such writers born at the end of the century as Eliot and Pound. And there was something else in Dickens's Birmingham speech, arguably the most important speech he had yet made, which deserves consideration, since it touches upon the very essence of his conception of art. He spoke of painting but he could have been speaking of his own medium; " . . . it cannot hope to rest on a single foundation for its great temple—or the mere classic pose of a figure, or the folds of a drapery—but it must be imbued with human passions and action, informed with human right and wrong . . ." A statement which, according to the newspaper reports, was greeted with "*Cheers.*"

Throughout much of his life, and long thereafter, Dickens was himself widely regarded as a paragon of bourgeois virtue—the calm, kindly paterfamilias shown in portraits and photographs with buttoned waistcoat and sagely beard. Even today, readers who know little or nothing about Dickens are likely to link him vaguely to children, animals, holiday dinners, and resilient good cheer. In many ways Dickens does fit the stereotypical image of the middle-class Victorian, being (at times) squeamish about sex, and much concerned with propriety. Shaw liked to note, for example, that despite his own passion for drama, Dickens refused to allow his own daughters to pursue acting careers, warning them that by doing so they would rub shoulders with a host of unsavory characters. One recalls too the very curious episode—recounted by Myron Magnet in *Dickens and the Social Order* (1985)—in which England's leading novelist insisted on pressing charges against a girl of seventeen because he found her swearing loudly as she swaggered merrily with some male friends down a London street. Dickens had cultivated friendships with several London cops; and, if anything, had become more fascinated with crime and punishment as the years went by. And now, as Magnet notes, Dickens duly turned up in court, "armed" with his personal copy of the Police Act, and "was satisfied to see the girl sentenced to ten shillings or ten days."

Dickens was not then Father Christmas. He was not instantly loved by all who crossed his path. One of his daughters, Kate, once asked Shaw to "make the public understand that my father was not a joyous, jocose gentleman walking about the world with a plum pudding and a bowl of punch." Edmund Wilson, in 1939, did precisely that. Writing at a time when psychological interpretations of literature were becoming much in vogue, Wilson argued that common assumptions regarding the nature of Dickens's life were wildly simplistic—as simplistic, and inaccurate, as those assumptions regarding the nature of his art. "It was not merely that his passion for the theatre had given [Dickens] a taste for melodramatic contrasts," Wilson argued, "it was rather that the lack of balance between the opposite impulses of his nature had stimulated an appetite for melodrama. For emotionally Dickens *was* unstable. . . . He seems almost as unstable as Dostoyevsky." Wilson's Dickens was, as John Gross notes, "a subversive and uncomfortable writer, inwardly hostile to the age which acclaimed him and seeking relief from the strain of his double life in fantasies of crime and violence." Ackroyd's *Dickens*, probably the best biography to date, doesn't go as far, but it similarly shows Dickens as a tormented and indeed "strange" figure in whose fiction we find the exorcism of many personal demons. Edmund Wilson found Dickens "capable of great hardness and cruelty." He points out that Dickens's daughter Kate, late in her life, told Gladys Storey, the author of *Dickens and Daughter* (1939), that "'my father was a wicked man—a very wicked man.'" Robertson Davies, writing in the 1970s, called Dickens "a ripsnorting, raging, egotistical cad."

Davies goes too far. Close readings of Ackroyd's biography, and Fred Kaplan's fine *Charles Dickens* (1988), make clear that the author of *Barnaby Rudge* and *Bleak House* was an enormously complex and often very unhappy man, perhaps a manic-depressive, dogged by periods of intense anxiety and restlessness throughout much of his life. In the early 1850s, Dickens told Forster that his head would "split like a fired shell" if he kept still for too long; he described himself elsewhere—at the height of his success—as "wandering—unsettled—restless—uncontrollable," as "infirm of purpose as Macbeth, as errant as Mad Tom, and as rugged as Timon." Such phrases nicely illustrate Dickens's wonderful instinct for exaggeration. But Dickens was, in fact, notoriously impatient and abrupt. He was driven, compulsive, and rather vain. He seems rather to have relished the role of the victim, the wronged party, and for years nursed his wounds and regrets. He was highly sensitive to criticism, tending to insist that things go his way—or not at all. Henry James, seeing Dickens during the 1860s, sensed "an automatic hardness" in the man, and was struck particularly by his "merciless *military* eye." Dickens was not, of course, the only prominent figure of the Victorian era to work so intensely in such an utterly unrelenting way. Much of Carlyle's work extols an ethic of severe, unrelenting labor. One thinks of the nearly superhumanly energetic Gladstone on one end and the manic Bram Stoker on the other, and one can only conclude that, well, *something* was in the air. Dickens's obsession with work, with motion, with hard activity on a hundred fronts, is testimony not only to his own great, unceasing energy, but also perhaps to a compulsion for self-escape and even self-destruction.

Dickens was then—as the saying goes—a great bunch of guys. Different people saw different sides. Many would come to recall this domineering, sharp-tempered, and often taciturn figure; others, as Ackroyd shows, would always remember Dickens's kindness, gentleness, and geniality. Little evidence suggests that Dickens was himself prone to a pattern of vile hypocrisy; that he was a closet

Scrooge full of stinginess, ill will, and greed. Despite his sometimes hot temper, Dickens was not particularly mean-spirited—not driven by envy, malice, or spite. ("Novels," as André Maurois noted some years ago, "are not written by saints; at the most, they inspire them. But Dickens's books offer proof of a sensitiveness so acute that it is impossible for us reasonably to accept an accusation of cruel or dishonest character." "Evil character is generally rooted in unimaginativeness," Maurois astutely adds, "and that was not a defect from which Dickens suffered.") In fact, Dickens's lifetime of charitable acts show, as do his novels, that he was consistently, unusually capable of empathy and generosity: one would be hard pressed to name another writer of significance who, in peacetime, gave so much of himself for what he believed to be the common good. Arnold Kettle, for one, is grateful that Wilson in "The Two Scrooges" made it "impossible for the sentimental-hearty view of Dickens to be maintained." But Kettle, writing twenty years after Wilson's essay, also regretted that one of its "chief effects" was "to provide the stuffy, respectable Dickens-figure with a few good sadistic neuroses very much to the taste of the post-Freudian western reader." Without denying that Dickens had his "psychological problems" and "eccentricities," Kettle fairly stresses that Dickens's "acceptance of an active and practical public life, his thoroughgoing commitment not, in the twentieth-century intellectual's manner, to certain *ideas* about reality but to reality itself, to facing the world and changing it, counteracted to a profound extent his personal frustrations." Kettle insists—also rightly—that "the sensibility behind" Dickens's novels "is essentially sane, balanced and un-neurotic," adding that "the traditional description of Dickens as a comic novelist, though it has sometimes veiled his greatness, is right; the elements of violence and extremity in the books—which are immensely important—involve no more than an imaginative penetration into the realities of the life he knew. If they are not 'nice' books it is because he did not live in a nice world." And as Edmund Wilson notes, Kate Dickens also told Storey that "'I loved my father better than any man in the world—in a different way of course. . . . I loved him for his faults.'"

*　　　*

The early years of Charles John Huffam Dickens tell all; rarely has a great writer altered so little from when he was a boy. Dickens was born in Portsmouth on February 7, 1812. His mother, Elizabeth, had been reared in a comfortable middle-class milieu; her father, Charles Barrow, had risen rapidly in the navy's pay office, becoming its chief conductor of monies. Dickens's father, John, grew up on a country estate, where his parents worked—as seward and housekeeper—for the Marquis of Crewe. Helped by the Crewe family's connections, John Dickens became at nineteen a pay clerk in the Navy Pay Office in London, where he met the Barrows. After a two-year courtship, he and Elizabeth were married, moving first to Portsmouth, where John Dickens continued his clerking duties and where, in 1810, their first child Fanny was born. Charles was next. Over the next thirteen years, six more children followed, but two—a boy and a girl—died in infancy.

Soon after their marriage, John and Elizabeth learned that John Barrow, Dickens's maternal grandfather, had discreetly but systematically robbed the navy of over five thousand pounds. Michael Allen notes—in his thoroughly documented *Charles Dickens' Childhood* (1988)—that the event seems "to have made little difference to the material position" of John and Elizabeth Dickens. But it was surely a source of considerable, if quiet, familial shame. As an adult, Dickens almost never spoke of the darker periods of his younger years. His novels, however, repeatedly show dishonor and deceit lurking just below the surface of respectability: over and over they show that crime can strike close to home.

And so can poverty. When Dickens was small, his family moved frequently, and lived in a nearly constant state of financial turmoil. Dickens would recall the years in Chatham—between 1817 and 1822—with special fondness. For here, his family lived in a rather spacious house and employed a couple of servants, one of whom—a nanny called Mary Weller—was especially skilled at telling tales of ghosts and murderers that Charles liked to hear. (Dickens paid tribute to his nanny in *The Pickwick Papers*, passing her name onto Sam Weller, one of the novel's most popular characters—and another teller of macabre tales.) Chatham, as Forster put it, was "the birthplace" of Dickens's "fancy"; here, he attended a good local school, and read voraciously. The works and characters and titles that Dickens loved as a boy were the same works and characters that young Copperfield loved, and listed: "Roderick Random, Peregrine Pickle, Humphry Clinker, Tom Jones, the Vicar of Wakefield, Don Quixote, Gil Blas, and Robinson Crusoe"—as well as *Arabian Nights*, a work of huge popularity in Britain throughout the nineteenth century, making Sinbad as popular in his way as Ulysses. Angus Wilson has suggested that the episodic structure of *Arabian Nights* particularly influenced Dickens, who—like the Sultana Scheherazade—proved himself to be a compulsive teller of stories that, published serially, were designed to leave those who heard them in complete suspense. "The pattern of Scheherazade's narration," writes Wilson, "so familiar to him from childhood, must have inclined him towards the acceptance of this periodical, direct relationship with his readers which gave him such great satisfaction. The printer's boy at the door, waiting for the next installment, was a sort of threatening executioner."

Dickens's father was a loquacious, industrious man with a rather charming theatrical flair. He could not, however, manage his own financial affairs. He was forever borrowing, forever behind. Crisis came when Charles was ten. John Dickens, still working for the navy, was transferred back to London. But his salary was cut—and his bills continued to soar. Now the family found itself pawning books and furniture in a futile effort to stay afloat. Finally, in early 1824, John Dickens, in debt up to his ears, was arrested and sent to the Marshalsea—a London jail for debtors and smugglers that, in *Little Dorrit*, is described as "an oblong pile of barrack building, partitioned into squalid houses standing back to back, so that there were no back rooms; environed by a narrow paved yard, hemmed in by high walls duly spiked at top." As Trey Philpotts has recently revealed in "The Real Marshalsea," the prison truly was "cramped and constricted," and something of a fire trap; it was reasonably clean but not without sanitation problems. Philpotts, drawing on commission reports compiled around the time of John Dickens's imprisonment, notes that officials found the Marshalsea "to be 'tolerably clean' and noted that 'no infectious disorder' had occurred,'" but that "the prison yard overflowed with waste water and that the open drains were 'sometimes choked and offensive' and smelled bad." They observed too that the prisoners themselves were "generally healthy"; that "the most prevalent diseases were 'those arising from debauchery, dissipation, and drinking.'" Some of the prison's rooms "were even let out for prostitution"—a fact Dickens does not mention in *Little Dorrit*; indeed, writes Philpotts, a certain "licentiousness seemed to pervade the prison." "Set in this context," he adds, pointing to several of the novel's main characters, "William Dorrit's desire for Amy to flirt with young John Chivery in exchange for favors from his turnkey father and the general air of disrepute that surrounds Fanny"—Amy's sister—"take on added meaning." Dickens, then, "renders the sordidness of the real Marshalsea, but only indirectly, his characters, as it were, protected by mid-Victorian morality."

The Dickens family found a way for their own daughter, another Fanny, to stay on as a student at the Royal Academy of Music. But Charles wasn't so fortunate. Unlike his sister, he was pulled from school and put to work at a factory, a "crazy, tumbledown old house," as Dickens would later recall it—a place "literally overrun with rats." Here, Dickens endured endless days sticking labels on pots of black polish. There were, of course, worse fates for twelve-year-old boys in Victorian London. Dickens was not starving. He did not sleep huddled up in the streets. But he earned little, and most of that went back to his family. He lived alone in a cheap rented room, separated from his younger siblings, who stayed with his parents in cramped quarters at the Marshalsea. Michael Allen has convincingly shown that Dickens probably spent nearly a year working for Warren's Blacking Factory—not just three or four months as previous scholars tended to believe. Whatever the duration, Dickens's stint as a child laborer in a dingy factory had a searing effect on his emerging sensibility. Like most clever children of his class, Dickens had imagined a happy future for himself, a steady ascent through school to some sure and respected place in society. But now, verging on adolescence, Dickens felt abandoned and stuck. Known at the factory as "the little gentleman," he worked side by side with unschooled boys who were born poor—and doomed to stay that way. Years later, Dickens told Forster, one of his closest friends as well as his first biographer, that

no words can express the secret agony of my soul as I sunk into this companionship; compared these everyday associates with those of my happier childhood; and felt my early hopes of growing up to be a learned and distinguished man crushed in my breast. The deep remembrance of the sense I had of being utterly neglected and hopeless; of the shame I felt in the position; of the misery it was to my young heart to believe that, day by day, what I had learned, and thought, and delighted in, and raised my fancy and my emulation up by, was passing away from me, never to be brought back any more; cannot be written. . . . My whole nature was so penetrated with the grief and humiliation of such considerations, that even now, famous and caressed and happy, I often forget in my dreams that I have a

dear wife and children; even that I am a man; and wander desolately back
to that time of my life.

Dickens, writes Ackroyd, "had never escaped his past—he knew
that as well as anyone—he had merely prevented it from swallowing
him up." Dickens the man retained then, at some level, that fear of
collapse and disconnection, of complete and total abandonment—
what Ackroyd calls "that childhood terror of vagabondage." And not
just vagabondage. The experience seems to have left Dickens
acutely sensitive to confinement of any kind.

It might have been "shame" and "humiliation" that kept Dickens
from chatting freely about his childhood's darkest days. But he
wrote about them repeatedly, in varying ways, in novel after novel.
This is not to suggest that, like less imaginative writers, Dickens
simply recycled events and episodes from his life, touching them up
a bit; none of his novels—not even *Copperfield*—should be read
simply as thinly veiled autobiography. Still, Dickens's novels are
filled with wanderers, debtors, outcasts; with oppressed workers and
prisoners of all kinds. They feature wayward fathers—and characters
who experience sudden loss and misfortune and financial insecurity;
they repeatedly show orphans and other suffering children left
vulnerable in an often brutal world they could not have made, and
find hard to understand.

After several months at the Marshalsea, John Dickens—helped by
a small legacy—reached an agreement with his creditors and was
released from jail. (Incidentally, imprisonment for debt would
remain rather common for some decades; one major reform, the
"Bankruptcy Bill" of 1861, passed six years after the first
appearance of *Little Dorrit*, limited such imprisonment for no more
than a year.) Although the family's finances would remain shaky,
Charles was now freed from the factory and returned to
school—despite the objections of his mother, who had come to
count on his small but steady contributions to the household fund,
and who thus, however unwittingly, reinforced the fear of
abandonment the young Dickens already so keenly felt. ("I never
afterwards forgot," Dickens later wrote, "I never shall forget, I never
can forget, that my mother was warm for my being sent back.")
Dickens, hiding the facts of his recent hardship, did well during his
two years at the Wellington Academy in London—although the
place seems to have triggered his loathing for the crude and often

brutal pedagogical methods that still prevailed in Britain's schools. Dickens called the headmaster "by far the most ignorant man I have ever had the pleasure to know, who was one of the worst-tempered men perhaps that ever lived, whose business it was to make as much out of us and to put as little into us as possible"—a description that was later confirmed, Ackroyd notes, by those who were Dickens's contemporaries at the school.

At fifteen, Dickens left the Wellington House Academy. His formal schooling—what Dickens himself called his "irregular rambling education"—was now complete. And he now signed on as a low-level clerk for Ellis & Blackmore, a London legal firm. Here, as at school, Dickens was viewed by his supervisors and mates as a cheerful, dutiful fellow fast with the jokes. But here too Dickens seems to have seethed, quietly forming a hypercritical view of those who make their living in the law—a view that surfaces repeatedly in his fiction. By now, John Dickens—having lost his government job—had settled into a second career, as a reporter covering the House of Commons. Charles followed suit. And like Copperfield he soon mastered "the mystery of shorthand writing and reading"—then a must for any boy entering the journalistic field. After a stint as a freelance covering London's courts, Dickens joined the staff of the *Mirror of Parliament* (which his uncle John Barrow owned), and was soon widely hailed for his prompt and accurate parliamentary reports. Although Dickens's peers in the Parliament press corps— they numbered nearly one hundred—respected his precocious skills, Dickens, easily bored, soon wearied of what Copperfield calls "the dreary debates," the "music of the parliamentary bagpipes," the "old drone."

During this period Dickens's love for the theater continued to grow. In later years, he recalled that he now "went to some theatre every night," always "studying the bills first, and going to see where there was the best acting," but generally watching productions that were not, as Ackroyd puts it, "of the first rank"—including "Gothic melodrama, corrupted Shakespeare, sentimental comedy, domestic farce, romantic drama, burletta, extravaganza, the whole gamut of early nineteenth-century drama in which sentimentality was matched only by grotesquerie, pathos by sensationalism." At this point, Dickens still planned for a stage career of his own. He was, his friends would remember, unusually skilled at imitating Charles Matthews and other leading actors and singers of the day. In fact,

Dickens's talent as a mimic was legendary among his friends, and is of course clearly evident in his fiction, where vividly drawn characters become convincing through the precise depiction of carefully chosen tendencies and quirks. In early 1832, Dickens landed an audition at Covent Garden after informing the manager that "I believed I had a strong perception of character and oddity, and a natural power of reproducing in my own person what I observed in others." But on the day of the audition Dickens found himself sick with a cold. He stayed home. Ackroyd suggests that "never can there have been a more fortunate illness," for Dickens never renewed his application, and was drawn further into the world of letters instead. What of Dickens's actual acting skills? John Forster wrote that Dickens "had the powers of projecting himself into shapes and suggestions of his fancy which is one of the marvels of creative imagination, and what he desired to express he became." But Forster also notes that Dickens's strength "was rather in the vividness and variety of his assumptions than in the completeness, finish, or ideality he could give to any part of them"—implying, then, that Dickens was better at imitation and improvisation than at acting in the more classic sense. Ackroyd thinks that Dickens "would not have been a great stage actor; he was too small for romantic leads, and there was a certain spareness and lightness about him which would have made him suitable really only for servants, dandies and assorted comic roles."

Around this time Dickens fell deeply in love with Maria Beadnell, the daughter of a London banker. Maria was a stunner, and widely considered a prize catch. Dickens wooed her earnestly, passionately; indeed, decades later, when Dickens and Maria began again to correspond, he told her that "you made me wretchedly happy . . . the most innocent, the most ardent, and the most disinterested days of my life had you for their Sun." But his efforts were in vain. Maria kept a flock of suitors, enjoyed playing the flirt and, in due course, married a man who ran a sawmill in Finsbury. And while Maria's parents were always on cordial terms with young Charles (or "Mr. Dickin" as Mrs. Beadnell distractedly called him), they never deemed him a serious candidate for Maria's hand. His father was, after all, a bankrupt. Dickens's own prospects seemed limited: he was presumably destined to remain a scrapping Fleet Streeter with scarcely a quid to his name. This class-based rebuff—this dousing of strong desire—also marked Dickens for

years to come. He told Forster that his failure with Maria left him
with "a habit of suppression" that "I know is no part of my original
nature, but which makes me chary of showing my affections, even
to my children, except when they are very young." His novels often
include unsuitable suitors pining for girls they cannot win—one
thinks of Kit Nubbles in *The Old Curiosity Shop*, for example, and
Young John Chivery in *Little Dorrit*. The Beadnell affair, one
assumes, propelled Dickens into an early—and unfortunate—
marriage. It also pushed him even harder to succeed.

That success was remarkably close at hand. Dickens was now
broadening the range of his writing, placing a series of light and
witty features in various places, including the *Morning Chronicle*,
where he was now reporting full time. Some of these pieces were
included in Dickens's first book, *Sketches by Boz* (1836), which also
features drawings by George Cruikshank—one of the period's best-
known illustrators. In later years, Dickens described these "first
attempts at authorship" as "extremely crude and ill-considered, and
bearing obvious marks of haste and inexperience." In fact, they do
show something of the same sort of stylistic self-consciousness and
mocking bravado that one often finds among clever and perceptive
undergraduates who—having stepped forever out of childhood—
have started to suspect that much about adult life is pathetic and
absurd. In *Sketches by Boz*, Dickens's sentimental side is somewhat
more subdued; often he is cheeky and ironic as he starts to display
his continuing ability to examine the world from an odd perch, a
different angle—almost as if he were seeing it for the first time.
"Boz" is like an anthropologist, or like an extraterrestrial, zeroing in
with brilliant precision and richly accumulative detail on what the
less astute or more jaded might well ignore. For Boz, as for the very
best essayists, the familiar often looks foreign: the world is exotic
and odd, and described with gusto. He takes us, for example, to
"brokers' shops," these "second-hand furniture repositories" that run
along London's backstreets and that brim with "goods adapted to the
taste, or rather to the means, of cheap purchasers" and where "you
walk through groves of deceitful, showy-looking furniture, and
where the prospect is occasionally enlivened by a bright red, blue,
and yellow hearth-rug, embellished with the pleasing device of a
mail-coach at full speed, or a strange animal, supposed to have been
originally intended for a dog, with a mass of worsted-work in his
mouth, which conjecture has likened to a basket of flowers." Boz

goes as well to a pawnbroker's shop, where he watches "the jewelled shopman," and the "old sallow-looking woman" at the counter, telling him to "make haste," for "my two grandchildren's locked up at home, and I'm afeer'd of the fire." He sees a young prostitute at the shop, her dress "miserably poor but extremely gaudy." And he is sympathetic as he shows her "rich satin gown with its faded trimmings, the worn-out thin shoes, and pink silk stockings, the summer bonnet in winter, and the sunken face, where a daub of rouge only serves as an index to the ravages of squandered health never to be regained, and lost happiness never to be restored." Elsewhere Boz strolls down an alley near "the back of Fleet Street." It is night: he notes the gutter that "ran down the centre of the alley—all the sluggish odours of which had been called forth by the rain." *Sketches by Boz* is thick with details of this sort—with rich proof of Dickens's scrupulous note-taking skills: his brilliant attentiveness to the city's citizens, its sights and sounds and smells.

In these "sketches" we find a series of still-recognizable human types, reminding us of Dickens's delight in classifying and cartooning. Some of these portraits have an edge—are less sympathetic than cruel. Some are simply amusing; many are relevant, reminding us that while centuries pass certain types endure; that there are, perhaps, but a finite number of blossoms on the great human stalk. Thus we meet, among others, "The Poetical Young Gentlemen," all intensity and affectation, a figure whose "countenance is of a plaintive and melancholy cast," and whose "manner is abstracted and bespeaks affliction of soul"; he "often talks about being an outcast and wanting a kindred spirit." Meanwhile "The Couple Who Dote upon Their Children" will, Boz observes, pass an entire evening going on and on about their offspring, who "are either prodigies of good health or prodigies of bad health; whatever they are, they must be prodigies." Such people are, of course, incorrigible bores, who "cannot be said to be actuated by a general love for these engaging little people (which would be a great excuse); for they are apt to underrate and entertain a jealousy of any children but their own. If they examined their own hearts, they would, perhaps, find at the bottom of all this, more self-love and egotism than they think of. Self-love and egotism are bad qualities, of which the unrestrained exhibition, though it may be sometimes amusing, never fails to be wearisome and unpleasant. Couples who dote upon their children, therefore, are best avoided."

Dickens's later works offer a sustained attack on "self-love and egotism" in more virulent forms. In this regard, he joins the ranks of countless writers of his age—from Tocqueville to George Meredith to Thomas Huxley—who in varying ways addressed the moral and ethical implications of selfishness or "individualism" in all of its forms. These sketches also signal Dickens's abiding interest in crime and punishment. Boz offers a sober visit to the notorious Newgate Prison, and to London's criminal courts, where a woman "of decent appearance, though evidently poor, and a boy of about fourteen or fifteen," her son, have had to face once more the hard fact of the law. "Their little history," Dickens writes, was far from unusual in the teeming, impoverished quarters he would soon depict more fully in *Oliver Twist*; it was, in fact "obvious." The boy "had formed dissolute connexions; idleness had led to crime." When Dickens spots this pair, the boy is fresh from his release, and the mother, "still hoping to reclaim him, had been waiting at the gate to implore him to return home." Dickens's depiction of this troubled mother and her troublesome son again reveals his instinctive capacity for sympathizing with people who must struggle on the margins of "respectable" society; it has a sharp, photographic quality unfaded by time. What Boz sees, we too see:

We cannot forget the boy; he descended the steps with a dogged look, shaking his head with an air of bravado and obstinate determination. They walked a few paces, and paused. The woman put her hand upon his shoulder in an agony of entreaty, and the boy sullenly raised his head as if in refusal. It was a brilliant morning, and every object looked fresh and happy in the broad, gay sunlight; he gazed round him for a few moments, bewildered with the brightness of the scene, for it was long since he had beheld anything save the gloomy walls of a prison. Perhaps the wretchedness of his mother made some impression on the boy's heart; perhaps some undefined recollection of the time when he was a happy child, and she his only friend and best companion, crowded on him—he burst into tears; and covering his face with one hand, and hurriedly placing the other in his mother's, walked away with her.

Dickens's big break came when, in 1836, William Hall, an aspiring publisher, asked him to come up with a text of some sort meant to accompany a series of comical drawings featuring the hapless members of a Cockney sporting club. Dickens accepted the deal, but only if the drawings complemented *his* words—not the other way around. Hall agreed, and arranged to publish what became *The Posthumous Papers of the Pickwick Club* as a monthly serial, following a format employed earlier in Pierce Egan's *Life in London; or, the Day and Night Scenes of Jerry Hawthorne, Esq. and Corinthian Tom*—known otherwise as *Tom and Jerry.* Egan's work, published between 1821 and 1823, had been hugely popular. But *The Pickwick Papers* proved more so. After a slow start, sales of *The Pickwick Papers* went ballistic, and Dickens's first novel, which appeared in twenty parts, became one of the most successful ventures in British publishing history, sparking many imitations and dramatizations—even consumer products linked, however tenuously, to Dickens's fictional figures. Pickwick, indeed, became all the rage. There were scores of imitations: *Pickwick Abroad, Posthumous Notes of the Pickwickian Club, The Pickwick Comic Almanac, The Pickwick Treasury of Wit.* There were Pickwick hats, Pickwick coats, Pickwick cigars—even a "Boz" cabriolet. Dickens's fluid plot and likable characters clearly played the largest part in the book's wide appeal; its sales started to fly soon after the appearance of Sam Weller, Pickwick's street-smart valet. Weller is humorous, the classic Cockney type; but Dickens gives him a certain dignity too. Without his valet, Pickwick the "gentleman" would in fact be quite lost in a world that, as Dickens shows, abounds with lovely and happy things, but is also quite full of duplicity, disappointment, and loss. Moreover "this book," writes Ackroyd, "was in fact *reaching* the people whom it idealized, the locksmith in Liverpool no less than the doctor in London." It appealed "to a national audience at precisely the time when it could effectively and cheaply reach such a national audience; in these first decades of the nineteenth century new ways of manufacturing paper, the accelerated speed of printing, improvements in transport and in the network of distribution meant that the demands of a middle-class public could more easily be met." The method of serial publication proved particularly shrewd. "Serialisation," writes Ackroyd, "encourages suspense and maintains the continuity of interest which more conventional publication *in toto* would have precluded, and there is no doubt also that serial publication encouraged precisely the kind of breathless, and almost topical, excitement which the newspapers also satisfied." From *Pickwick,* Dickens and his publishers learned a lot. All of his

subsequent novels first appeared in weekly or monthly parts. Before
Pickwick, "Boz" was a writer to watch. Now he was a household
word.

Dickens was now setting up his own household as a newly
married man. His wife, Catherine, was the daughter of the journalist
and critic George Hogarth, who in years past had been a friend of
one of Dickens's greatest literary heroes: Walter Scott. Dickens
quickly felt at ease with the Hogarths. They took books seriously.
They were, in a sense, "shabby genteel"—more like his own family
than the wealthy Bardells. Dickens was certainly drawn to Mary
Hogarth, Catherine's younger sister. His fondness for Catherine
herself is made plain in letters written before and during their
marriage, which lasted for more than twenty years and produced ten
children (Dickens, it seems, simply liked having a baby about), and
whose names, at least the boys among them—Charles, Walter
Landor, Francis Jeffrey, Alfred Tennyson, Sydney Smith, Henry
Fielding, and Edward Bulwer-Lytton—give us a good indication of
Dickens's literary tastes. But as Edgar Johnson notes, Dickens's
early letters to Catherine also show certain "reservations." Before his
marriage, writes Johnson, Dickens seems to have viewed Catherine
"from a certain judicial if affectionate elevation." As the years
passed, these "reservations" became irritations as the many
differences—and similarities—between the two became clear. Both
were prone to long, dark moods. But Catherine, unlike her husband,
could not also hit the high notes. She had little of his spontaneous
energy. Nor did she share his zest for carrying out all tasks in an
orderly, punctual way. Like many children deeply disturbed by
disorienting change and disorder, Dickens as an adult grew obsessed
with household tidiness: in later years he would subject his family
to barrackslike inspection sessions meant to insure that all was quite
clean and right in its place. And he would come to complain
particularly of Catherine's "indescribable lassitude of character."

Dickens's marriage is a complex story and, like any intimate
relationship, can never be fully understood by anyone squinting in
from outside; moreover, as Angus Wilson once complained, "the
sexual life of Charles Dickens, like that of most Victorians, has
become a shop-soiled subject." But Wilson himself would note, not
unfairly, that Dickens was "a strongly sensual man, he had a deep
social and emotional need for family life and love, he had a
compensating claustrophobic dislike of the domestic scene, and he

woke up to these contradictions in his sexual make-up very late."
William J. Palmer picks up on these tensions in his entertaining
fictional re-creations of Dickens-as-detective. In *The Highwayman
and Mr. Dickens*, for example, Palmer's narrator—the novelist
Wilkie Collins—notes: "I realise now, looking back upon those days
when we feared nothing, that Dickens and I were constantly shaking
the bars of our cells trying somehow to escape all the restrictions
and hypocrisies of the age of Victoria. And yet, our sexual
possession was a prison as well. His beloved Ellen [the actress who
played so large a role in Dickens's later life], my Meg, they were
the pages of our passion to be free, and yet they made us prisoners
of their fire."

One sees these conflicting strains in Dickens's novels. Often, they
show marriage to be a necessary refuge for sensitive souls in a cold
and brutal world. But they do not abound with happily married men.
Some of these husbands, like Bumble in *Oliver Twist*, are part of the
long comic tradition of the hapless, henpecked sap. But *David
Copperfield*—Dickens's greatest novel—is to a large extent the
account of one man's miserable marriage—and so, in its way, is
Great Expectations (1861), wherein one watches Joe Gargery
stoically, if not stupidly, endure the daily abuse of Pip's shrewish
sister, perhaps the least-likable figure in all of Dickens's later
fiction. Copperfield presumably finds happiness with Agnes
Wickfield. And so does Arthur Clennam with Amy in *Little Dorrit*.
But significantly, Dickens declines showing these unions in bloom.
Clearly Agnes and Amy are meant to be attractive women. But they
remain the wooed—not the won. They do not really become wives.

The success of both *Pickwick* and *Oliver Twist* (which started to
run in *Bentley's Miscellany* even before the *Pickwick* series came to
a close) not only enabled Dickens to start his marriage prosperously,
but gave him a new sense of financial security he would
understandably prove reluctant to lose. In the winter of 1837,
Dickens rented a house on Doughty Street, in Bloomsbury, now the
home of a Dickens museum. Here, Dickens's first child, Charles
Culliford Boz Dickens, was born in January 1837. And here, only
a few months later, Mary Hogarth died suddenly, at seventeen, of
what doctors termed heart failure. (Although more recently, the late
William Ober, a pathologist with a long interest in literary subjects,
noted that "the presenting symptoms and subsequent course" of
Mary's case "are typical of a sudden subarachnoid hemorrhage, a

lesion that was not appreciated in the 1830s.") Dickens had grown increasingly attached to Mary, who, with his brother Fred, had been a part of the Doughty Street household. Her death had a deep effect on his still-maturing sensibility, as well as on his still-developing art. As Ackroyd puts it, Dickens now endured "the most powerful sense of loss and pain he was ever to experience." It is impossible, of course—and unnecessary, really—to know precisely why Dickens felt so strongly about his sister-in-law. The roots of his attraction very probably did stem, at least in part, from his growing sense that it was Mary, not Catherine, who was his more perfect mate. In any event, Mary did become his "idealised image of the female"— "young, beautiful, and good," to use the words that Dickens himself ordered for her gravestone. She was the model for the many virtuous, virginal young women who now began to appear repeatedly in Dickens's fiction, including Little Nell in *The Old Curiosity Shop*, who like Mary dies young, and who like Pickwick earned international fame.

Both *The Old Curiosity Shop* and *Barnaby Rudge* (1841), Dickens's fifth novel, first appeared in *Master Humphrey's Clock*, a "miscellany" he now established roughly on the model of such famous eighteenth-century periodicals as the *Tatler*, the *Spectator*, and Goldsmith's *Bee*. But *Master Humphrey's Clock* stopped with *Barnaby Rudge*, an historical novel based loosely on events surrounding the Gordon Riots, or the "No Popery Riots" of 1780—a chaotic but costly series of disturbances in London lead by one Lord George Gordon, who was rabidly anti-Catholic, and rabidly opposed to the looming prospect of extending Catholic rights in an officially Protestant nation. Dickens depicts Gordon as "stiff, lank, and solemn"—a strange figure in his "Puritan attire," shown at one point sitting "bolt upright upon his bony steed, with his long, straight hair, dangling about his face and fluttering in the wind; his limbs all angular and rigid, his elbows stuck out on either side ungracefully, and his whole frame jogged and shaken at every motion of his horse's feet; a more grotesque or more ungainly figure can hardly be conceived."

Dickens spent several years researching and writing *Rudge*. The book has its merits, starting with the title character, a vividly drawn simpleton, as restless as Gordon is rigid, who knows nothing of politics but is lured nonetheless into the mayhem—into the burning and pillaging that goes on for days and that Dickens sets down with precise detail and plain relish. Some critics, including Angus Wilson, have discerned in the more ambitious structure of *Barnaby Rudge* signs of Dickens's growing artistic maturity. But the novel sold poorly—at least when compared to his previous works. Its plot is slow, and today's readers will find it a particularly rough road to hoe. *Barnaby Rudge* does not sustain the immediacy and intensity of Dickens's best work. Barnaby, with his clever pet raven, can hold one's interest, and so does the Varden family, around whom much of the action revolves. But there is something oddly secondhand about *Barnaby Rudge*, which also features several stock figures who appear to have been drawn less from life than from the pages of other historical and Gothic novels. *Rudge* owes, in fact, to Scott's *Heart of Midlothian* (1818).

By the end of 1841 Dickens found himself—not for the last time—drained. Convinced that a long trip would bring rejuvenation, Dickens accepted his publisher's offer to undertake, and then write about, an extensive tour of the United States. Thus in January 1842, Dickens, along with Catherine and her attendant, Anne Browne, boarded the steamship *Britannia*—Cunard's first transatlantic liner—and embarked on a six-month journey that took them not only to Boston, New York, Baltimore, and Washington, but to such exotic "western" locales as Louisville, St. Louis, and Sandusky, Ohio, and then more briefly into Canada. Dickens began the journey burning with enthusiasm and hope. Like many Europeans before and since, he was eager to explore a new nation founded on the ideals of liberty and equality, an ocean away from Europe's ancient corruptions and feuds. Because Dickens was so hopeful about the wonders and delights that awaited him in America, his disappointment proved particularly keen. This is not to say that Dickens loathed everything about the United States. He established friendships with several notable natives, including Washington Irving and Henry Wadsworth Longfellow. As his *American Notes* reveals, Dickens loved Niagara Falls, but not the off-color jokes and scrawls—the "ribaldry" he found in the visitor's registry. ("It is humiliating enough," Dickens writes in the *Notes*, "to know that there are among men, brutes so obscene and worthless, that they can delight in laying their miserable profanations upon the very steps of Nature's greatest altar.") He admired Boston's public facilities—including its prison system and its asylums, finding them both efficient and humane. In Cincinnati he met "intelligent, courteous,

and agreeable" people: he found this still-new Ohio city "beautiful
and thriving." Dickens was especially impressed by Cincinnati's
public school system—"one of the most interesting in America."
But Dickens's complaints grew as the trip wore on. This new
nation was, he rather quickly realized, rough, excessive, crude—and
the home, then as today, of the world's largest collection of bores.
Many, moreover, were relentless chewers of tobacco who spat,
without restraint, everywhere. And they lacked discretion, often
assembling to gape at Dickens the celebrity when Dickens the man
simply wanted to be left alone. The American press, Dickens
learned, was no more discreet; it was both sensationalistic and
unfair, inclined to dish up a steady diet of scandal, gossip, and
violence—and worse, to run repeated attacks on Dickens himself.
These attacks were triggered by Dickens's decision, from the very
start of his tour, to raise over and over the issue of international
copyright. Dickens was angry because American publishers and
periodicals repeatedly reprinted, without compensation, the works of
numerous British authors, including himself. This was piracy, he
reasonably argued, and should be stopped. But of course, there was
scant support for international copyright protection among American
editors and publishers, who in the midst of hard economic times
were in a fierce fight for readers at a time of growing press
competition. They found some merriment, thus, in depicting the
young author of *Pickwick* and *Oliver Twist* as a greedy charlatan
and an ungrateful guest. (At least one paper wrote disapprovingly of
Dickens's "get-up," his red waistcoats and gold jewelry, noting that
"his whole appearance is foppish, and partakes of the flash order.")
Dickens, always sensitive to criticism, was deeply hurt by the more
vicious of these attacks; "I vow to heaven," he wrote one friend,
"that the scorn and indignation I have felt under this unmanly and
ungenerous treatment has been to me an amount of agony such as
I never experienced since my birth." By the end of his trip, Dickens
was homesick, weary, and quite certain that he had seen the
limitations of democracy—at least in its American guise. In
America, and writing home to his friend, the actor William
Macready, Dickens observes: "I infinitely prefer a liberal Monarchy
. . . to such a Government as this. . . . And England, even England,
bad and faulty as the old land is, and miserable as millions of her
people are, rises in the comparison."

Dickens's own criticism of America was unbuckled in *Martin Chuzzlewit* (1844), his sixth novel, which also includes two of his most memorable creations, the oily Seth Pecksniff and the well-oiled Sairey Gamp. Sales of *Chuzzlewit* never hit the heights, but Dickens's high place in the world of English letters was never really in question, and throughout the decade he remained an increasingly visible man of letters whose circle of friends and acquaintances came to include many of the period's most prominent literary and theatrical figures. The pompous but loyal Forster, for one, Dickens's biographer, was a barrister with a literary bent, and with much literary influence. Forster was a prominent reviewer; his *Life and Adventures of Oliver Goldsmith* (1848) was a successful study of an author who was not only greatly admired by the diverse likes of Dr. Johnson and Lord Byron, but whose popularity remained strong throughout much of the nineteenth century. Dickens was now also on close terms with, among others, Tennyson, Leigh Hunt, Mark Lemon, and Edward Bulwer-Lytton, with whom he helped organize "An Association for the Protection of Literature" that, throughout the 1840s, worked to assure that authors received fairer compensation for their published writings, in Britain as well as in the United States. Most notably, Dickens became friends with Thomas Carlyle (1795-1881), the greatest "prophet" of his age, and the writer who most influenced the ideational content of Dickens's own work.

Because today he is largely ignored, it is difficult for readers to appreciate the range and depth of Carlyle's influence in Britain among writers and intellectuals during the middle decades of the nineteenth century, and particularly in the 1840s, when the long list of his friends and followers included not only Dickens, but Thackeray, Browning, Elizabeth Gaskell, Charles Kingsley, and Thomas Arnold. Among his contemporaries, many assumed—with Harriet Martineau—that Carlyle "most essentially modified the mind of his time." Obviously, one cannot assert that Carlyle accounts for, say, 70 percent of Dickens's own political and social thought. Dickens read Carlyle selectively—a fact that may account for the condescending attitude that Carlyle tended to show when discussing Dickens's own published writings. But Dickens never hid his admiration for—or indebtedness to—the author of such works as *Sartor Resartus* (1833) and *The French Revolution* (1837). Dickens once told Forster that he would "go at all times much farther to see

Carlyle than any man alive." He told his son, Henry Dickens, that Carlyle was "the man who most influenced him." He told Carlyle himself that "I am always trying to go your way."

This, for many, is an odd pairing. After all, Dickens is still billed as Britain's "best loved" writer of fiction. And there seems little that is lovable about Thomas Carlyle. He has few readers—and far fewer champions. True, Carlyle is still studied—often grudgingly and in brief snatches—in English Literature Surveys and graduate seminars. Students discover a brilliant, original, unsystematic, and sometimes puzzling writer. Throughout his career, Carlyle is often ecstatic and rhapsodic as he writes of the spiritual mysteries of the universe. He is sincerely concerned with the suffering of the poor. He is impressively passionate in his earlier works when he condemns war, or mocks the useless and parasitic aristocracy. But in his later works, Carlyle grows rather more belligerent, more hostile to democracy, more elitist, more enthralled with the idea of dictatorship as a means of solving social problems with both grandeur and efficiency. Carlyle's *Latter-Day Pamphlets* (1850) attack the idea of universal suffrage, and dismiss the notion that much social good will ever grow out of, for example, philanthropy and prison reform. He still supports universal education; but he also likes the idea of a bigger army—one filled from the ranks of the unemployed and kept at the command of a right-thinking, God-fearing strongman.

Carlyle thus can also be stern, didactic, and gruff—striking one as a curious mix of John Calvin and Karl Marx; of D. H. Lawrence and Benito Mussolini. Students thus meet a figure who produced long shelves of unique prose that is at once dense and colloquial, and whose growing obsession with "great men" and "hero-worship" played at least some part in creating a growing intellectual climate that—some decades later—proved just right for the rise of fascist ideology. At various times, Carlyle hailed not only Goethe and Robert Burns, but also Otto von Bismarck, Frederick the Great, and José Gaspar Rodríguez Francia—aka *El Supremo*—the dictator who ruled Paraguay from 1814 to 1840. We read Carlyle asserting that "all human society is founded on 'Hero-worship,'"; that "We all love great men; love, venerate, and bow down submissive before great men—nay, can we honestly bow down to anything else?" One recognizes the truth in this; indeed, it seems self-evident. Still, in light of this century's history one grows uneasy.

Dickens, for his part, was not especially attracted to Carlyle's theory of heroes. He did not share Carlyle's nostalgia for an idealized, preindustrial, medieval past. But again, Dickens did have his own strong authoritarian streak; he identified with the ideals of democracy, but—like Carlyle—feared that in the long run it might lead to social disorder on a wide, intolerable scale. Dickens was deeply drawn to Carlyle's enraged analysis of Britain's social and moral ills. Britain's power and wealth in the nineteenth century has often been exaggerated; as the Boer War would finally reveal, it was—for much of the century—a nation stretched thin. Still, there was more and more money about, and more visibly wealthy people, and an expanding middle class. There was of course growing industrialization, more scientific innovation—and a growing sense, backed by the nation's growing press, that human progress was centered in Britain, and that the United Kingdom was destined to lead the world.

Still, as such works as *Past and Present* (1843) made clear, Carlyle was not impressed. Despite its growing wealth and prosperity and influence, Britain was, Carlyle believed, a sick society—its values grossly distorted and tragically misplaced. It had lost its sense of unity, of wholeness, and had become instead a nation of grasping individuals pursuing dubious individual aims. As a result, "our life is not a mutual helpfulness," but rather, "cloaked under dire laws-of-war, named 'fair competition' and so forth, it is a mutual hostility." Carlyle's Britain was full of rapaciousness and greed, driven largely by what he called "Mammon-worship," a "melancholy creed" based on the notion that "Cash-payment" is "the sole relation of human beings." It was a place where too many were left spiritually empty and economically crushed. "England," he wrote, "with its plethoric wealth, has as yet made nobody rich; it is an enchanted wealth, and belongs as yet to nobody. We might ask, Which of us has it enriched? In Poor and Rich, instead of noble thrift and plenty, there is idle luxury alternating with mean scarcity and inability. We have sumptuous garnitures for our Life, but have forgotten to *live* in the middle of them. It is an enchanted wealth; no man of us can yet touch it. The class of men who feel that they are truly better off by means of it, let them give us their name!"

Carlyle in his adulthood cannot be described as an orthodox Christian; indeed, many of his contemporaries, like Dickens, "found relief," notes A. L. Le Quesne, "in Carlyle's outspoken denunciation of the Churches as mere hollow shells of what had once been authentic symbols of the divine instinct in men." But like Lawrence, Carlyle was in his way not only a preacher, but a deeply religious writer—and one much influenced by the conservative Protestant training he had received as a child. Carlyle, reared in a small Scotch village in the Western Lowlands, wrote often of the importance of work and the value of dignified labor. Dickens certainly shared this view, although not to a puritanical extreme. Dickens stands as one of the most industrious fellows of his century; but—as noted above—his fiction consistently attacks the deadening notion, still at the core of Anglo-American middle-class culture, that work is, basically, all there is to life, and that one's identity is—and must be—tied inextricably to one's job. Thus Wemmick, one of the more sympathetic figures in *Great Expectations*, rigorously maintains—far from his dull and dubious duties as clerk to the shady Jaggers—a "Castle" where he can engage happily in innocent pleasure and play. Still, when Carlyle calls life "a most earnest thing" and a "serious matter," he is using phrases that Dickens would repeatedly echo. Carlyle's view of the world, like Dickens's, clearly reflects a rather diverse combination of philosophical and theological strains; but in the end it is highly Romantic, stressing even more than the value of sound work and discipline an intense celebration of life's beauties and mysteries—of natural wonders that, Carlyle believed, are the result of a divine purpose that is well above and far beyond the mechanistic systems of daily living, and that only a fool or a charlatan would claim fully to understand. "Science," Carlyle writes, "has done much for us; but it is a poor science that would hide from us the great deep sacred infinitude of Nescience whither we can never penetrate, on which all science swims as a mere superficial film. This world, after all our science and sciences, is still a miracle; wonderful, inscrutable, *magical* and more, to whosoever will *think* it."

Again, one cannot convincingly contend that it was from Carlyle that Dickens derived *all* of his biases and beliefs; that, in the last analysis, Dickens simply remolds Carlyle's philosophy into a more accessible fictional form. Carlyle had his own distinctive, highly idiosyncratic voice. Dickens did not have Carlyle's erudition, his deep grounding in German philosophy and literature. Moreover, the nature of the cultural criticism that both men practiced was common enough in their era; many novelists, poets, and prose writers—in both Britain and America—were similarly concerned with cultural changes that swirled in the wake of the industrial revolution, including the growing obsession with status, efficiency, and wealth. In Britain, John Ruskin—as influential in his way as Carlyle—wrote repeatedly, often movingly, against the spread of materialism and the cult of efficiency, warning of the rise of those who "look to wealth as the only means of pleasure," as well as of those who through indifference or by design add to "the degradation of the workman," and thus to the cheapening of human life. In America, Henry Thoreau, for one, similarly observed that increasingly, "this world is a place of business"; that, everywhere, "it is nothing but work, work, work"; that "there is nothing, not even crime, more opposed to poetry, to philosophy, ay, to life itself, than this incessant business." "There is no more fatal blunderer than he who consumes the greater part of his life getting his living," wrote Thoreau in "Life Without Principle" (1863)—a statement that applies perfectly to many of Dickens's characters, including Scrooge and Mr. Dombey. Robert Louis Stevenson—born four years after *Dombey and Son* first appeared—spoke throughout his career for a host of Dickensian virtues, perhaps most famously in "An Apology for Idlers," where he observes that "there is a sort of dead-alive, hackneyed people about, who are scarcely conscious of living except in the exercise of some conventional occupation." "Perpetual devotion to what a man calls his business, is only to be sustained by perpetual neglect of many other things." This too is Scrooge: the cramped, obsessed figure forced to learn what Stevenson too would come to know—namely, that "a happy man or woman is a better thing to find than a five-pound note."

A *Christmas Carol* appeared in a richly illustrated edition in December 1843, as *Martin Chuzzlewit* continued its serial run. A *Christmas Carol* sold well, but proved to be something of an economic bust, for it was rather badly advertised, and its low sale price did not quite cover its unusually high costs of production. Though often called "timeless," A *Christmas Carol* is very much rooted in its time, with direct references, for example, to the controversial Poor Law Act of 1834; or the proposed Sunday Observance Bill, which aimed to shut certain shops and places of recreation on Sundays—a bill Dickens, not surprisingly, strongly opposed. (Decades later, in 1864, Dickens—to his eternal credit—was still attacking those do-gooders, busybodies, and prudes who would set curbs on the leisure activities of working people; thus, in one letter, we find him urging "working men" to "declare" that "they want social rest and social recreation for themselves and their families"; and that the various "clubs" then being charitably established for their use "do not need educational pretences or flourishes." After a week of work, Dickens insisted, one should not "be afraid or ashamed of wanting to be amused and pleased.") For Scrooge, "business" is the most important activity in life. He muses hopefully that the poor will soon die off, and so "decrease the surplus population": a direct reference to an increasingly popular apocalyptic tract, Thomas Malthus's *Essay on the Principle of Population* (1803), which argued—among other things—that Britain would sooner or later find itself faced with masses of paupers it had no means to feed. One also finds in *A Christmas Carol* certain images and themes that would surface repeatedly in Dickens's work; in "Stave One," for instance, the ghost of Marley is shown dragging chains, telling Scrooge that "I wear the chain I forged in life"; that "I made it link by link, and yard by yard; I girded it on of my own free will, and of my own free will I wore it." In *Little Dorrit*, this prison motif is even more noticeable; in fact this novel often seems to suggest that simply to be born is to be imprisoned, fettered by relations and obligations that lead to misery more often than not. ("I am quite weighed down and loaded and chained in life," is how Dickens once put it to Forster, when both strangers and family members were demanding his attention and his financial aid.)

In light of the disappointing return on *A Christmas Carol*, and faced with mounting financial strains that included his father's continuing debts, Dickens decided to move his growing family for several months to Italy, then a cheaper place to live. When he returned to Britain in the summer of 1845, Dickens did not start another novel straightaway. Instead he took roles in a pair of amateur stage productions (including Bobadil in *Every Man in His Humour*), and began a series of negotiations that, in the early weeks of 1846, led him to assume the editorship of the *Daily News*—further proof that even now, well into his career as a writer of fiction, Dickens still felt close to his journalistic roots. Many of his friends warned Dickens that running a daily paper designed to compete with both the *Times* and the *Morning Chronicle* would leave him little time for writing fiction. But Dickens, ever stubborn, wanted to work for—or, more precisely, *control*—a major publication that represented what he now termed his "decidedly liberal" political biases; that backed massive educational reform, for starters, and stood against both the growing crusade for "total abstinence" and the grotesquely popular spectacle of public hangings. As Fred Kaplan notes, Dickens had long seen "the relationship between criminality and lack of education"—a theme he first struck up in *Oliver Twist*. He opposed the banning of alcohol not only because, obviously, it would deny the majority of people the pleasure of drinking moderately, but because he was "angered," in Kaplan's words, "by the widespread assertion that drunkenness was the cause of many evils rather than a result of already existing ones." "Beginning with his earliest sketches," writes Kaplan, Dickens had commonsensically and "unequivocally claimed that societies with high levels of poverty and ignorance created the conditions that encouraged high levels of crime and alcoholism."

The *Daily News* was backed largely by Bradbury and Evans, the publishers of Dickens's novels. Its staff included many of the leading lights of London journalism. It provided jobs for members of Dickens's family, including his father-in-law, George Hogarth (as music and drama critic), his uncle John Barrow (as India correspondent) and, perhaps not surprisingly, Dickens's own father, who had long been using his celebrated son's name to cadge money from all sorts of places, and who was now given a proper job supervising the paper's reporters. The *Daily News* struggled, but survived, holding its niche for many decades to come; long enough, indeed, to run slamming reviews of D. H. Lawrence's early novels. But Dickens was soon calling it the "Daily Noose," for, he realized that—as Kaplan puts it—"he had taken on tedious detail, infinite vexation, and the unanticipated frustration of problems with incompetent printers and nervous investors," some of whom opposed Dickens's reformist political views. So Dickens quit the paper within weeks of starting his job. He retained a loose affiliation; his *Pictures from Italy*, for example, first appeared serially in the *Daily News*.

Dickens's next novel, *Dombey and Son*, did well from the start, winning praise form reviewers and from Dickens's rivals, including Thackeray, who thought the lyrical, lugubrious chapter describing Paul Dombey's death was both "stupendous" and "unsurpassed." "There's no writing against such power as this," Thackeray exclaimed. "One has no chance!" Still, Dickens's place as England's leading novelist could no longer be taken for granted. New novels

by Thackeray and the Brontës, among others, were also drawing
enthusiastic readers and glowing reviews. Dickens's relationship
with Thackeray himself was sometimes tense, but the two generally
remained on cordial terms, with Thackeray sometimes recording his
open admiration for Dickens's work and its wide appeal. "All
children ought to love him," Thackeray wrote in "Charity and
Humour," first published in 1853.

I know two that do, and read his books ten times for once that they peruse
the dismal preachments of their father. I know one who, when she is happy,
reads Nicholas Nickleby; when she is unhappy, reads Nicholas Nickleby;
when she is in bed, reads Nicholas Nickleby; when she has nothing to do,
reads Nicholas Nickleby; and when she has finished the book, reads
Nicholas Nickleby over again. This candid young critic, at ten years of age,
said: "I like Mr. Dickens's books much better than yours, papa"; and
frequently expressed her desire that the latter author should write a book
like Mr. Dickens's books. Who can? Every man must say his own thoughts
in his own voice, in his own way; lucky is he who has such a charming gift
of nature as this, which brings all the children in the world trooping to him,
and being fond of him.

Dickens, who aimed always to stay cool in the most stressful
situations, never wrote—and rarely spoke—critically of his more
gifted rivals. But after *Dombey and Son* his novels do become more
ambitiously structured, showing his recognition that as the
competition intensified, he was in no position to coast. Sales of his
later novels remained strong, aided not only by his growing
reputation, but by the strong push of publicity his publishers tended
to provide. (*Dombey*—a real "weepie" as they used to say in
Hollywood—far outsold *Vanity Fair*; and, while not leaving Dickens
vastly rich, did provide him with a cushion of financial comfort he
would henceforth maintain.) Now, however, reviewers more
frequently expressed the wish to see again the more rompish air of
Dickens's earlier novels—what one called that "natural, easy," and
"Pickwickian" style.

    With *David Copperfield* appearing in monthly numbers, Dickens
began plans for a general interest magazine. He appointed himself
editor, and found in W. H. Wills an assistant as ultra-industrious as
himself. The result, *Household Words*, became a major financial and
popular success as a weekly mix of fiction, features, travel writing,
and social criticism that—as Ackroyd notes—"was not in any sense

'intellectual,'" but "rather took its place among the magazines which heralded or exploited the growth of the reading public throughout the period." From the start, Dickens was more than a figurehead. He worked closely with contributors, printers, and distributors, aiming always to ensure that the magazine remained, in Ackroyd's words, "cheerful, bright, informative and, above all readable."

The premier issue of March 30, 1850, included "A Preliminary Word" that reveals much about Dickens's aesthetic assumptions and moral aims. *Household Words* will, he promises, seek a wide audience while maintaining an optimistic tone. It will be the "comrade and friend of many thousands of people, of both sexes, and of all ages and conditions." It will bring, "into innumerable homes, from the stirring world around us, the knowledge of many social wonders, good and evil, that are not calculated to render any of us less ardently persevering in ourselves, less tolerant of one another, less faithful in the progress of mankind, less thankful for the privilege of living in this summer-dawn time." And it will avoid parochialism, treating not simply "the hopes, the enterprises, triumphs, joys, and sorrows, of this country only, but, in some degree, of those of every nation upon earth. For nothing can be a source of real interest in one of them, without concerning all the rest." This goal stems from the broader, rather more cosmopolitan view that Dickens undoubtedly derived, in part, from those eighteenth-century writers he most admired, and that deepened in the wake of his ever more frequent European jaunts. (One thinks, for example, of Addison in "The Royal Exchange" proclaiming himself—in 1711—"a citizen of the world" and celebrating a vision of the world's nations "united together by their common interest.") Indeed, as both a novelist and a journalist, Dickens rarely attacks the beliefs and practices of other nations. "Never anywhere," George Orwell writes—overlooking, perhaps, the minor case of *A Child's History of England*—does Dickens "indulge in the typical English boasting, the 'island race,' 'bulldog breed,' 'right little, tight little island' style of talk." Dickens "is very much an Englishman, but he is hardly aware of it—certainly the thought of being an Englishman does not thrill him," a singular trait at a time of growing British power. "A Preliminary Word" in *Household Words* also promises not to assume a "harsh tone," nor serve simply as a catalogue of "grim realities." It will not reflect some "mere utilitarian spirit"—but will "tenderly cherish that light of Fancy which is inherent in the human breast." *Household Words* will show "that in all familiar things, even in those which are repellant on the surface, there is Romance enough, if we will find it out"—a notion that not only informs most of Dickens's fiction (including, in a major way, his later works), but that shows his aesthetic links both to Carlyle and to the most influential poetry and prose published in England during the first decades of the nineteenth century. Dickens was a "Romantic" in almost every sense of the word. But he was also very much a Victorian—as the closing segment of his magazine's manifesto makes clear. Here Dickens celebrates movement, motion, endurance, transcendence, *progress*—values we tend to associate with Tennyson's poetry and Arnold's prose. Even *Pictures from Italy*, one of Dickens's travel books, concludes by proclaiming that "the wheel of Time is rolling for an end, and the world is, in all great essentials, better, gentler, more forbearing, and more hopeful, as it rolls!"

As it rolls to a close, Dickens's "Preliminary Word" in *Household Words* alludes to "the adventurer in the old fairy story," who "climbing towards the summit of a steep eminence on which the object of his search was stationed, was surrounded by a roar of voices, crying to him, from the stones in the way, to turn back."

All the voices *we* hear, cry Go on! The stones that call to us have sermons in them, as the trees have tongues, as there are books in the running brooks, as there is good in everything! They, and the time, cry out to us Go on! With a fresh heart, a light step, and hopeful courage, we begin the journey. The road is not so rough that it need daunt our feet: the way is not so steep that we need stop for breath, and, looking faintly down, be stricken motionless. Go on, is all we hear, Go on! In a glow already, with the air from yonder height upon us, and the inspiriting voices joining in this acclamation, we echo back the cry, and go on cheerily!

Household Words would remain bright, optimistic, and direct. Off the stands for more than a century, it remains a delight to read, providing a fascinating look at many of the trends, forces, and events that shaped Britain during the middle decades of the nineteenth century. It informs and entertains without also being patronizing or sensationalistic—an achievement that relatively few general interest magazines can match today. "Valentine's Day at the Post Office," for example—which Dickens himself wrote with Wills—offers a lively, highly informative "behind-the-scenes" look at how mail handlers of the day dealt with, among other things, bad penmanship and insufficient postage. One also finds a lengthy account of "The Troubled Water Question," which shows something of the magazine's "investigative" edge, as well as Dickens's preoccupation with issues of public health. Reading it reminds one that safe water was long one of London's major problems—and one of Dickens's chief concerns—and that, particularly in the city's poorer quarters, little had changed since 1836, when a Select Committee of the government reported that, daily, the Thames ("a deadly sewer," as Dickens called it in *Little Dorrit*) received among other cheery things, "the filth and refuse of many hundred factories; the foul and gory liquid from the slaughter-houses; and the purulent abominations from hospitals and dissecting rooms, too disgusting to detail." In issue after issue, *Household Words* highlights the worsening plight of Britain's poor. Like Dickens himself, the magazine—reform-minded, but not revolutionary—called repeatedly for the sort of significant, and now seemingly obvious, reforms in (for example) labor law and education that were eventually enacted, and not only made England a safer and more civilized place, but kept the lid on swelling social discontent. Dickens, wrote Maurois

has not only remained the great popular writer of a race: it may be said that he took a great part in shaping that race. M. Cazamian has well said that Dickens can be counted among the causes of moral order whereby England was spared a revolution. If certain shades of gentleness and sentiment have become the predominant colours in English family life, if the brutality of certain spectacles, such as public hangings, or if certain usages, such as imprisonment for debt, have vanished from British life, if the children of the poor are treated in England with some respect and kindness, these things are in part the work of Charles Dickens.

In 1851 Dickens moved his family to a house near Tavistock Square, in the Bloomsbury district of London. It was here, at "Tavistock House," that Dickens's last child was born. Here he wrote *Bleak House*, his most ambitious novel to date, and *Hard Times*, which he published in weekly installments in *Household Words*. Such productivity suggests that Dickens had become a sort of Victorian Isaac Asimov, roped to his desk, his life focused almost entirely on his editing duties and the writing of books. Nothing could be less true. Dickens was prolific because his power of discipline matched his power of imagination; over the years he stuck to a strict routine that limited his writing to one well-defined segment each day—although this segment tended to swell as a deadline loomed. Thus, at one point during the writing of *Bleak House*, Dickens was also editing *Household Words*, and adding to its pages *A Child's History of England*. But he was also again rehearsing and acting with an amateur theatrical group whose performances raised funds for one of his favorite causes: a "Guild of Literature and Art" established to provide housing and financial help for deserving artists and writers who found themselves destitute. Dickens was actively involved in public health issues (and particularly the Great Ormond Street Hospital, devoted to children's care); and, like Gladstone, he worked to help London's prostitutes, especially those seeking to reform. Thus he continued to assist Angela Burdett-Coutts—a noted philanthropist—with the administration of Urania Cottage, a "Home for Homeless Women," many of them prostitutes, in Shepherd's Bush. ("The workshop of the world gave way every night in central London to the whoreshop of the world," wrote J. B. Priestly about the city at mid-century. "An hour spent in or around Haymarket after midnight would have left any member of our own 'permissive society' speechless from shock. Foreign visitors were staggered by it. Once respectability was left behind, they were in Venusberg. Even Dostoyevsky, no wandering innocent, cried in astonishment at the prostitutes gathering in the thousands.") Undoubtedly, Dickens's decision not to hole up in his study but to stay active in his world contributed much to his success as editor, and enabled him to bring to his fiction a sense of vitality and immediacy that readers still recognize. Indeed, Dickens, a chronic and tireless walker, regularly filled his fiction and journalism with images and scenes he took in while walking incognito through London's streets, often at night.

In "Night-Walks," a later piece written for *All the Year Round*, Dickens offers an intriguing account of these wanderings—one triggered, he somewhat disingenuously records, by a prolonged bout of sleeplessness that he sought to conquer by "the brisk treatment of getting up directly after lying down, and going out, and coming home tired at sunrise." As a result of these wanderings, Dickens—aiming only "to get through the night"—found also that this state of "houselessness" brought him "into sympathetic relations with people who have no other object every night in the year." Of course, as Dickens's earlier works repeatedly show, he had long maintained much sympathy for all sorts of outcasts and wanderers: the state of restlessness, nocturnal or otherwise, was one with which he could readily identify. Here, Dickens notes the "restlessness of a great city, and the way in which it tumbles and tosses before it can get to sleep"—an image that shows well the impulse for personification that persists, often splendidly, throughout his career. And here, Dickens the reporter shows once more a particularly sharp eye for the pathetic, the grotesque—the decidedly *un*sentimental. He spots drunks in the night, who "appeared to be magnetically attracted towards each other; so that we knew when we saw one drunken object staggering against the shutters of a shop, that another drunken object would stagger up before five minutes were out, to fraternise or fight with it." "When we made a divergence from the regular species of drunkard," he adds, "the thin-armed, puff-faced, leaden-lipped gin-drinker, and encountered a rarer specimen of a more decent appearance, fifty to one but that the specimen was dressed in soiled mourning. As the street experience in the night, so the street experience in the day: the common folk who came unexpectedly into a little property, come unexpectedly into a deal of liquor."

Dickens's persistent interest in the odd workings of the mind—and in the grim fact of human failure and decline—is also displayed in this rich sketch, particularly when he muses on the "very curious disease" of "Dry Rot in men": an ailment which, he notes, can strike one quite in "the prime of life," even when one appears to be "clever" and "popular" and "suitably married." The Dry Rot, as Dickens defines it, produces "a certain slovenliness and deterioration which is not poverty, nor dirt, nor intoxication, nor ill-health, but simply Dry Rot"—a state that he seems to link closely to a fondness for "strong waters," and that results, inevitably, in "a looseness respecting everything," and finally a "crumbling to pieces." Dickens's other works similarly suggest that this fear of disorder, laxity, flabbiness was one of his most abiding concerns. Certainly he was intrigued by madness, and at times seemed rather fearful of the firmness of his own mental state; in "Night Walks" he connects himself, and everyone else, with the inhabitants of a mental asylum he passes along the way, noting that: "Are not the sane and the insane equal at night as the sane lie a dreaming? Are not all of us outside the hospital, who dream, more or less in the condition of those inside it, every night of our lives?" "Said an afflicted man to me," Dickens recalls, "when I was last in a hospital like this, 'Sir, I can frequently fly.' I was half ashamed to reflect that so could I—by night."

As his daily duties multiplied, Dickens often felt stretched and pressed by the awful fact of looming deadlines—felt, as one does, like a man tied to the tracks and fumbling with the ropes while hearing, with growing clarity, the ominous rumble of an approaching train. In April 1853 he was writing a friend: "I had got up at 5, and gone furiously to work, so that about noon I was comparatively insensible." Around the same time, he noted in a letter that too many would-be writers supposed that the creation of literature was "the easiest amusement in the world," not realizing that it required "such elements as patience, study, punctuality, determination, self-denial, training of mind and body, hours of application and seclusion."

Dickens, rather sickly as a child, was now simply, slowly, burning himself out. But he could still muster enough force not only to produce some of his best fiction—including *Little Dorrit*, and *Great Expectations* (1860-61). He continued to travel to the Continent and elsewhere, and to deepen his involvement in the theatrical world. In fact, as he worked on his final novels, Dickens's involvement with the stage was at its peak. In January 1857, for example, he took on the staging of *The Frozen Deep*, a rousing melodrama inspired by the exploits of the polar explorer Sir John Franklin, and written by his close friend Wilkie Collins—who is today best known for his "sensation" novels, and particularly the mystery, *The Woman in White* (1868). Dickens produced the play—its first performance was at Tavistock House itself—and took on the role of Richard Wardour, who dies so that a rival in love might live. *The Frozen Deep* was ambitiously staged and proved a great success; a private showing was arranged for the queen, who was apparently much amused. In the summer of 1857 Dickens and his troupe took the play on the road, aiming to raise funds for the family of Douglas Jerrold, the recently deceased playwright. As a result of these performances, Dickens met Ellen Ternan, eighteen, the daughter of Fanny Ternan, a well-known professional actress hired for a role in *The Frozen Deep*. Dickens fell in love with Ellen, who had a smaller part in the play; she was smart, charming, resilient—and superbly concealed. Claire Tomalin called her 1991 biography of Ternan *The Invisible Woman*, for her relationship with

Dickens was, until well into the twentieth century, almost completely hidden from public view. Of course, many who knew Dickens or his family were aware of the affair, which—in more recent years—has been chronicled and analyzed in many books and biographies. Ackroyd contends that Ellen's relationship with Dickens remained Platonic; Tomalin suggests, more convincingly, that she bore him a child.

In any event, Dickens spent much time with Ellen during the final thirteen years of his life, providing her—and her family—with various means of financial support. His marriage ended more formally not long after Ellen entered his life. Dickens and Catherine were, by the summer of 1858, living apart. She was settled in Regent's Park, having accepted a generous settlement of six hundred pounds a year. Dickens continued to reside in the spacious house he had recently purchased at Gad's Hill, in Kent. One of his sons accompanied Catherine; the others remained at Gad's Hill, largely under the watch of Georgina Hogarth, Catherine's sister, who—like Mary before her—had become an integral part of Dickens's household, and one of his strongest allies. At his death Dickens left Georgina all of his private papers, calling her "the best and truest friend man ever had."

Dickens was never eager to air the facts of his troubled marriage—for of course his own image as a novelist and editor had long been widely, if perhaps imprecisely, associated with the pleasures and rewards of domestic life. Dickens thus grew irate when, during the spring of 1858, rumors regarding his private life started to fly. Some, he now learned, were spreading tales of his friendship with Ellen; others claimed he was carrying on with Georgina herself. Seething ("My father was like a madman," his daughter Kate would recall), Dickens dashed off a direct address to his readers and ran it smack on the front page of *Household Words*. This brief, vague, and impassioned piece denies all charges of wayward conduct and alludes vaguely to long-standing marital woes. It probably sparked more questions than it answered, for of course most readers of *Household Words* lived well beyond London's literary or theatrical circles, and had no clue as to Dickens's difficult domestic affairs.

His odd and clumsy handling of the Ternan affair caused Dickens to quarrel with Bradbury and Evans, his longtime publishers and the printers of *Household Words*. As a result, he cut his relations with the firm and launched a new weekly magazine, *All the Year Round*, published by Chapman and Hall. By the time it appeared in April 1859, Dickens had already embarked on the fierce schedule of public readings—both for charity and for his own profit—that would dominate this last phase of his career. Thus, in August 1858, he appeared in Clifton, Exeter, Plymouth, and Worcester, as well as in Dublin, Belfast, and Cork. In September, Dickens played Huddersfield, Wakefield, Scarborough, and Hull. In the months that followed he was in Dundee, Glasgow, Nottingham, Derby and Leeds, among other places—and was a huge hit wherever he went. These were, in fact, more performances than "readings," for Dickens, ever the actor and stage manager, picked from his works those passages and scenes he knew would most probably prompt laughter and tears, taking on the voices and gestures of his most colorful characters.

A Tale of Two Cities, long one of Dickens's most popular titles, began its serial run in the spring of 1859, gracing the first issue of *All the Year Round*, which became as successful in its way as *Household Words*. (Dickens's own journalistic contributions to the magazine are collected in the *Uncommercial Traveller*, a collection that was published in various editions throughout the 1860s and that, in effect, shows "Boz" in his maturity, roaming about and keenly observing.) As countless high school students can attest, *A Tale of Two Cities* deals with the French Revolution, and features what are very probably the most famous opening and closing sentences in all of British fiction. It is also much informed by contemporary concerns; Parliament throughout the decade had been slow to address a host of pressing social issues, including those involving public health. Cholera was, for example, a constant concern: there were major outbreaks of the disease in 1849, 1853, and 1865. There were also continuing problems with TB, small pox, dysentery, and scarlet fever.

Again Dickens sensed danger in the air, telling one friend, the 1850s, that the continuation of "aristocratic insolence or incapacity" could well ignite in the nation "a conflagration as never had been beheld before." Actually, the novel reveals much about Dickens's political sensibility; it shows the horrors of revolution while also attacking the sources of social power and social corruption. It functions too as a warning, reminding Britain's leaders and elites, its shapers of opinion and policy, of the simple and basic and often forgotten truth that contempt breeds contempt and violence breeds violence; that, in the long run, social oppression brings barbarism and death.

On the one hand, Dickens never forgot his own social roots. He was the grandson of servants, a former factory hand who became a "self-made" man and who, as both his letters and novels plainly show, had no interest in sentimentalizing the ruling class. In one letter, dated 1855, Dickens refers to "all our English tuft-hunting, toad-eating" and "accursed gentility"; in another, to John Forster, dated a few weeks later, he complains of "a non-working aristocracy, and a silent parliament, and everybody for himself and nobody for the rest." In another letter to Forster, written in September of 1855—the same year as *Little Dorrit* and only a four years before *A Tale of Two Cities*—Dickens goes so far to suggest that "representative government is become altogether a failure with us, that the English gentilities and subserviences render the people unfit for it, and that the whole thing has broken down since that great seventeenth-century time, and has no hope in it."

A Tale of Two Cities is, in some ways, something of a potboiler, lacking the depth of his other later novels and showing a more overt return to his more melodramatic ways. As Barbara Hardy notes, *Two Cities* intriguingly conveys "something of the prison mood and claustrophobia of *Dorrit*"; but it also shows "no satiric or comic power, and very little character-interest"; it is "stark in moral action, simple in feeling, quite a good novel to read in childhood, but one which does not wear well into adult life." The book draws much of its inspiration and information from Carlyle's *French Revolution*—a work Dickens greatly admired, and read repeatedly over the years. It is also "strikingly similar," as Ruth Glancy points out, to Watts Phillips's *The Dead Heart*, "an obscure but at the time popular play" that was written, but in limited circulation, a few years before *A Tale of Two Cities* appeared. Both works, notes Glancy, draw on the same historical background; in Phillips's play "the young hero, Landry, is imprisoned in the Bastille by an aristocrat who abducts his fiancée." Landry, like Dickens's Manette, is "released 18 years later, and in both works the phrases 'buried alive' and 'recalled to life' are used to describe their imprisonment." Landry ends up taking another's place before the executioner, as does Sydney Carton, the hero of *A Tale of Two Cities*. Carton is Dickens's supreme example of selflessness—the key virtue in all of his novels.

Something of a failure in life, Carton is redeemed when, near the book's close, he dies for Charles Darney, convinced that "it is a far, far better thing that I do, than I have ever done; it is a far, far better rest that I go to than I have ever known."

Dickens's next novel, *Great Expectations*, began serialization in December 1860. It was a popular and critical success, boosting the sagging sales of *All the Year Round* while also winning over reviewers who found that it echoed certain of Dickens's earlier works—particularly the much-loved *Copperfield*. Dickens was only forty-eight when he began *Great Expectations*. His legendary vitality appeared undimmed. He was writing away—better than ever, some believed—while still directing a weekly magazine. He kept on with his legendarily long walks, and continued to refresh himself with visits to France and elsewhere, often with Ellen Ternan at his side. He also continued to pitch himself into his readings, adding and carefully adapting new material from *Copperfield* and *Nickleby* into his repertoire and accepting dates in cities large and small. In October 1861, Dickens began a series of nearly fifty readings that took him to Norwich, Ipswich, Dover, and Edinburgh; to Preston, Manchester, and Liverpool. By the summer of 1862, he was seriously considering an offer of ten thousand pounds to tour Australia—a trip that, if made, would consume months and, as Forster among others argued, keep him even further away from his writing. Three years had passed between the completion of *Great Expectations* and *Our Mutual Friend* (1864-65), the last of his completed novels.

There were other distractions. Dickens was still, after all, the head of a large family, and his older children were now starting their own lives—and not always with ease. Indeed, several of his sons were proving themselves members in good standing of the John Dickens school of personal economics—much to their father's growing distress. In early June 1865 Dickens himself narrowly escaped death when the train in which he and Ellen Ternan were riding jumped the tracks between Dover and London, killing ten and injuring fifty more. At the scene of the wreck, Dickens appeared calm, and helped attend to the hurt and the dying. But the incident, sudden and violent, shook him badly. In the following months, Dickens—whose health had long been marked by various odd complaints—now felt frequently dizzy, and began suffering from a severe swelling of his left foot. The accident may have been a factor in this ailment; he was, moreover, prone to arthritis and gout. William Ober, reading several symptoms, suggests: "It's very likely that Dickens was hypertensive, though the sphygmomanometer had not yet been invented." Dickens's own doctor, in the summer of 1866, detected "degeneration of some functions of the heart," and prescribed iron, digitalis, and quinine. But Dickens, being Dickens, pressed on with his usual activities while also managing to complete *Our Mutual Friend*, one of his more ambitious—and least-readable—novels.

Long, dense, and thickly textured, *Our Mutual Friend* has become one of Dickens's most widely analyzed works. But perhaps most readers will find that it brings sleep not stimulation, and will be hard pressed to slog on much past chapter 5. Of course the book has its virtues. It shows real intellectual ambition, and represents Dickens's deepest (and darkest) thoughts about the corrosive, contaminating effects of life in a culture obsessed with social status and, particularly, money—which is here famously equated with rubbish and dung. Bella Wilfer is one of Dickens's most convincingly depicted women; the murderous Bradley Headstone, in his "decent black coat" and his "decent white shirt," makes a fine villain, one of Dickens's best. But the Veneerings—his "bran-new people in a bran-new house in a bran-new quarter of London"—are, for example, drawn with rather too heavy a hand, suggesting that Dickens is rather tired creatively, but freshly aware, from his many readings, that he can always sustain the attention of an audience through blunt exaggeration and a strong dose of the grotesque. Forty years ago Julian Symons observed that *Our Mutual Friend* showed "power and interest." But he also found, around its edges, hints of hysteria—even madness. The later novels, Symons suggested, perhaps too dramatically, "are the work of an author who has increased his power of portraying the visual world, in its minutest detail, but is slowly losing his sense of reality." "Life," Symons wrote, "life is not like this. People are not like this; these flashes of lightning illuminate nothing but the room of distorting mirrors in which Dickens lived. The characters in his last novels bear the same relation to those in the early work that a gargoyle by an artist of genius bears to a comic cartoon by a draughtsman with a good sense of line. They come from the mind of a man defeated, a man possessed."

Despite persistent problems with his health, Dickens sailed again to North America in late 1868—not as a tourist this time but as a performer who, everywhere he went, packed halls. His American reading tour and its related schedule of appearances was both lucrative and successful; but its pace would have taxed Vic Tanny in his prime. In fact, it is tiring simply to *read* of Dickens's varied activities on this whirlwind tour.

He meets with Henry Wadsworth Longfellow, Ralph Waldo Emerson, Oliver Wendell Holmes. He gives a speech at a Boston boy's school. He reads triumphantly in New York. He resists a cold, ignoring his doctor's order to rest. He plays Philadelphia, Washington, and Baltimore. He meets President Andrew Johnson. The cold persists. He reads in Providence, Hartford, and—again—in Boston, where, still ill, he partakes in something called the "Great International Walking Match." ("If I couldn't walk fast and far," Dickens once told John Forster, "I should explode and perish.")

He goes again to Niagara Falls. He plays Springfield, Worcester, and New Haven. He travels once more to Hartford, where one morning he is finally so drained that he simply cannot drag himself from his bed to catch an early-morning train. But again, somehow, Dickens gears up. Suffering from chronic sleeplessness and catarrh, he still refuses to rest, heading for New York where he gives more readings and is feted at a huge farewell dinner hosted by the city's press. By now, Dickens's troubled foot is so swollen that he can no longer force it into a boot, and instead drags it along swathed in a kerchief of some sort. In the end—April 1868—he endures a rough ocean crossing, and goes home with close to twenty thousand pounds.

Dickens was now, even with all of his financial obligations, a wealthy man. But he wasted no time setting up yet another British reading tour, this time adding to the bill that scene from *Oliver Twist* in which Bill Sikes murders the pathetic prostitute Nancy—a scene that, by all accounts, he performed with particular brio. Meanwhile, he kept writing, constructing the first chapters of *The Mystery of Edwin Drood*, which are set in Cloisterham, a cathedral town that owes much to Rochester, one of Dickens's favorite places. In this dark, unfinished novel, we find John Jasper, a choirmaster addicted to opium. There are the Landless twins—Neville and Helena—who have lived in Ceylon and whose lives are mysterious. Drood himself is engaged to Rosa Bud, whom he calls, perhaps regrettably, "Pussy." Landless also loves Rosa. And so does Jasper, Rosa's guardian. Drood disappears, and only bits of his clothing are found by the river. Was he murdered? And if so, why? By whom? Dickens left few clues. Legend says that a month before his death, Dickens, while chatting with Queen Victoria, offered to reveal the ending that is now forever concealed. But the queen didn't care who murdered Edwin Drood.

Dickens died on June 9, 1870. He had spent the afternoon working on *Drood* (leaving it about half complete) and writing letters. That evening, at supper, he was stricken with an aneurysm of the brain and never regained consciousness. He died the next day. In his will, Dickens "emphatically" expressed the desire "that I be buried in an inexpensive, unostentatious, and strictly private manner; that no public announcement be made of the time or place of my burial; that at the utmost not more than three plain mourning coaches be employed; and that those who attend my funeral wear no scarf, cloak, black bow, long hat-band, or other such revolting absurdity."

In fact, Dickens's body was brought by a special train from his house in Gad's Hill to Charing Cross Station and then by hearse to Westminster Abbey. And there Dickens was buried, in Poets' Corner, the statue of Shakespeare looking down. The funeral service itself, on June 14, was limited to all but family members and certain friends; the stone that marks his place of rest bears little more than his name and the dates of his life. Five days later a public service was held, in Westminster Abbey, with Dean Stanley presiding. And then the stream began. "There was a constant pressure on the spot," the Dean would record, "and many flowers were strewn upon it by unknown hands, many tears shed from unknown eyes."

A year later, the *Times* of London recalled, however, that Dickens "was often vulgar in manners and dress, and often overbearing." The paper—which then spoke to and for "respectable" society—noted too that he was "ill at ease in his intercourse with gentlemen; that he preferred being a King in very low company; that even in his early days he lived rather in a clique than in society; that he was something of a Bohemian in his best moments—all these are truths."

But let Vladimir Nabokov, who knew something about making novels, have the last word. In his lecture on *Bleak House*, Nabokov suggested that, in reading the book, we should relax and let our spines take over. Although we read with our minds, the seat of artistic delight is between the shoulder blades. That little shiver is quite certainly the highest form of emotion that humanity has attained when evolving pure art and pure science. Let us worship the spine and its tingle. Let us be proud of our being vertebrates, for we are vertebrates tipped at the head with a divine flame. The brain only continues the spine: the wick really goes through the whole length of the candle. If we are not capable of enjoying that shiver, if we cannot enjoy literature, then let us give up the whole thing and concentrate on our comics, our videos, our books-of-the-week. But I think Dickens will prove stronger.

2

Good and Evil

The Pickwick Papers, Oliver Twist, Nicholas Nickleby,
The Old Curiosity Shop, Martin Chuzzlewit

Dickens's first novel doesn't get off to a sparkling start. The opening sentence of *The Pickwick Papers*, unfurling slowly, features words like *perusal* and *indefatigable* and *assiduity*, no doubt prompting many to conclude that the author has just discovered how to use a thesaurus, and that something pretty dull is about to occur. In fact, what follows next is a tedious but mercifully brief account of the "Transactions of the Pickwick Club," whose founding member, Samuel Pickwick, has just delivered a paper compellingly called "Speculations on the Source of the Hampstead Ponds, with Some Observations on the Theory of Tittlebats." Pickwick now proclaims that—accompanied by his colleagues, the Messrs. Tupman, Snodgrass, and Winkle—he is about to set forth on a bold exploration of the wider world. And the world, one suspects, is full of readers who after slogging through chapter 1 have gone no further in Pickwick's path. *The Pickwick Papers*, they know, is supposed to be funny—hilarious, even. But by page 6 they are bored stiff, suspecting they were born about a century too late to get the jokes. For them, *Pickwick* remains a closed book, stuck on a back shelf with *Humphry Clinker* beneath a layer of dust.

But those readers should press on. *Pickwick* soon picks up the pace. In its opening pages, Dickens is still finding his voice as he parodies that aura of pomposity that tends to descend whenever the self-important come together, whether they be Pickwickians or MPs. By the time he reaches chapter 2—and gets Pickwick out on the road—Dickens has finished clearing his throat; he's found the right levers and switches, and is letting his imagination fly. The result is a novel that, on one level, owes much to the tradition of picaresque fiction, with its questing "hero" and charming improvisational air. *Pickwick* is in fact, despite its sprawl, superbly paced: its dialogue is funny, convincing, and brisk, and shows that had he been born a century later, Dickens would have found quick success writing for the screen—the perfect partner for S. J. Perelman. With its mix of slapstick, satire, and familiar comic types, *The Pickwick Papers* reads at times like a Victorian version of *The Cocoanuts* (1929), say, or *A Night at the Opera* (1935); it is, in fact, one piece of nineteenth-century fiction in which the Marx Brothers could feel perfectly at home. Not surprisingly, in 1952, Noel Langley stuck closely to Dickens's text as he turned *The Pickwick Papers* into one of the better film adaptations of any Dickens novel.

In fact, after seeing Langley's film it is nearly impossible to read the novel and not see the rotund and bespectacled James Hayter whenever Pickwick's name appears. That Pickwick should look so little like Dickens himself might surprise those who assume that all first novels must show a vivid autobiographical thread. Dickens was twenty-four when he began *The Pickwick Papers*—a small, long-haired, boyish figure who was freshly married and well known for his theatrical flair. But there is Pickwick: a rheumatic bachelor in late middle age. He is also, particularly in the early chapters, a bit of a buffoon, the comic butt: he is seen chasing his hat, Chaplin-like, as it "rolled over and over as merrily as a lively porpoise in a strong tide." Moments before, Pickwick finds himself facing a regiment of soldiers with bayonets. In this case, "Mr. Pickwick gazed through his spectacles for an instant on the advancing mass, and then fairly turned his back and—we will not say fled; firstly, because it is an ignoble term, and, secondly, because Mr. Pickwick's figure was by no means adapted for that mode of retreat—he trotted away, at as quick a rate as his legs would convey him." Pickwick is forever being knocked about: Sam Weller, in one scene, boosts him a bit too heartily over a garden wall, and "that immortal gentleman" goes flying, "crushing three gooseberry-bushes and a rose-tree" before "he finally alighted at full length."

Pickwick is funny because Dickens has made him a bit pompous and a little vain, prone to fancy himself something of a scientist, and likely to show up for a dance—as he does in chapter 28—sporting "speckled silk stockings" and "smartly-tied pumps." But then, so was Dickens a bit pompous and a little vain. Despite their differences in age and appearance, Dickens and Pickwick do share certain traits: even their names faintly rhyme. Pickwick, like Dickens, is far from sedentary; he can rarely "resist so tempting an opportunity of studying human nature"; he is keenly curious about the world and sets forth boldly to explore it, notebook in hand. He certainly exhibits many of the virtues Dickens would often extol. He is neither selfish nor neurotically self-absorbed. Although Pickwick voices no religious maxims, he certainly exhibits what Dickens believed to be the key Christian virtues: generosity, compassion, forgiveness, and the willingness to help those who bring him nothing but grief. These include the con man Alfred Jingle, and the housekeeper Mrs. Martha Bardell—who, mistakenly convinced that Pickwick has backed out of a proposal of marriage, takes "that immortal gentleman" to court, egged on by that august pair of legal minds, the Messrs. Dodson and Fogg. Pickwick is no grim ideologue—no dour Puritanical zealot. He is "open to conviction," and far from stuffy and prim, displaying the sort of "juvenility of spirit" that, for example, prompts him to plunge into a round of blindman's bluff "with the utmost relish." Moreover, Pickwick's spirits are "elastic": he is resilient and stubbornly cheerful; he does not stew; he carries on in situations "which might well have depressed the spirits of many a man." Indeed, he overflows with "kindly feelings and animal spirits"—and sometimes with spirits of another kind. Thus one finds him early in the book with his head "sunk upon his bosom," snoring away, contentedly awash with wine.

Pickwick leads the way for many other kindly, avuncular figures who will turn up in Dickens's fiction; as Fred Kaplan writes, he foreshadows "the man of Benevolence, who in his idealized form, such as the Cheeryble brothers in *Nicholas Nickleby* and Mr. Brownlow in *Oliver Twist*, matches his innate moral sentiments with moral acts." Pickwick is, then, very much the kind of hero one might expect to get from a young writer who loved *The Vicar of Wakefield* and long admired Henry Fielding. According to Fielding, "Good-Nature is that benevolent and amiable Temper of Mind which disposes us to feel the Misfortunes and enjoy the Happiness of others; and consequently pushes us on to promote the latter, and prevent the former." Pickwick—"the very personation of kindness and humanity," as the narrator calls him—is in sum everything Dickens's vilest characters are not. He's a million miles from Edward Murdstone.

The narrator of *The Pickwick Papers* also frequently hails its
hero's vast intelligence and his "gigantic brain." But then, the
narrator is Dickens, and so prone to irony. For despite his wide-
ranging curiosity and his many good intentions, Pickwick is quite
hopelessly vague about the ways of the world. Indeed, as the novel
proceeds to show, this man who had "agitated the scientific world
with his Theory of Tittlebats," would be quite lost without his valet,
Sam Weller, "a gentleman of great gallantry in his own way" and
certainly no stranger to life on the streets.

Thus, in several respects, Pickwick resembles other protagonists
in Dickens's early fiction. Obviously, unlike Oliver and Little Nell,
he has money, in fact "far more than a man at my age can ever live
to spend." But like them, Pickwick similarly ends up on the move
and rather vulnerable, meeting up with characters whose motives are
far from pure. Like Oliver and Nell, he finds violence, corruption,
and deceit in the wider world. In "Dingley Dell & the Fleet,"
included in *The Dyer's Hand* (1962), the always perceptive W. H.
Auden suggests that

the real theme of *Pickwick Papers*—I am not saying Dickens was
consciously aware of it and, indeed, I am pretty certain that he was not—is
the Fall of Man. It is the story of a man who is innocent, that is to say,
who has not eaten of the Tree of the Knowledge of Good and Evil and is,
therefore, living in Eden. He then eats of the Tree, that is to say, he
becomes conscious of the reality of Evil but, instead of falling from
innocence into sin—this is what makes him a mythical character—he
changes from an innocent child into an innocent adult who no longer lives
in an imaginary Eden of his own but in the real and fallen world.

In the world of *The Pickwick Papers*, the irrational and the
unpredictable often appear to be the order of the day. In one of its
first scenes, Pickwick strikes up a chat with the driver of a hansom
cab. Made suspicious by Pickwick's persistent questions, the driver
grows mean and smacks "the learned man" in the face, sending his
spectacles flying. A "mob" duly forms, but Pickwick gets away and
soon finds himself "ruminating" on "the strange mutability of human
affairs"—a particularly apt phrase to appear at the start of the first
novel by a writer whose subsequent work will show a continuing
interest not only in violence, but in the abruptness of change and the
hard swiftness of time. Indeed, later in *The Pickwick Papers*,
Dickens takes the reader to a happy skating party that ends abruptly

when "a sharp smart crack" is heard and Pickwick drops through the ice, nearly drowning. He is duly warmed up at a merry gathering of friends featuring the free flow of laughter and punch. "The party," the narrator notes, "broke up next morning. Breakings up are capital things in our school days, but in after life they are painful enough. Death, self-interest, and fortune's changes, are every day breaking up many a happy group, and scattering them far and wide; and the boys and girls never come back again."

Pickwick in the main prompts laughter. Jingle is convincing, colorful, and one of Dickens's best comic creations. And so are the Wellers, *fils et pére*. Several of the novel's moments are among Dickens's most enduringly funny; one thinks especially of the courtroom scenes in which Serjeant Buzfuz—stating Mrs. Bardell's case—depicts Pickwick as a "serpent" who was "on the watch," a "Being, erect upon two legs, and bearing all the outward semblance of a man, and not of a monster," who one day "knocked at the door of Mrs. Bardell's house," rented some rooms there, and so began his dark plotting, his "systematic villainy." But, as the sad skating party coda suggests, Dickens's first novel hints of dark undercurrents that become clearer—darker—as his career proceeds. At one point Pickwick finds himself in the Fleet, a debtor's jail filled with misery and squalor. One sees that Dickens's obsession with indebtedness and imprisonment is there from the start. Certainly, much of the novel's satire has a razor's edge. Dickens might have been fond of odd individuals, and of the idea of "the common man," but from the start his works show this fear of mob behavior. His depiction in *Pickwick* of the Eatenswill elections—of the contest between Fizkin and Slumkey, the Buffs and the Blues—makes vividly clear Dickens's view of politics in action. The politicians are bombastic, their handlers corrupt; the crowds they play to are volatile and easily swayed. And for all of its sunniness, *The Pickwick Papers* signals Dickens's continuing fondness for the grotesque and the macabre. "The Stroller's Tale," for instance, is the grisly account of the death of a "low pantomime actor" who was also a "habitual drunkard." This brief, self-contained narrative—one of several interspersed through the text—is agonizingly detailed, showing a man with "bloated body and shrunken legs" suffering the assaults of delirium tremens, "writhing under the torments of a burning fever," and hallucinating, believing "the walls and ceiling" to be "alive with reptiles," and seeing too "the faces of men he knew, rendered

hideous by gibing and mouthing." They were "searing him with
heated irons, and binding his head with cords till the blood started;
and he struggled madly for life." Such scenes appear to have been
dropped into the narrative primarily to stun readers, to push them
into their own ruminations on life's cruelties and horrors. Like the
narcoleptic Fat Boy who graces the book's early chapters, Dickens
"wants to make your flesh creep," it appears. Consider as well the
curious anecdote related by Sam Weller in chapter 31 of a man who
invents a sausage-making machine that, as Sam puts it, would
"swaller up a pavin' stone if you put it too near, and grind it into
sassages as easy as if it was a tender young babby." The inventor is
himself ground to bits in his own device, and unwittingly devoured,
Weller relates, by a "little old gen'l'm'n, who had been remarkably
partial to sassages all his life." (E. A. Poe, not surprisingly, found
much to admire in the early Dickens; certain of Poe's
stories—including "The Man of the Crowd"—show direct
Dickensian links.)

Like *The Pickwick Papers*, *Oliver Twist* also comes to a happy
close. But far more than *Pickwick*, which takes place just prior to
the start of the Victorian era, *Twist* is a dark novel—a fact some
might find surprising. Dennis Walder, in *Dickens and Religion*
(1981), suggests that the "overall mood" of *Oliver Twist* is like "one
long, oppressive nightmare." In *Charles Dickens: The World of His
Novels* (1958), J. Hillis Miller finds it filled with "images of dark
dirty rooms with no apparent exit." "No novel could be more
completely   dominated   by   an   imaginative   complex   of
claustrophobia," Miller writes, pointing to Oliver's imprisonment at
various times in a coal cellar, a "dark and solitary room," and a
"cell"—all of them dirty, confining places within a dirty, confining
world. But in the wake of many popular adaptations, many have
probably come to assume that *Oliver Twist* is, despite certain sad
parts, a blithe little book full of characters who from Fagin on down
are rough but endearing.

For example, Carol Reed's 1968 film adaptation of Lionel Bart's
play is in its own way a moving and memorable work, capturing
well the novel's clear comic strains. But to watch *Oliver!* is to
glimpse only a fraction of Dickens's artistic aims. He wanted this
novel—the first to bear *his* name and not the pseudonym Boz—to
stand as a scathing indictment of the ways in which an increasingly
prosperous nation was dealing (or rather *not* dealing) with the vast

fact of urban poverty and its growing list of related problems. In other words, he wanted his better-off readers to look poverty straight in the face. The "fundamental aim" of *Oliver Twist*, Walder suggests, is "to move us, as Mr. Pickwick was moved in the Fleet, into sympathy and charity for the poor."

In the early chapters of *Oliver Twist*, Dickens's most specific target is a new series of regulations surrounding the "Poor Law Amendment Act"—regulations put into effect by Parliament a few years before the novel began to appear. He continued to believe that the new law—which aimed to reduce, or at least discourage, public assistance to the poor—was both badly conceived and badly administered. At that time, welfare (such as it was) was administered indifferently and often chaotically through church parishes and, thus, by parish beadles or constables who were otherwise responsible for maintaining order during church services and performing other similarly menial church-related tasks. As the portrait of Bumble suggests, the local beadle was not likely to be a well-trained, sensitive soul wholly devoted to alleviating human suffering and improving civic life. Writing nearly thirty years after *Oliver Twist*, in a postscript to *Our Mutual Friend*, Dickens was still attacking the Poor Law and its effects. "I believe there has been in England, since the days of the Stuarts," he wrote, "no law so often infamously administered, no law so openly violated, no law habitually so ill-supervised."

The effect of the Poor Law—or, more precisely, laws—was to make workhouses, which were the last refuge for the thoroughly desperate, more prisonlike; this was achieved by cutting food rations and—in hopes of cutting the birth rate—by separating men from their wives. ("Thin gruel," is the way Dickens describes poorhouse grub in chapter 2, where he also notes that these "wise and humane" regulations "kindly undertook to divorce poor married people.") Oliver, not yet ten, is thus a figure representative of the countless neglected citizens forced to scrape and scrap for survival in a social and legal system that Dickens, not surprisingly, found incongruent with Christian virtues. Oliver is "the orphan of a workhouse." He is "cuffed and buffeted" within a legal system that the novel notes might well send a man to jail simply for playing the flute. *Oliver Twist* suggests that in a system so dependent on fear and punishment—so devoid of the promise of compassion and hope—poverty and resentment will not be reduced, and crime certainly will not abate but instead will thrive.

Oliver Twist remains one of Dickens's most popular titles, and not, one assumes, because readers retain a lively interest in social policy debates stretching back to the days of Earl Grey. (Although of course similar debates continue to rage.) As in Dickens's other fiction, the key concerns of *Oliver Twist* are more primal than topical: Oliver, after all, seeks nothing more than food, shelter, and consoling love. ("More than any other author," Dickens, Anatole Broyard once wrote—perhaps thinking of *Twist*—"makes you feel weather, reminds you that you are an animal in an environment, a prey to wet and cold. Nobody builds fires better in the imagination.") *Oliver Twist* is bluntly melodramatic and highly accessible, showing the battle between good and evil in the starkest of terms. Some years after completing the book, Dickens said he "wished to show, in little Oliver, the principle of Good surviving through every adverse circumstance, and triumphing at last."

Because he is a symbol of innocent goodness, Oliver is not—at least not for adult readers—particularly complex or compelling. Mr. Brownlow, Oliver's kindly friend and Dickens's apostle of good, is also something of a blank: the forerunner of other, better-drawn benevolent gentlemen—John Jarndyce and perhaps Arthur Clennam—who help the helpless in Dickens's later novels. Nancy, the pathetic prostitute trapped in Fagin's den, was hailed as a masterpiece of characterization in Dickens's day: Wilkie Collins called her "the finest thing" Dickens ever did. "He never afterwards saw all sides of a woman's character—saw all around her." Contemporary readers might not agree. Nancy is perhaps one of the more "realistic" characters in Dickens's early fiction; but she is obviously not more deeply interesting—dramatically or psycho-logically—than (say) Esther Summerson, a major figure in the more mature and artful *Bleak House*. Nancy is something of a type increasingly common in both popular and serious literature of the nineteenth century: the whore with a heart o' gold. Dickens avoids bluntly mentioning Nancy's profession, as Humphry House pointed out in *The Dickens World* (1941), a popular and influential study. As House notes, Dickens stressed in a preface to *Twist* that he sought to describe "the dregs of life 'so long as their speech did not offend the ear.'" Indeed, in early Dickens particularly, "everything," writes House, "was written with an eye on decency." Thus, he "does

not merely omit incidents and words and phrases that might be put
in, but conceives the whole plot in a way that underestimates the
brutality, squalor, and filth of the setting in which it is supposed to
develop." Nancy, then, "is supposed to be a thorough-going whore
who is working full-time for Fagin and Sikes: one of her jobs is to
keep an eye on the apprentice thieves, and apparently also to recruit
for the gang." All of this, House demonstrates, is "historically
right"—indeed, "Nancy's job would certainly have been to use her
sex as much as possible with boys like Charley Bates and the
Dodger; and the whole atmosphere in which Oliver lived in London
would have been drenched in sex; but Dickens does not hint at such
a thing"—nor, adds House, does he make clear that "the filth" and
the "filthy odours" that filled London's streets were there because
"the street was full of the emptyings of pots and privies."

House has a point: Dickens did write around certain unpleasant
facts and circumstances, even as he sought to shed light on the
urban horrors and social evils of his time. From the start he was
more "wholesome" and less frank than those eighteenth century
writers he so admired; in this respect, at least, he was sometimes
closer to Walt Disney than Henry Fielding. Indeed, as critics have
long noted, such discretion clearly contributed to the massive appeal
of *The Pickwick Papers*, which mixed a maximum of comic
rompishness with a minimum of ribaldry. (In the book's preface,
Dickens promised that "no incident or expression occurs which
would call a blush into the most delicate cheek.") As a result, "the
frankness of Fielding and the coarseness of Smollett," as Norman
Page puts it, "have been refined and sentimentalized." House
reminds us that this "constant censorship that Dickens imposed upon
his work can partly be explained by the common practice in
Victorian society, in all classes, of reading books and periodicals in
the family circle; he had children always in mind." As his letters
show, Dickens also had in mind—particularly as he matured—the
goal of raising the stature of the novelist in society; and he reckoned
that many middle class readers would simply dismiss the seriousness
of his message if they were also put off by the bluntness of his
images, or the coarseness of his words.

But these letters also tend to show that while Dickens himself
was discreet in sexual matters, he was by no means a prude. As his
affection for Fielding suggests, he was no Thomas Bowdler, who,
in 1818, gave the world his sanitized Shakespeare. In fact, in *Our*

Mutual Friend, the last of his completed novels, Dickens mocked this obsessive impulse to shield the young from supposed improprieties, calling it "Podsnappery" after one of the novel's pompous duffers. David Paroissien rightly observes, in his edition of the *Selected Letters of Charles Dickens* (1985), that all things considered, Dickens in his fiction actually faced up to a rather wide range of potentially offensive and controversial topics; for in fact, "Victorian standards of the acceptable were perhaps less uniform and more flexible than a modern writer like [Virginia] Woolf might assume." (Woolf, Paroissien notes, had once observed: "What books Dickens could have written had he been permitted! Think of Thackeray as unfettered as Flaubert or Balzac!") "Even in the case of Dickens," writes Paroissien, "who readily agreed to write novels and edit journals suitable for 'family fare,' the most cursory glance at his work reveals a catalogue of illegitimate children, prostitutes, seducers. . . ." For Dickens then, as for most mainstream novelists and dramatists until quite recently, "the issue was perhaps less a matter of avoiding the forbidden and more of a manner in which controversial subjects were treated."

In *Oliver Twist*, as in *Oliver!*, the figure of Fagin possesses a weird, mesmerizing appeal—villains often do. Still, Fagin generates no sympathy or affection. He has no redeeming qualities: not a hint of the kind of compassion or fellow feeling that Dickens's most admirable characters tend so readily to display. (His life revolves around what is, for Dickens, an unpardonable crime: the destruction of youth and the corruption of innocence.) Fagin has lured Nancy to her ruin, and now seeks nothing less than the fatal poisoning of Oliver's soul. To that end, he hands the boy a well-thumbed "history of the lives and trials of great criminals"—a sort of pornographic anthology of "dreadful crimes" presumably meant to whet his appetite for similar activities. Like Squeers, Quilp, and Edward Murdstone, Fagin is much drawn to the use of intimidation and force. He threatens and beats his charges, from whom childhood has prematurely fled. When Oliver first sees them, they are "smoking long clay pipes" and "drinking spirits with the air of middle-aged men." "Make 'em your models," Fagin tells Oliver upon introducing him to the Artful Dodger and his crew, "tapping the fire-shovel in the hearth to add force to his words."

This theme of lost childhood is crucial to Dickens's work, and clearly stems, in part, from his own shattering experience, at twelve, of the rough reality of poverty and neglect. It is there, for example, in *Sketches by Boz*, when during "A Visit to Newgate," Dickens describes a young prostitute visiting her mother in the prison, a girl who "belonged to a class—unhappily but too extensive—the very existence of which should make men's heart's bleed." The girl is "barely past her childhood," but she was "one of those children, born and bred in neglect and vice, who have never known what childhood is: who have never been taught to love and court a parent's smile, or to dread a parent's frown." She is "thinly clad, and shaking with the cold." She has been forced to "enter at once upon the stern realities and miseries of life," never experienced "the thousand nameless endearments of childhood, its gaiety and innocence." Indeed, this theme links *Oliver Twist* not only to *Dombey and Son* (where Dombey the younger, a sensitive soul, is shoved roughly through childhood by his father), but to *Bleak House* (where the pathetic Jo must pass his childhood sweeping up—and sleeping on—London's streets) and to *Hard Times* (where the imaginations of Gradgrind's children are "murdered" beneath the weight of dull, ruthless "facts").

But neither Dombey nor Gradgrind are beyond the pale. Dombey, for one, is obtuse and spiritually impoverished, twisted by the perverse values of an overly materialistic society. Fagin *is* evil; by placing him with a fire shovel at the hearth, Dickens links him directly to the devil—as he does elsewhere in the novel. At one point, for example, the cruel and shadowy Bill Sikes—Nancy's murderer—tells a beaming Fagin that "there never was a man with such a face as yours, unless it was your father, and I suppose he is singeing his grizzled beard red by this time, unless you come straight from the old 'un [i.e. Satan] without any father at all betwixt you; which I shouldn't wonder at, a bit." Dickens also speaks of Fagin in animalistic terms, suggesting—as he does with Daniel Quilp in *The Old Curiosity Shop*—that such supremely selfish behavior has severed him forever from the human community.

Of course Fagin is even more frequently referred to as "the Jew" or "the Old Jew" or "the wily old Jew"—labels that become particularly troublesome when, in chapter 15, Dickens brings on another Jew, "younger than Fagin, but nearly as vile and repulsive in appearance." Fagin owes something, apparently, to an actual criminal, Ikey Solomon, a notorious London fence. He can be linked to other wily, slinking, demonized villains in the very popular "penny dreadfuls" of the day; he derives too from the stage tradition of the villainous—and sometimes rather comical—Jew whose best-known example is Shakespeare's Shylock.

Dickens was, as Ackroyd and others have shown, entirely capable of making stupid statements regarding Jews and other non-Europeans. But his subsequent works are not obsessively racist or anti-Semitic, and even Fagin is not much worse than other stereotypically nefarious Jews who turn up in the Victorian fiction of, among others, Anthony Trollope and Thackeray. (Some readers will indeed detect elements of sympathy in Dickens's closing depiction of Fagin as he waits, trapped in a jail cell, fearfully awaiting his end.) In any event, in later years, Dickens realized that his portrait of Fagin had caused much offense: Jews he knew had told him so. As a result, he made a point of depicting Jews more sympathetically—although some might also say condescendingly—in *Our Mutual Friend*, which began serialization in 1864, six years after Jews were, for the first time, admitted to Parliament. Here we find the figure of Riah, who is wronged by the gentile Fascination Fledgeby, a sleazy moneylender who makes sneering anti-Semitic cracks: "Your people need speak the truth sometimes," he tells Riah, "for they lie enough." (The issue of anti-Semitism in Dickens's work was revived in 1948, when—just three years after Hitler's war—David Lean's film version of *Oliver Twist* appeared, with Alec Guinness playing Fagin's vileness to the hilt. Several prominent Jewish groups were, understandably, outraged; in New York the film was banned.)

Dickens's later novels continue to feature sharp photographs of dreary, decaying, and impoverished quarters; in *Oliver Twist*, through a particularly sharp lens, he looks frequently at London's sadder faces and sorrier places. Here, as in *Bleak House* and elsewhere, Dickens makes a direct assault on the sort of smug complacency that tends to characterize the middle class during periods of economic prosperity: he attacks what John Kenneth Galbraith, writing about the 1980s, called "the Culture of Contentment." Dickens confronts the common assumption that men with power and money can always be trusted to know what is best for society—and that moreover, as a rule, poor people just like being poor, or have no initiative to change their wretched state. In fact, one of the single best summaries of Dickens's earlier political attitudes can be found in a letter he wrote to the *Morning Chronicle* in July 1842, at a time when Britain's political leaders were finally beginning to respond to commission reports that exposed the massive and systematic abuse of workers, many of them women and children. Dickens here speaks specifically to "the Mines and Collieries Bill"—an act that would, among other things, prohibit small children and women from working in the coal pits, where injury and even death were common and the pay notoriously low. Dickens begins by noting that it is "well known to every one" that England's mines have long been

utterly out of legislative mind; that for so many years all considerations of humanity, policy, social virtue, and common decency, have been left rotting at the pit's mouth, with other disregarded dunghill matter from which lordly colliers could extract no money; that for many years, a state of things has existed in these places, in the heart and core of a Christian country, which, if it had been discovered by mariners or missionaries in the Sandwich Islands, would have made the fortune of two quarto volumes, filled the whole bench of bishops with emotion, and nerved to new and mighty projects the Society for the Propagation of the Gospel in Foreign Parts.

In *Bleak House* and elsewhere, Dickens would pointedly observe that in Britain Christianity was more preached than practiced; that social compassion comes cheap when it is showered upon people who live far from one's own city or country—and preferably on continents at least one ocean away. Dickens notes that "collier lordships" continue to contend that "there are no discomforts, no miseries whatever, in the mines; that all labourers in mines are perpetually singing and dancing, and festively enjoying themselves; in a word, that they lead such rollicking and roystering lives that it is well they work below the surface of the earth, or society would be deafened by their shouts of merriment."

In such novels as *Oliver Twist*, Dickens wants his readers to see the absurdity of such beliefs. He wants them to *see* the sad and neglected figures they were likely to pass—and shun—every day. The stakes were high. "In these times," he wrote in this letter of 1842, "a gulf has opened between the rich and poor, which instead of narrowing, as all good men would have it, grows broader daily." And the nation's "strength and happiness," even its "future existence" required that "these two great divisions of society" should

not be allowed to drift further apart—or be pushed apart by those
driven by little more than self-interest and greed.

In *Oliver Twist*, Dickens the novelist and Dickens the editorialist
often contend for space: *look* at "our" city, our society he repeatedly
demands. In chapter 23 he describes the night as "bleak, dark, and
piercing cold," and adds: "It was a night for the well-housed and fed
to draw round the bright fire and thank God they were at home; and
for the homeless, starving wretch to lay him down and die. Many
hunger-worn outcasts close their eyes in our bare streets, at such
times, who, let their crimes have been what they may, can hardly
open them in a more bitter world." In many of London's police
stations, things are barely better. "In our station-houses," he asserts
in chapter 11, "men and women are every night confined on the
most trivial *charges*—the word is worth noting—in dungeons,
compared with which, those in Newgate, occupied by the most
atrocious felons, tried, found guilty, and under sentence of death, are
palaces." In chapter 4, Dickens describes a starving Oliver eating
with much relish some scraps of meat meant for the Sowerberry
family's dog. "I wish," he shouts, "some well-fed philosopher"—
some maker of public policy—"whose meat and drink turn to gall
within him; whose blood is ice, whose heart is iron; could have seen
Oliver Twist clutching at the dainty viands that the dog had
neglected. I wish he could have witnessed the horrible avidity with
which Oliver tore the bits asunder with all the ferocity of famine.
There is only thing I should like better; and that would be to see the
Philosopher making the same sort of meal himself, with the same
relish."

Creating Bumble, the parish beadle, Dickens lightens up on the
diabolical imagery he lavishes on Fagin; in fact, at times,
particularly when he appears as the henpecked husband, Bumble
supplies the novel's comic relief: he is there because—as Dickens
notes in chapter 17—it is "the custom on the stage, in all good
murderous melodramas, to present the tragic and the comic scenes,
in as regular alternation, as the layers of red and white in a side of
streaky bacon." (A comment that also reminds one that, as an artist,
Dickens was acutely self-aware: he always *knew* when he was being
melodramatic and when he was not—sometimes parodying the
form's conventions when not adapting them for his own artistic
ends.) Bumble, very fleetingly, shows a certain sympathy for
Oliver's plight. But as the novel proceeds, Bumble—his name

suggesting both "muddle" and "mumble"—becomes more bluntly disgusting; Dickens wants him to stand for all that is cruel and unfeeling about the system he seeks to attack. At one point Bumble, shielded from the cold by his "blue great-coat" and cape, but greatly put off by the presence of "two paupers, who persisted in shivering, and complaining of the cold, in a manner which, Mr. Bumble declared, caused his teeth to chatter in his head." Morally, Bumble is hopelessly thick, the novel makes clear; after becoming cozily warm again, and stuffing himself with a "temperate dinner of steaks, oyster sauce, and porter," he thinks again of those shivering paupers, and fills his head "with sundry moral reflections on the too-prevalent sin of discontent and complaining." Dickens notes elsewhere that Bumble "had a decided propensity for bullying" and "derived no inconsiderable pleasure from the exercise of petty cruelty." But he is also "a coward"—just like most "official personages." Dickens in chapter 37 invites the reader to heed Bumble's true nature, which his uniform conceals. Remove that uniform—that "laced coat" and that "mighty cocked hat"—and Bumble is "no longer a beadle," but just another pompous jackass who savors too keenly what little power he has. In fact, in one of the novel's more effective editorial asides, Dickens—ever the actor, ever aware of the power of costume—reminds his readers that there are "some promotions in life, which independent of the more substantial rewards they offer, acquire peculiar value and dignity from the coats and waistcoats connected with them." "A field-marshall," he observes, "has his uniform; a bishop his silk apron; a counsellor his silk gown; a beadle his cocked hat." "Strip the bishop of his apron," he declares in one of the novel's most incendiary passages, "or the beadle of his cocked hat and gold lace, what are they? Men, mere men. Promote them, raise them to higher and different offices in the state; and divested of their black silk aprons and cocked hats, they shall lack their old dignity and be somewhat shorn of their influence with the multitude. Dignity, and even holiness too, sometimes, are more questions of coat and waistcoat than some people imagine."

As his fiction shows, Dickens's interest in dress and image making would always be strong. And so was his interest in the mind's mysterious workings. In his twenties, Dickens first became keenly interested in hypnotism—or "mesmerism" as it was called at the time. This interest is not surprising. A person hypnotized can experience a state of mind very similar to that of a fiction writer engaged in intense creation. In both cases, one exists simultaneously in the world and outside of it; one is relaxed, unfettered, open to suggestion; one can assume other identities that are, for the moment, as real as one's own. Dickens does not write explicitly of mesmerism in *Oliver Twist*; he does not show the title character involved in the act of imaginative creation. But he does show Oliver experiencing altered psychological states, floating in that intriguing zone between consciousness and sleep. In early 1838, at the start of his writing career, Dickens took in one of John Elliotson's demonstrations, at the University of London, on the power of "mesmerism." Dickens and Elliotson (who also pioneered the use of the stethoscope in Britain) soon became friends. And within a few years, Dickens—at parties and in private sessions—was showing off his own skills at putting people under: in 1842, in America, as Fred Kaplan records, Dickens once "magnetized Catherine 'into hysterics'"—to use Dickens's own phrase—"within six minutes of making hand passes about her head, and then, to his alarm, into mesmeric trance. He successfully repeated the experience the next night." He became "increasingly fascinated by his own powers," mesmerizing "friends and members of his family, sometimes for their social amusement, sometimes to alleviate illness."

Given this, two passages in *Oliver Twist* are especially worth noting. In the first (chapter 9) Dickens describes Oliver coming out of sleep, in that "drowsy state, between sleeping and waking, when you dream more in five minutes with your eyes half open, and yourself half conscious of everything that is passing around you, than you would in five nights with your eyes fast closed, and your senses wrapt in perfect unconsciousness." "At such times," he observes, "a mortal knows just enough of what his mind is doing, to form some glimmering conception of its mighty powers, its bounding from earth and spurning time and space, when freed from the restraint of its corporeal state." Later, in chapter 34, Dickens again describes Oliver, tired on a sultry day, giving in to that "kind of sleep that steals upon us sometimes, while it holds the body prisoner, does not free the mind from a sense of things about it, and enable it to ramble at its pleasure." In this state one is overpowered by "heaviness," by an "utter inability to control our thoughts or power of motion"; and yet, Dickens notes—clearly fascinated by the psychological terrain he is newly crossing—"we have a consciousness of all that is going on about us, and, if we dream at such a time, words which are really spoken, or sounds which really exist at the moment, accommodate themselves with surprising readiness to our visions, until reality and imagination become so strangely blended that it is afterwards almost a matter of impossibility to separate the two."

In Dickens's next published novel, *Nicholas Nickleby*, evil again wears a recognizably human face. Ralph Nickleby, Nicholas's uncle, thinks of money obsessively, in ways that warp the soul. He decides early in life that "riches are the only true source of happiness and power, and that it is lawful and just to compass their acquisition by all means short of felony." To that end, he takes up lending money at exorbitant rates—a practice that, the novel's narrator wryly notes, "cannot be too strongly recommended to the notice of capitalists, both large and small, and more especially of money-brokers and bill-discounters. Indeed, to do these gentlemen justice, many of them are to this day in the frequent habit of adapting it with eminent success."

Ralph Nickleby ends up a suicide, shattered by a sense of remorse and loss; he stands at the front of a long line of characters in Dickens designed to show how money corrodes and destroys: he is, like Scrooge, selfishness personified. In fact, he is a melodramatic villain—a "double dastard" Nicholas calls him—who tempts and torments the virtuous and the innocent in what critics have long called Dickens's most "theatrical" novel. As Ackroyd writes, "theatrical effects suffuse" *Nicholas Nickleby*; it is a novel "written by someone whose understanding of appearance, of gesture, of speech and of character has been very strongly influenced by his experience of acting"—and who, it is known, spent countless hours intently watching the popular stage productions of his time. *Nickleby*, Ackroyd writes, features some "obviously theatrical scenes"—including "the rescue of Madeline Bray from the clutches of the hideous miser Arthur Gride," and "the discovery that Smike is really Ralph Nickleby's son." Gride, like Ralph Nickleby, is completely odious; Smike is wholly pathetic; Kate—the hero's sister—is quite without stain. Her scenes seem particularly well suited for the melodramatic stage. At one point she confronts her sleazy uncle who, stunned, "literally gnashed his teeth." Kate, "with flashing eyes and the red blood mantling in her cheeks," boldly asserts: "If I have a girl's weakness, I have a woman's heart."

Elsewhere, facing the lecherous Sir Mulberry Hawk—who is holding her dress—Kate, "her heart swelling with anger," actually says: "Unhand me, sir."

But of course, nothing Dickens ever wrote is *simply* melodrama; *Nicholas Nickleby* is also in its way a dark book strongly flavored with key elements of Dickens's distinctive style. Consider Wackford Squeers—a mixed pleasure indeed. By doing so, one gets a good sense of just what "Dickensian" means: one sees it as the fantastic and the realistic, the extravagant and the concrete, the comic and the sinister, the political and the grotesque—all combined in a splendid, inimitable way. Squeers, like Hawk, Ralph Nickleby, and Arthur Gride, is a predator—and by far the worst of this sorry lot. For Squeers preys on children, and for this one must imagine him deep down in a Dickens hell, sweating amidst the cinders with, among others, Fagin and the Murdstones. Squeers's Yorkshire "school" is in fact nothing more than a dumping ground for unwanted boys, many born out of wedlock. Such places were common in Dickens's day; indeed, before writing *Nickleby*, Dickens posed as a prospective client and investigated a similar "academy" in Yorkshire run by a man called William Shaw. Shaw was notorious; some of his pupils suffered from diseases brought on by years of neglect. *Nicholas Nickleby*, then, even more than *Oliver Twist*, is roughly akin to what is called today "investigative journalism." Drawing on firsthand research, it aims to expose an intolerable social ill requiring immediate attention—and immediate fixing.

And yet, little in *Nicholas Nickleby* qualifies as objective reportage. Those sections dealing with Squeers and his "school" do not recall Upton Sinclair's *The Jungle* (1906), say, or other well-known novels of social protest or "social realism" published during the first decades of this century. Nor was Dickens's style like that of Honoré de Balzac, or Mrs. Elizabeth Gaskell, or Thomas Hardy. Dickens, a brilliant user of realistic details, also found the impulse to exaggerate hard to resist; he was always drawn to the comic and the grotesque. Thus could Lord Clark, for one, note that "for all his generosity of spirit, Dickens took a kind of sadistic pleasure in the horrors he described." And in fact, in the end, it is surely this impulse for slapstick and comic hyperbole that has kept many from taking seriously Dickens's intellectual and moral views: a writer who gives his characters names like Squeers, Bumble, Sweedlepipe, and Toots will simply never get credit for moral gravity, will never be grouped with Tolstoy, Mann, and Solzhenitsyn. In any event, as Peter Ackroyd neatly puts it, "Dickens is rarely if ever a 'realistic' writer in any accepted sense; all of his polemic and observation are at the service of the larger themes or moods with which he animated his narrative. What he saw, and remembered, was determined by what he felt; his temperament, grave or gay, filled the world with its own shapes."

Descriptions of Squeers and his family are underscored with the sort of weighty irony one always finds in Dickens's work; Squeers's grotesque son—"a striking likeness of his father"—is called "amiable." Mrs. Squeers, as horrid as her husband, is an "amiable helpmate"; at one point she force-feeds her pathetic pupils from "an immense basin of brimstone and treacle" that the narrator calls "a delicious compound," and is part of a diet that also includes "a brown composition which looked like diluted pincushions without the covers, and was called porridge." Of course, Squeers and his clan are themselves amply nourished; and—like Bumble, and other monstrous hypocrites Dickens would come to create—they justify their grossly selfish and insensitive acts with self-serving moral precepts. Soon after arriving at Dotheboys Hall, Nicholas sees Squeers dispense small amounts of nourishment to his charges, and announce: "'Subdue your appetites, my dears, and you've conquered human nature. This is the way we inculcate strength of mind, Mr. Nickleby,'" he explains, "turning to Nicholas, and speaking with his mouth very full of beef and toast." Again, Dickens is particularly blunt when he wants to remind his readers that Squeers's victims have—like Fagin's—been robbed of their childhood and a chance for normal physical and mental growth. At one point, as Nicholas surveys the "pale and haggard faces" in his class, he sees "children with the countenances of old men." These, he realizes, were:

little faces which should have been handsome, darkened with the scowl of sullen, dogged suffering; there was childhood with the light of its eye quenched, its beauty gone, and its helplessness alone remaining; there were vicious-faced boys, brooding, with leaden eyes, like malefactors in a jail; and there were young creatures on whom the sins of their frail parents had descended, weeping even for the mercenary nurses they had known, and lonesome even in their loneliness. With every kindly sympathy and affection blasted in its birth, with every young and healthy feeling flogged and starved down, with every revengeful passion that can fester in swollen hearts eating its evil way to their core in silence, what an incipient Hell was breeding here!

In his description of Squeers himself, one finds the essence of Dickens's early style: an adroit, distinctive blend of detail, under-statement, and hyperbole. Squeers is, like many of Dickens's characters, perfectly named—in this case a serpentine, sinister *s* is simply but aptly stuck in front of "queer." Squeers's "appearance" one is told, "was not prepossessing." He "had but one eye, and the popular prejudice runs in favor of two. The eye he had was unquestionably useful, but not ornamental: being of a greenish grey, and in shape resembling the fan-light of a street door." (Who but Dickens could see, in porridge, "diluted pincushions," and, in an eye, the fanlight of a street door?) "The blank side" of Squeers's face "was much puckered up, which gave him a very sinister appearance, especially when he smiled, at which times his expression bordered closely on the villainous." ("Sinister," "villainous": again the language of melodrama, but combined with an image of blankness—nothingness—that is not only scary, but very fitting for an evil, idiotic man hollow at the core.) Squeers's hair "was very flat and shiny, save at the ends, where it was brushed stiffly up from a low protruding forehead, which assorted well with his harsh voice and coarse manner." ("Stiffly" is of course perfect for the rigid Squeers, and so is the "low forehead," with its suggestion of an obdurate, simian stupidity.)

The novel's title character is neither hugely interesting nor particularly complex. Nicholas Nickleby is earnest, good, and naive—like many young heroes of the Victorian stage. One is inclined to like him instantly, and particularly when he shows kindness to the lame and "hopeless" Smike who, although "eighteen or nineteen years old," and "tall for that age," is first shown wearing "a skeleton suit, such as is usually put upon very little boys"—and who becomes, very possibly, the most movingly pathetic figure in all of Dickens's fiction. Like all heroes, Nicholas must do battle with—and vanquish—several foes: he ends up smacking Squeers around the schoolroom, after informing "the ruffian" that "my indignation is aggravated by the dastardly cruelties practised on helpless infancy in this foul den." As Squeers's daughter Fanny would later relate, in a lengthy letter to Ralph Nickleby—and one of the most hilarious bits in all of Dickens—this "nevew that you recommended for a teacher" left the schoolmaster "one mask of brooses both blue and green likewise two forms are steepled in his Goar. We were kimpelled to have him carried down into the kitchen where he now lays."

Nicholas also ends up throttling Sir Mulberry in another scene that surely pleased Dickens's readers. For although Nicholas grandly calls himself "the son of a country gentleman," he must, like most people—like Dickens himself—work to survive; for Hawk, pampered since youth, life is no struggle, but a game. Thus at one point Sir Mulberry is found "lounging on an ottoman" and "the worse—if a man be a ruffian at heart, he is never the better—for wine." Elsewhere he is in his private apartment in Regent Street, "reclining listlessly" on a sofa at three o'clock in the afternoon, worn from "the debauch" of the night before. In subsequent works, Dickens, following Carlyle, criticizes the aristocracy and other members of the monied classes for failing to lead, and putting decadent self-indulgence above social responsibility. Indeed, here Dickens appears to hate Sir Mulberry as much for his idleness as his lechery. As Carlyle wrote in *Past and Present*, "One monster there is in the world—the idle man." These are not words Sir Mulberry would readily understand—but that would certainly ring true with most of those reading Dickens's works. Fiction writing is, after all, a public act; no novel begins to succeed unless it finds an audience greater than one. In his own day Dickens had a vast audience, but based largely in the rising middle class or, in Julian Symons's words, "the ascending bourgeoisie," whom he sought both to amuse and attack: to move, tease, and inspire. Certainly as Symons once observed, Dickens's "feelings"—as expressed in *Sketches by Boz* and all that followed—seemed always to be "perfectly at one with those of his chosen audience"; indeed, "in conscious belief he adhered utterly to its scale of values." Thus

the lower class, in his work, are comic figures when well treated by their masters; when badly treated by unjust masters they are pathetic. The aristocracy may be selfish or stupid, and very often they have a family secret to hide in the form of some blemish of birth or crime. The professional class are seen, with very few exceptions, as a parasitic growth upon the upper class. But the central characters of Dickens's novels, both heroes and villains, belong generally to the bourgeoisie. They are merchants and shopkeepers, near-gentlemen and white-collar office workers, young men with a position in society rendered dubious by the source, or the lack, of their income.

Sir Mulberry, the rakish aristocrat, could have strolled straight out of any number of novels and plays popular in Dickens's day. But *Nicholas Nickleby* does show Dickens maturing somewhat as a creator of character; even such secondary figures as Mr. Mantalini and Mrs. Nickleby are delightfully individuated, the latter apparently owing much to Dickens's own mother. The villainous Ralph Nickleby, one learns, has disowned his son Smike and left him to the mercies of Squeers. He regards his brother's family with nothing but contempt. He tries to pimp his niece. But even *he* gains some depth, if not much decency, as the novel proceeds. Ralph can be fawning as well as condescending; sometimes, fleetingly—in scenes that foreshadow somewhat his guiltracked end—Ralph shows hints of remorse, of a long-buried humanity. Sir Mulberry vows revenge on Nicholas, promising to drag "that pattern of chastity, that pink of prudery, his delicate sister, through—" And the narrator notes: "It might have been that even Ralph's cold blood tingled in his cheeks at that moment. It might have been that Sir Mulberry remembered, that, knave and usurer as he was, he must, in some early time of infancy, have twined his arm about her father's neck."

Nicholas Nickleby first appeared in monthly parts under the full title, *The Life and Adventures of Nicholas Nickleby, Containing a Faithful Account of the Fortunes, Misfortunes, Uprisings, Downfallings, and Complete Career of the Nickleby Family*. As Norman Page notes, this allusion to "life and adventures" in the title brings to mind "the eighteenth-century authors whom Dickens, like David Copperfield, read as a child"; and *Nickleby* certainly is, like *Pickwick*, "picaresque in structure and spirit. Like Smollett's *Roderick Random*, Nicholas is an impoverished young man of good family driven by circumstances to make his own way in the world." As the novel proceeds, Nicholas does deepen a bit; one see hints of his own idiosyncrasies. Like his mother, he has a dreamy, self-deluding, highly romanticizing side; indeed, Mrs. Nickleby decides initially that Sir Mulberry would make the perfect mate for Kate—the very man she would have picked "if she had been picking and choosing from all mankind." And so Nicholas is seen early on preparing to teach at Squeers's "school" and entertaining a "thousand visionary ideas." Nicholas tells his sneering uncle that he half expects that "some young nobleman who is being educated at the Hall" will "take a fancy" to him and, perhaps, "get his father" to find him "some handsome appointment." Of course, Nicholas—like so many of Dickens's heroes—loses much of his innocence as his story proceeds: few novelists have been so consistently drawn not only to the picaresque tradition, but to the spirit and structure of the *bildungsroman*. Nicholas starts the novel "wholly unacquainted with what is called the world." But near its close, in a remarkable passage, Dickens shows Nicholas—not a particularly contemplative fellow—considering the harsher realities of life, and so anticipating the concerns of *The Old Curiosity Shop*, a work full of dark shadows. Pacing the streets, aching to talk to his love Madeline but fearing that she will soon enter the "clutches" of the slimy Arthur Gride, Nicholas is struck by how "regularly things went on, from day to day, in the same unvarying round; how youth and beauty died, and ugly griping age lived tottering on; how crafty avarice grew rich, and manly honest hearts were poor and sad; how few they were who tenanted the stately houses, and how many those who lay in noisome pens, or rose each day and laid them down each night, and lived and died, father and son, mother and child, race upon race, generation upon generation, without a home to shelter them or the energies of a single man directed to their aid."

Suddenly Nicholas has shown a political side. And what follows recalls the many narrative outbursts of *Oliver Twist*. It similarly retains its power because it strikes one as something Dickens has not faked, or stuck crudely into the narrative in order to appear—to use the tired contemporary phrase—"politically correct." One suspects, indeed, that much of the affection and admiration that Dickens still inspires comes largely from the fact that passages such as these, put down by a writer still in his twenties, are so *un*selfconscious, so plainly sincere, so alive with honest anger. Nicholas now thinks of how, in the surrounding city, many were doomed to live "a most wretched and inadequate subsistence," including children who, in time, will "drive most criminal and dreadful trades." He thinks also of how "ignorance was punished and never taught," of

how jail-doors gaped and gallows loomed, for thousands urged towards them by circumstances darkly curtaining their very cradles' heads, and but for which they might have earned their honest bread and lived in peace;

how many died in soul, and had no chance of life; how many who could scarcely go astray, be they vicious as they would, turned haughtily from the crushed and stricken wretch who could scarcely do otherwise, and who would have been a greater wonder had he or she done well, than even they had done ill; how much injustice, misery, and wrong there was, and yet how the world rolled on, from year to year, alike careless and indifferent, and no man seeking to remedy or redress it.

Twice Nicholas thinks of this missing "man" coming to "aid" the poor and the suffering. But the novel does not strongly suggest that Nicholas himself will pick up this challenge; "he felt, indeed, that there was little ground for hope." Nicholas decides abruptly to think of other things, for—as the narrator notes—"youth is not prone to contemplate the darkest side of a picture it can shift at will." The passage thus seems to confirm the charge that, when it comes to politics, Dickens wants to have it both ways. Here, he catalogues a series of severe social problems—hard realities that no doubt most of his readers would prefer to ignore—but in the end says little more than, in effect, this is really quite awful and somebody ought to do something about it. Dickens does not supply—here or elsewhere—a rousing, extensive depiction of a man seriously bent on wide social reform. Nicholas marries Madeline, and then enters business with the Cheeryble brothers, hardly a pair of flaming revolutionaries. The Cheerybles stand for capitalism's more benevolent side; for that Pickwickian strain of goodness and decency that Dickens's novels often hold up as the only real and lasting solution to the sort of horrors that Nicholas describes. "The truth is that Dickens's criticism of society is almost exclusively moral," writes George Orwell, from the political left, in 1939. "Hence the utter lack of any constructive suggestion anywhere in his work." For Dickens's real target, always, "is not so much society as 'human nature.'" It "would be difficult," Orwell adds, "to point anywhere in his books to a passage suggesting that the economic system is wrong *as a system*. Nowhere, for instance, does he make any attack on private enterprise or private property." Of course one can infer from such later novels as *Hard Times* and *Our Mutual Friend* "the evil of *laissez-faire* capitalism." But even in the former, there is not "a line" that "can properly be called Socialistic; indeed, its tendency if anything is pro-capitalist, because its whole moral is that capitalists ought to be kind, not that workers ought to be rebellious." "As far as social criticism goes," Orwell writes, "one can never extract much more from Dickens than this, unless one deliberately reads meanings into him." (As T. A. Jackson tended to do in *Charles Dickens: The Progress of a Radical*.) Dickens's "whole 'message' is one that at first glance looks like an enormous platitude," Orwell concludes. "If men would behave decently the world would be decent."

Like *Hard Times*, *Nicholas Nickleby* very clearly celebrates the importance of the imagination—and those who, against the odds, bring the pleasures of escape and play to a post-Puritan culture where such pleasures are not valued (at least not in the "respectable" classes) and are often crushed beneath the realities of money getting and grueling labor. Vincent Crummles—an impresario and ham—is obviously one of the more sympathetic figures in *Nicholas Nickleby*; he performs what Dickens clearly sees as crucial, soul-saving work. He is also, of course, something of a con man, prone to shameless hype, packaging his daughter as an "infant Prodigy" when she is obviously neither. But Crummles displays many of the virtues Dickens most likes to praise. Unlike Ralph Nickleby, Crummles has channeled his talents and energies not into the making of profit, but into the making of play—or more precisely, plays. Crummles is cordial and nonjudgmental: he gives Smike, as well as Nicholas, a crack at the stage. Crummles is not rich; but like his similarly eccentric wife—herself an actor—he is generous and kind. Mrs. Crummles promptly offers to feed Nicholas a meal at their first meeting. "We have but a shoulder of mutton with onion sauce," she tells him, "but such as our dinner is, we beg you to partake of it." "You are very good," Nicholas replies, quite rightly. As Angus Wilson writes, the Crummles episodes permit Dickens to pay "splendid tribute to the theatre" as represented in this "little world of the fourth-rate touring company." "Vanity," Wilson notes, "is their mainspring, as it must be for all theatre people who are offering what is so poor; but they also know that what they offer has its spring in fancy and imagination, which make it worth more than all the values of the wretched local bourgeoisie to whom they have to beg for patronage." In this light, Nicholas's early chat with Crummles and wife is worth noting. "Are they theatrical people here?" Nicholas asks, referring to those in the surrounding town.

"'No,' replied Mr. Crummles, shaking his head, 'far from it—far from it.'

'I pity them,' observed Mrs. Crummles.

'So do I,' said Nicholas; 'if they have no relish for theatrical entertainments, properly conducted.'"

The Old Curiosity Shop also features appearances by various itinerant showmen, including one Vuffin, who manages a "giant," a "little lady without legs or arms" and, not least, a "silent gentleman" who "had rather deranged the natural expression of his countenance by putting small leaden lozenges into his eyes and bringing them out at his mouth." In chapter 19 these figures assemble at the Jolly Sandboys, where they talk shop; Vuffin—a specialist in entertainers of a certain size—concedes that his giant is getting bad knees: bad news indeed. "Once get a giant shaky on his legs," Vuffin admits, "and the public care no more about him than they do a dead cabbagestalk." The fickle public will, of course, take quickly to an old, "well-wrinkled" dwarf, but will simply not put down good money to see a giant "weak in the legs and not standing upright."

This *Old Curiosity Shop* brims with strange beings and grim events, showing well the fascination with the morbid and grotesque that would always be part of Dickens's art. Its main villain, Daniel Quilp, is the novel's most striking character—and the role Danny DeVito was born to play. Quilp is compellingly monstrous, and not simply because of his curious physical attributes—Dickens notes that he was "quite a dwarf, though his head and face were large enough for the body of a giant"—but because of his ceaseless proclivity for mischief and cruelty. (Quilp is prefigured, one thinks, by a figure Dickens brings very briefly into chapter 32 of *Oliver Twist*, a "little demon" who sets up "a hideous yell, and danced upon the ground, as if wild with rage.") Quilp, another of Dickens's wicked moneylenders, is so malevolently alert, so self-absorbed, so quick with the cutting quip, and so hotly fueled by envy, lust, and greed, that he prompts attention and amusement every time he appears. Here's Quilp at play:

Among his various eccentric habits he had a humorous one of always cheating at cards, which rendered necessary on his part, not only a close observance of the game, and a sleight of hand in counting and scoring, but also involved the constant correction, by looks, and frowns, and kicks under the table, of Richard Swiveller, who being bewildered by the rapidity with which his cards were told, and at the rate at which the pegs traveled down the board, could not be prevented from sometimes expressing his surprise and incredulity.

Quilp leers and bites. He beats and abuses his wife. Quilp craves "the secret store of money" he wrongly believes that Little Nell's grandfather hoards—and he craves Nell herself with an intensity that is hard to miss: "Be a good girl, Nelly," he tells her, "and see if you don't come to be Mrs. Quilp of Tower Hill." Like Shakespeare, and all great writers, Dickens clearly likes his darker characters, or at least some of them; indeed Quilp, small and driven and volcanic, possesses certain traits that recall Dickens's own. One finds Quilp compelling—as do many of the women he meets. "With the exception of Little Nell," writes Fred Kaplan, "women respond to this Quilpian urge, and it is irresistible. Mrs. Quilp has learned on the bed and with the bruises of experience the close relationship between repulsion and attraction, the conspiracy between dominating male and subjugated female, between operator and subject, that flourishes in a certain psychological-sexual ambiance so common to both fairy tales and the actual arrangements of Victorian culture."

Quilp is, whatever else, the embodiment of animal energy and instinct—"I'm as sharp as a ferret," he boasts at one point, "and as cunning as a weasel." Elsewhere one sees Quilp's "hawk's eye" and his "dog-like smile." He is an "evil spirit" who at one point does "a kind of demon-dance" around a dog he cruelly torments. Here then, Dickens underlines Quilp's animal viciousness by placing him eye to eye with another beast. We also see Quilp's "extraordinary greediness" when, in another scene, he shovels down "hard eggs, shell and all," as well as "gigantic prawns with the heads and tails on." Quilp also enjoys the simultaneous chewing of tobacco and watercress, and washing his grub down with "boiling tea" that he drinks "without winking."

This curious and largely ignored novel is full of such grotesqueries, with images and instances of cruelty and caprice, with sadness and suffering. Its two most sympathetic figures, Nell Trent, who is "nearly fourteen," and her grandfather—a chronic gambler— find themselves far from home, "alone in the world" and destitute, longing for the "peace of mind and happiness they had once enjoyed." Nell dies, but not before Dickens has her witness the slow death of another child, the "Little Scholar." Before that Dickens sends Nell to a cemetery, where she examines the headstone of a young man dead for half a century. There she meets his widow, now withered with age, who notes that "death doesn't change us more than life, dear." Throughout the novel, life is portrayed as one long, grim losing battle—a battle full of vile predators and vulnerable prey. No wonder Mr. Codlin, the circus owner and misanthrope, considers himself "doomed to contemplate the harsh realities of existence."

And yet, *The Old Curiosity Shop* does not seem to have struck Dickens's contemporaries as unduly depressing. Quilp—like Squeers and like Fagin—is monstrous; but he also has an absurd comicality that reminds us of the circus, of vaudeville, of tall tales, and such infamous figures as Punch and Rumpelstiltskin. The novel's scenes of long illness and lingering death are balanced by its many references to an afterlife—to the "bright and happy existence" that awaits "those who die young." (And many did die young in the London of 1839; nearly half of all funerals were for children under ten; the average life span in this city of two million was around twenty-seven.) "Think what earth is," the narrator comments in the wake of Little Nell's death, "compared with the World to which her young spirit has winged its early flight; and say, if one deliberate wish expressed in solemn terms above this bed could call her back to life, which of us would utter it!" As Dennis Walder notes, some readers—including Harriet Beecher Stowe—complained that in spirit and imagery the book was not sufficiently Christian; that, as Stowe put it, Dickens "did not appear to recognise 'such a person as Jesus Christ,' or 'such a book as the Bible.'" In fact, as Walder writes, "nowhere" in the novel does Dickens "appear to provide explicit support for the central Christian belief in Christ as mediator and redeemer." And yet, there are those repeated references to life after death, to—as Walder writes—"resurrection, when man will come face to face with God, the source of all light." *The Old Curiosity Shop* again reminds us not only that Dickens's expressed religious beliefs were in the main quite orthodox, but that throughout most of his career he was reluctant to strand his readers in the gloom: there was always, at some point, light.

Moreover, readers of *The Old Curiosity Shop* could find within its pages certain Pickwickian echoes—bits of improvised horseplay and sudden showers of gratuitous detail that do nothing to advance the novel's plot, such as it is, but that certainly enrich its atmosphere. In chapter 39, for example, one suddenly finds, tossed casually into a dinner scene, the figure of Kit's baby brother, "sitting up in his mother's lap," while "trying to force a large orange into his mouth, and gazing intently at the lights in the chandelier."

Much of the novel's horseplay is, quite literally, horseplay. Whisker, Mr. Chuckster's willful pony, provides much of the novel's comic relief, heading this way and that as he deems fit; he must thus be reasoned with, and repeatedly warned "on the extreme impropriety of his conduct." Dickens delights in giving animals human traits—a practice that enhances this fairy-tale or folktale quality of much of his earlier fiction (where, for example, as Norman Page notes, Oliver Twist can be viewed "as a male Cinderella or princess disguised as a goosegirl"). In *The Old Curiosity Shop*, that fairy-tale flavor is most clearly enhanced by the surreal presence of Quilp; by Codlin's Fellini-like circus; by Richard Swiveller and his love affair with a maidservant, "The Marchioness," whom he comes to call Sophronia Sphynx. Swiveller is the sort of character who would always fascinate Dickens: he is a shabby clerk on the fringe of London life who fancies himself something of a gentleman and so cultivates a certain style—the result being both comic and pathetic. Although inimitable in his own right, and a rather convincing combination of shadiness and charm (Quilp calls him a gentleman of "great expectations"), Swiveller is something of a rough sketch for the more deeply drawn Wilkins Micawber, who in *David Copperfield* is made similarly memorable by his inflated language and his theatrical flair. "And say," Swiveller tells Quilp at one point, "say, sir, that I was wafted here upon the pinions of concord; that I came to remove, with the rake of friendship, the seeds of mutual wiolence and heart-burning, and to sow in their place, the germs of social harmony."

In *The Old Curiosity Shop*, Quilp stands as Dickens's figure of supreme selfishness: he is brutal greed run amok. Dickens wanted *Martin Chuzzlewit* to be an assault on selfishness through his depiction of Seth Pecksniff and assorted members of the Chuzzlewit family, whose long history he facetiously but tediously recounts in an opening chapter that also stresses that "violence and vagabondism" have long been part of the human scene; that the Chuzzlewits themselves—though quite certain of their "immense superiority" to the rest of mankind—were long "actively connected with diverse slaughterous conspiracies and bloody frays." Actually, no Dickens novel—not even Pickwick—takes this long to unwind; there is, at the start of chapter 2, a rather overblown description of the wind, which is personified as being wilful and rather wild. The early Dickens is, in fact, noticeably fond of personifying nature and time—a technique that would have seemed familiar and perhaps rather clever to readers in his own day, but that surely strikes most of us today as unnecessarily "poetic" and fey. (Ruskin, of course, had little use for this sort of practice; his famous 1856 discussion "Of the Pathetic Fallacy" attacks that literary impulse that would allow Charles Kingsley in *Alton Locke* (1850), to describe foam as "cruel, crawling"; that would drive Samuel Coleridge to make "the one red leaf, the last of its clan," not only "dance," but "dance as often as dance it can." Coleridge, Ruskin complained, "has a morbid, that is to say, a so far false, idea about the leaf; he fancies a life in it, and will, which there are not; confuses its powerlessness with choice, its fading death with merriment, and the wind that shakes it with music.") Dickens's description and deployment of the wind at the start of *Chuzzlewit* is more playful than morbid, albeit rather forced: Dickens finally employs it, successfully, to extinguish a candle and slam shut a street door against Seth Pecksniff, who—instead of entering his house—ends up tumbling down some steps, and receiving "that sort of knock on the head which lights up for the patient's entertainment an imaginary general illumination of very bright short-sixes." It is an inspired bit of slapstick that also serves to introduce Pecksniff's bouncing daughters, Mercy and Charity, who come to the aid of their father, and who—when helped to his feet—"continued to keep his mouth and his eyes very wide open and to drop his lower jaw, somewhat after the manner of a toy nutcracker." Thus the general tone of the novel is set: it too will include parody, satire, and a good bit of cartooning. Indeed one is relieved when Pecksniff and his daughters take the stage. At last, one thinks, Dickens ponderous will now give way to Dickens playful, and the Pecksniffs will stand as an especially rich gallery of hypocritical grotesques. We are told that Pecksniff— debunked even before he opens his mouth—"was a moral man"; that, in fact, "there never was a more moral man than Mr. Pecksniff." In fact, "he was a most exemplary man, fuller of virtuous precepts than a copy book." We are also told, however, that Pecksniff's manner is "soft and oily." He is an architect, according to the "brazen plate" upon his door. But Pecksniff's "genius," one learns, "lay in ensnaring" pupils who pay high premiums for zero results. Of Pecksniff's "architectural doings nothing was clearly known except that he had never designed or built anything." Still, "it was generally understood that his knowledge of the science was almost awful in its profundity." Here then is Squeers with a slicker veneer; here is another in a long line of Dickensian hypocrites, con men, and frauds. Pecksniff, like Merdle—the murky financier in *Little Dorrit*—is all surface, precisely the sort of man who can flourish in a society obsessed with status, propriety, and money, and where it matters far less who one is than what one *appears* to be.

Pecksniff, one of Dickens's most vivid creations, has entered the dictionary as a synonym for unctuous hypocrisy. But some readers will today find him—and his gruesome daughters—to be rather too bluntly drawn, more wearying than amusing, suggesting the sort of bat-on-the-head satirical overkill that marks Sinclair Lewis at his worst. In Sarah Gamp, midwife and "nurse," Dickens has created another enduring, although no more endearing, character: a "fat old woman" with "a husky voice and a moist eye" who drinks much, takes snuff, and rattles on always about her friend and ally, Mrs. Harris, glimpsed by none but Gamp herself. Dickens, through Mrs. Gamp, reveals again his acute understanding of the crucial role that imagination—and self-delusion—plays in human psychology. He shows through her colorful, comical, self-congratulating monologues a superb ability to convey convincingly not only the free flow of colloquial speech, but the ways in which thought itself unfolds. Mrs. Gamp's rich if rather disgusting character is revealed gradually, bit by bit, and is wholly convincing—as is her own creation of Mrs. Harris, her staunch ally. Mrs. Gamp is the perfect representative of Dickens's comedy, and that comedy, as V. S. Pritchett once shrewdly observed, is built upon the fact that London itself is, in many ways, "the chief character" of much of his fiction. "Its fogs," he writes, "its smoke, its noise, its courts, officers, bricks, slums and docks, its gentilities and its crimes, have a quasi-human body. London is seen as the sum of the fantasies and dreams of its inhabitants."

It is a city of speeches and voices. The comedy will be in the fusion of the city's dream life and its realities. So will the committal to moral indignation. What we precisely find in this comedy is people's projection of their self-esteem, the attempt to disentangle the self from the ineluctable London situation; they take on the dramatic role of solitary pronouncers. All Dickens's characters, comic or not, issue personal pronouncements that magnify their inner life. Some are crude like Podsnap, others are subtle like Pecksniff or poetic like Micawber, unbelievable like Skimpole, aristocratic casuists like the father of the Marshalsea, glossy like the Veneerings. All are actors; quip or rhetoric is second nature to them. They are strange, even mad, because they speak as if they were they only persons in the world.

Mrs. Gamp, continues Pritchett, lives by a "private idea or fiction"—by "the fiction of the approval of her imaginary friend Mrs. Harris." This "self-made myth"—as Pritchett calls her—turns up in only eight of the fifty-four chapters in *Martin Chuzzlewit*. But for many she is its dominant figure; one hears her distinctive and tipsy voice, her mispronunciations—"calcilations," "suppoge," "betwixt you and me"—long after one puts down the book. One can also learn much about the nature of Dickens's art by studying the way he brings her on and off the stage, and the way he lets her move from point to point in the sort of leaping but artful ramble that makes us think of any good comic monologist—or, indeed, of Joyce's Molly Bloom, whose interior talk would range similarly over the comings and goings of mankind. Joyce, one assumes, learned much from Dickens: the two viewed life in similar ways. But the difference between Dickens and Joyce is not only the difference between England and Ireland but between religious belief and tormented doubt. It is also the difference of seventy or eighty years. Dickens wrote *Chuzzlewit* before critics and other writers placed a premium on "realism" in fiction, and before novel-writing in Britain had achieved the status of *art*—at least in the sense that Henry James or Joyce would have used the term. Thus Dickens is still clumsy where Joyce would be supremely sophisticated; the author of *Pickwick* and *Twist* still senses the need to pop into the plot occasionally to make sure that even the dimmest souls in his audience catch his points—he even feels compelled to note that Mrs. Harris is very probably a figment of Mrs. Gamp's fertile, if boozy, imagination. Thus, in chapter 25, when Mrs. Gamp stops for breath, Dickens steps in. "Advantage may be taken," he writes, "to state that a fearful mystery surrounded this lady by the name of Harris, whom no one in the circle of Mrs. Gamp's acquaintance had ever seen; neither did any human being know her place of residence, though Mrs. Gamp appeared on her own showing to be in constant communication with her." He continues:

There were conflicting rumors on the subject, but the prevalent opinion was that she was a phantom of Mrs. Gamp's brain—as Messrs. Doe and Roe are fictions of the law—created for the express purpose of holding visionary dialogues with her on all manner of subjects and invariably winding up with a compliment to the excellence of her nature.

Dickens was, at the very least, the Robin Williams of his day, capable of assuming quite convincingly a wide range of characters and then improvising outrageously, hilariously. Mrs. Gamp's voice is certainly authentic: you can still hear it in certain British shops and buses. Dickens "could imitate," one friend would recall, "in a manner that I have never heard equaled the low population of the streets of London in all their varieties, whether mere loafers or sellers of fruit, vegetables, or anything else." Indeed, Mrs. Gamp is a Dickens classic; she is so vividly drawn that she has lived on, in various guises, even off the page. As recently as 1934 André Maurois could write, with both amazement and respect:

In every English-speaking country Dickens is still the great popular writer. This very evening, no doubt, in some music-hall of the London suburbs, in a programme of acrobats, low comedians, dancers, and ventriloquists, one might see that peculiar "turn" the "Dickens Impersonator," the man who can mime the Dickens characters. He invites the audience to suggest names, and from all parts of the house come the cries: "Pickwick!" "Sam Weller!" "Little Nell!" "Fagin!" "Mrs. Gamp!" "Pecksniff!" The performer extracts wigs and clothing from a basket, and, donning the outward semblance of each of these immortals in turn, imitates their speech for a few minutes. Would such a performance be possible in France? Can one imagine a working-class audience shouting for Vautrin or Baron Hulot, Madame Marneffe or Rastignac?

Martin Chuzzlewit would be hopelessly slow without Mrs. Gamp. It was, in fact, a sluggish seller. Jonas Chuzzlewit, as many critics have noted, is a rather interesting study in vile, selfish brutality: he schemes constantly, darkly, even trying to poison his father, Anthony, as a fast way of getting his share of the family's loot. The novel offers two Martin Chuzzlewits—and neither is hugely interesting. "Old Martin," Anthony's brother, is both a miser and a bore. His grandson, the other Martin, is somewhat more complexly drawn than Dickens's previous protagonists; he is self-centered as the novel begins and becomes less so as it proceeds. Still, Martin is no David Copperfield—and for many readers he will remain little more than a name on the page. Mark Tapley, Young Martin's kindly and ever-optimistic servant, is a dim echo of Sam Weller,

distinguished mainly by his habit of saying "jolly" a lot no matter
how trying his circumstances. Certainly the chapter in *Chuzzlewit*
entitled "Miss Pecksniff Makes Love" will disappoint those
thumbing the book to find an erotic interlude.

When Mrs. Gamp is away, the novel's most satisfying sections
take place when Martin and Mark visit America—a trip Dickens
rather abruptly arranged in the hope of sparking sales that hung for
months at around twenty-four thousand copies. (Sales of Dickens's
other novels averaged twice that.) Mark and Martin endure a rough
crossing on a ship pointedly called *The Screw*. Mark retains his
good humor, as do many of the immigrants they encounter in the
ship's steerage sections. These are poor people, "English people,
Irish people, Welsh people, and Scotch people, all with their little
store of coarse food and shabby clothes"; and nearly all "with their
families of children"—valiant souls braving danger and the unknown
in search of a second chance, a better life. Dickens pays them
tribute. "Every kind of domestic suffering that is bred in poverty,
illness, banishment, sorrow, and long travel in bad weather was
crammed into the little space and yet there was infinitely less
complaint and querulousness and infinitely more of mutual
assistance and general kindness to be found in that unwholesome ark
than in many brilliant ball-rooms."

As Martin and Mark discover, this place so far from England is
far from Utopia too. Dickens now uses the novel to mock all that he
found disagreeable during his first trip to the United States; in fact,
as Alexander Welsh, for one, rightly points out, many of Martin's
experiences in America would seem far more likely for "a
celebrity"—that is, for "a person in Dickens's situation"—than for
"an impoverished young man" hoping to find his fortune in the New
World. Martin, writes Welsh in *From Copyright to Copperfield*
(1987), is "consulted as a literary authority, begged to share his
influence with important people, and constantly grabbed by the hand
or stared at."

Readers and reviewers on both sides of the Atlantic quickly and
critically took note of the bile in these chapters. As Sidney P. Moss
records in his admirably researched book, *Charles Dickens' Quarrel
With America* (1984), the *London Athenaeum* saw little more than
"bad temper and prejudice" in these American episodes; the *North
American Review* found them "an unaccountable excrescence,"
presumably meant to "form a new and more pungent edition of the

American Notes, but with only the harshest censures distilled over and concentrated." Not surprisingly, the American press was, as Moss shows, particularly hostile—although some of these publications were in the ironical position of savaging a work they were simultaneously stealing. Dickens had, apparently, counted on such a paradox: he was still steaming over the lack of international copyright, and wanted these chapters in *Chuzzlewit* to function especially as a direct assault on American greed and hypocrisy.

Thus Martin, disembarking in New York, promptly notices that the newspapers—which Dickens subtly dubs the *Sewer* and the *Peeper* and the like—devote themselves largely to the sensationalized coverage of violence, mayhem, and scandal. One paper promises "an exclusive account of a flagrant act of dishonesty committed by the Secretary of State when he was eight years old, now communicated, at a great expense, by his own nurse." Throughout his career Dickens demanded high standards for the press, which he believed could—ideally—lead the world "onward in the path of knowledge, of mercy, and of human improvement." He was then consistently critical of publications, British or American, that strayed from this ideal, choosing instead to court the most doltish minds. Before coming to the States, Dickens seems to have believed, however naively, that he would find in the new nation, and in its organs of information, a renewed commitment to the same high political and aesthetic values. His disappointment was first expressed in his *American Notes*, where he observes that American journalism dealt largely in "round abuse and blackguard names," and liked "pulling off the roofs of private houses." It was forever "primping and pandering for all degrees of vicious taste"—a description that of course retains its relevancy at a time when the coverage of "news" in America has fallen increasingly to commercial television, which exists solely to generate large profits, and so supplies a daily fare of violence and titillation designed, presumably, to appeal in some elemental way to every human being alive, however vulgar or dim.

There is no doubt many in the States in Dickens's day found elements of truth in the more controversial chapters of *Chuzzlewit*; indeed, in many respects, they echo views published by other Europeans after earlier American tours; Alexis de Tocqueville, the best known of these, had similarly come across a good deal of coarse behavior not generally displayed in the more refined quarters of European society. "In democratic countries," he observed, "manners are generally devoid of dignity"; the "men who live in democracies are too fluctuating for a certain number of them ever to succeed in laying down a code of good breeding, and forcing people to follow it." Thus "every man," for better or worse, "behaves after his own fashion, and there is always a certain incoherence in the manners of such times, because they are moulded upon the feelings and notions of each individual, rather than upon an ideal model proposed for general imitation."

But Tocqueville tends to be balanced, circumspect; his more critical observations are tempered by complimentary words; he finds in most aspects of American life many things to praise. ("No man, upon the earth," he writes, "can as yet affirm, absolutely and generally, that the new state of the world is better than its former one; but it is already easy to perceive that this state is different.") Dickens, in *Chuzzlewit*, shows no inclination to be objective or detached. His criticisms of America are the stuff of lancing satire. Many reading *Chuzzlewit* today, alas, will find observations that continue to ring true in a nation that remains full of great possibilities and great contradictions—one that remains both proud and insecure, self-righteous and self-critical, grandly heroic and stunningly moronic, always willing to proclaim its achievements, but not eager to receive criticism from the outside. "Martin knew nothing about America," notes the narrator in chapter 16, "or he would have known perfectly well that if its individual citizens, to a man, are to be believed, it always *is* depressed, and always *is* stagnated, and always *is* at an alarming crisis, and never was otherwise, though as a body they are ready to make oath upon the Evangelists at any hour of the day or night that it is the most thriving and prosperous of all countries on the habitable globe." Thus one "shabbily dressed" citizen reminds Martin that America is "the envy of the World," the place where "the leaders of Human Civilisation" reside. As Martin discovers, boasting and social inflation are common in this new nation free for better or worse from cultural roots; it is full of all sorts of self-promoters and self-inventors, and Martin is forever meeting "one of the most remarkable men in our country." Thus, he also meets a great many bores. ("I am quite serious when I say that I do not believe there are, on the whole earth," Dickens told John Forster in a letter during his first American tour, "so many intensified bores as in these

United States. No man can form an adequate idea of the real meaning of the word, without coming here.") Americans, Martin realizes, are better at drinking than talking, more inclined to speechify than to converse: they show not only "an ineptitude for social and domestic pleasure," but an abiding preoccupation with making money. Indeed, in America, Dickens found taking shape all that he presciently feared about a future in which "Mammonism"— to use Carlyle's term—would grow increasingly pervasive and the commodification of virtually everything would finally take hold. "Dollars," a sadder but wiser Martin reflects. "All their cares, joys, hopes, affections, virtues, and associations seemed to be melted down into dollars. Whatever the chance contributions that fell into the slow cauldron of their talk, they made the gruel thick and slab with dollars. Men were weighed by their dollars, gauged by their dollars; life was auctioneered, appraised, put up, and knocked down for its dollars."

As the last sentence suggests, Dickens—like Tocqueville—was acutely aware of the moral travesty of slavery in the "Land of Liberty." Again, as Peter Ackroyd and others have shown, Dickens cannot be held up as a consistent foe of racist attitudes or colonialist practices: later in his life he showed clearer signs of racial chauvinism, cheering Governor Eyre's repressive measures in Jamaica, for example, and signaling his sympathy for the South in the American Civil War. But in his *American Notes* Dickens—at thirty—does write, at some length, about the "atrocities" of slavery. He condemns its upholders, saying that when they "speak of Freedom, [they] mean the Freedom to oppress their kind, and to be savage, merciless, and cruel." ("'Cash for Negroes,'" he records with disgust, "'Cash for Negroes, Cash for Negroes,' is the heading of advertisements in great capitals down the long columns of the crowded journals.") In *Martin Chuzzlewit*, Dickens uses the Norris family as the focus of this attack. Wealthy and snobbish, the Norrises are racists—and the sort of bores who cannot talk of their activities without also listing their achievements (they make a point of telling Martin that on their trips to England they have met with "all the great dukes, lords, viscounts, marquesses, duchesses, knights"). Martin, taking tea with this charming group, expresses his sympathy with the "repressed blacks"—and thus provokes laughter from one of the Norris girls, an airhead in fetching silk stockings. "The Negroes," she tells Martin, "were such a funny people, so excessively ludicrous in their manners and appearance that it was impossible for those who knew them well to associate any serious ideas with such an absurd part of the creation." The others in the family can only agree. "Mr. Norris the son," at the mere thought of interracial contact, "made a wry face and dusted his fingers as Hamlet might after getting rid of Yorick's skull, just as though he had that moment touched a Negro and some of the black had come off upon his hands." A few paragraphs later, Dickens underlines the family's self-righteous hypocrisy when—with his usual blunt irony—he brings in General Fladdock, a family friend, who has just come back from "that a-mazing Eu-rope" where he was sad to discover an "absence of a moral dignity" reflected in the "artificial barriers set up between man and man, the division of the human race into court cards and plain cards of every denomination—into clubs, diamonds, spades, anything but hearts!"

"'Ah!'" all the Norrises, disgusted, cry. "'Too true, General!'"

3

Facts of Life

Dombey and Son, David Copperfield, Bleak House, Hard Times

Dickens's indictment of the mindless, soul-killing pursuit of money continues in a novel that is largely—and not surprisingly—ignored today. Written in the wake of his relative failure with *Martin Chuzzlewit*, *Dombey and Son* was rather a struggle for Dickens, in part because its early chapters were written not in England but in Paris and Lausanne, where he had moved with his family in pursuit of the lower cost of living that the Continent, in those days, could still provide. At first Dickens enjoyed the change of scene: he "never grew tired," writes Peter Ackroyd, of "the icy mountains of the Alpine region." But especially as he began *Dombey*, Dickens realized that he missed the bustling atmosphere and creative stimulation that London always supplied. He was determined, however, to take particular care with structure and characterization. Dickens's earlier novels were more improvised, written hurriedly, sometimes rather slapdashedly, drawing inspiration from eighteenth-century models. He now wanted *Dombey* to confirm the seriousness of his artistry at a time when other writers—like Thackeray—were winning new readers and wide critical praise.

Some more recent critics, including John Lucas, have found much to praise in *Dombey and Son*. *Dombey*, writes Lucas in *The Melancholy Man* (1970), is "the first of Dickens's novels to be more or less thought through before begun." As a result, there is "brilliance" in its plotting; "hardly any of the narrative is irrelevant to the novel's concerns." Its treatment of the theme of time is both subtle and astute; *Dombey*, Lucas notes, "is after all about society in transition"—one in which power is shifting away from the

aristocracy to the middle class, of which Dombey stands as one
notable representative. But then Dombey himself is "a man of no
sure identity," a fact that contributes to the rigid, not-to-be-moved
role he has assumes in the world. "The real wonder of *Dombey and
Son*," Lucas writes, "is that it is so vast in range and yet so
coherent. To say that it is about England under Utilitarian ideas
would be absurd, but it is not absurd to point out that Dickens's
exploration of the effect of this spirit takes up ideas of self, great
expectations, money-interest and makes a wonderfully complex and
persuasively comprehensive statement. With *Dombey and Son*
Dickens becomes, I think, a really great creative critic of the modern
world. He also becomes the incomparably great master of the
English novel."

Kathleen Tillotson also finds much to admire in this rather
neglected work. *Dombey*, she notes, was the first of his novels in
which "a pervasive uneasiness about contemporary society takes the
place of an intermittent concern with specific social wrongs": the
first, in other words, to be concerned principally "not with the Poor
Law, or with boarding schools, but with the changing nature of
English life in its physical, social and moral aspects—a
preoccupation that was to develop and deepen in the great 'dark'
novels of his later period." *Dombey*, more than *Chuzzlewit*, and
more like *Bleak House*, "suggests"—in Tillotson's words—"the
gloom of wealth"; its "capacity to petrify or poison human relations,
in the family and in society."

Dombey and Son does show Dickens using images and symbols
in a much more self-conscious way. Its language is more obviously
artful and formal, and more "formulaic," too, as another critic has
noted, as well as at times "over-lush." Some readers are in fact
likely to conclude that much of this book is simply too deliberate
and carefully made; it feels labored, particularly in those early
chapters, as if Dickens is not only working without his usual
stimulus, but trying too hard to strike his themes and maintain a
serious tone.

At its most obvious, the book aims to indict Paul Dombey's
obsession with money and wealth while attacking as well his
"pride"—his continuing failure to consider fully any life besides his
own. Dombey is consistently shown to be aloof and rigid and as icy
as the Alps. His "presence," one learns at the start, strikes "like
damp, or cold air." At the christening of his son Paul, "on an iron-

grey autumnal day, with a shrewd east wind blowing," Dombey
"represented in himself the wind, the shade, and the autumn of the
christening": he seems "as hard and cold as the weather." Elsewhere
Dickens links Dombey directly with the object of his worship: he is
"one of those close-shaved close-cut monied gentleman who are
glossy and crisp like new bank notes." For Dombey himself, people
are commodities, objects to be moved about, owned. For him,
"*Cash-payment*"—in Carlyle's damning phrase—has become "the
sole relation of human beings." Early in the novel, Dickens—always
fond of pairing off opposites to make a point—shows Dombey
acting absurdly businesslike with more naturally passionate and
affectionate people, among them Polly Toodle, a wet-nurse, and his
own daughter, Florence. An idealized figure of tireless patience and
undoubted goodness, Florence must throughout the novel cope with
the bitter fact of her father's disdain. She regards him with
love—and fear. Had Dombey "looked with greater interest and with
a father's eye, he might have read in her keen glance the impulses
and fears that made her warmer; the passionate desire to run
clinging to him, crying, as she hid her face in his embrace, 'Oh
Father, try to love me!'" But always she felt "the dread of a repulse;
the fear of being too bold, and of offending him."

"The single most important organising concept" in Dickens's later
work, argues James M. Brown, and "the core" of "the social vision"
in these novels, is "the obsessively recurring metaphor of society as
one huge marketplace. This is the most consistently voiced and
strongly felt social theme of the later fiction, and it is impossible to
overemphasize its importance." Clearly one sees that concept—that
vision—taking shape in *Dombey and Son*. Here, too, social relations
including marriage are "mediated through an economic frame of
reference." In *Dombey and Son*, Dickens seeks to show that "social
behaviour in all areas of mid-Victorian society" had become
"conditioned by a degraded market-place logic." Brown continues:

In *The German Ideology* (1845/6) Marx had said of industrial society, "In
modern civil society all relations are in practice subordinated to the single
abstract relation of money and speculation," and it is precisely this insight
into mid-Victorian capitalism which is central to the social vision of
Dickens's mature fiction. His novels reflect the continuing importance for
the general relations of everyday social life of the relations of the economic
sphere. In all areas of social life, so the later novels assert, social behaviour

is in essence taking on the character of the new market relations of the economic sector.

Dombey—this stiff, cold, leaden presence—is a blunt symbol of cold capitalism or "Mammonism" run amok. But, being a symbol, he cannot also stand as one of the more compelling figures in Dickens's fiction. Fortunately, other figures enliven the novel's action. Little Paul, Dombey's son and presumed heir, is sensitive and perceptive; through him, Dickens effectively conveys a child's sometimes skewed, and sometimes astute sense of the world and its workings—as he would even more convincingly in *David Copperfield*. Paul—Dombey's "little poet son," as Bernard Shaw calls him—is, like Florence, a victim of his father's glacial stupidity. The elder Dombey, as Shaw puts it, "has no other conception of education than grinding a child into a middle class man." And so he "sends his boy to the most respectable and exclusive mill he can find. The result is that the child is ground to death." Over and over Dickens conveys this sense that, for too many people, life following the first years of childhood is and ought not to be a trial; that, for most, going to school differs little from going to prison, or working shifts at some brutalizing factory. As a journalist, philanthropist, and novelist, he often addresses issues of educational reform; in fact, schools and schooling figure prominently in *Dombey and Son*. In most schools as Dickens knew them, one buries one's self, one's "fancy"—to use one of his favorite words—and simply surrenders to the whims of those in control. As *Dombey* reveals, one can be profoundly scarred by a wretched "education": consider the fate of Polly Toodle's son, the pathetic Robin, who is sent to "the Charitable Grinder's School" and is turned into "Rob the Grinder," a petty criminal and spy. Those sections in *Dombey* that center on Doctor Blimber's Academy are among the novel's best; they also show something of Dickens's own horror, frequently conveyed in his fiction, of being trapped in some mechanical and idiotic group rhythm, compelled to obey directives not his own. Blimber, a hopeless pedagogue, has—like Mr. Dombey—lost all sense of what childhood is; he runs "a great hot-house, in which there was a forcing apparatus always at work" on his students. They do not think creatively, but are force-fed vast quantities of facts in a manner that recalls the rather less polished Squeers at Dotheboys Hall. The pompous Blimber is neatly described in machinelike terms: "His walk was stately, and calculated to impress the juvenile mind with solemn feelings. It was a sort of march; but when the Doctor put out his right foot, he gravely turned upon his axis, with a semicircular sweep towards the left; and when he put out his left foot, he turned in the same manner towards the right. So that he seemed, at every stride he took, to look about him as though he were saying, 'Can anybody have the goodness to indicate any subject, in any direction, on which I am uninformed? I rather think not.'"

Little Paul, a sickly child, tends to win the affection of those he meets; he is, in many ways, a memorable creation. Like Little Nell, Paul dies in childhood—in a series of scenes that deeply moved huge numbers of readers. Paul, who apparently owes something to Dickens's son Sydney (1847-72), is more deeply drawn than Little Nell. Perceptive and precocious, he has this "strange, old-fashioned, thoughtful way"; sometimes, "sitting brooding in his miniature arm-chair," he looks "like one of those terrible little Beings in the Fairy tales, who, at a hundred and fifty or two hundred years of age, fantastically represent the children for whom they have been substituted." Still, as such descriptions suggest, there is something not quite real about this "gentle, useful, quiet little fellow, always striving to secure the love and attachment of the rest." Indeed, at school, when he is not seen "at his old post on the stairs, or watching the waves and clouds from his solitary window," Little Paul can be found "among the other boys, modestly rendering them some little voluntary service." Little Paul, like Oliver Twist and Esther Summerson, is in effect an orphan; abandoned, he looks for love. He is also, like Little Nell, a little saint. And at times he seems too clearly designed to play the part of his father's foil—a function made famously clear when, in chapter 8, he repeatedly asks his father: "'Papa! What's money?'" Mr. Dombey is tongue-tied. Money, he insists, "'can do anything'"—except, he concedes, bring Paul's mother back to life.

Dombey remarries, and his second wife, Edith, is one of the novel's more interesting figures. She is trapped by her marriage; smothered by a whole series of social expectations she under-standably gasps for air. Dickens has long been criticized for the rather narrow range of his female characters. André Maurois, for one, observed sixty years ago that "it is particularly noticeable how faintly Dickens sketches the characters of the women in his novels";

"few," he wrote, "are convincing"; too many "are tiresome and silly, only intervening in the men's lives to carry on pointless and incoherent conversations." Indeed, "Dickens' treatment of women has had a bad press," writes Kate Flint, more recently. "The accusations leveled against him," she notes in *Dickens* (1986), "have been threefold: that he helped reinforce the dominant ideology that a woman's place is in the home, cheerfully supporting her husband, father or brother, and deftly supervising the running of the household; that allied to this, his writing shows slender sympathy for women who busied themselves with public causes; and thirdly, that he either denied women their sexuality, or treated it entirely from a male angle, with a malodorous relish which vacillated between the lascivious and the coy." John Carey, in *The Violent Effigy*, puts it more bluntly. Dickens's women, he suggests, fall almost always into one of two categories: "pure maid and frump." "The Victorian effort to restrict the role of women to such stereotypes," writes Carey, "both in fiction and real life, suggests a lurking awareness of woman's threat to male supremacy. The woman must be constrained to certain kinds of servitude—domestic pet, angel, mother, clown—to meet the male's need for entertainment or spiritual uplift."

Hints of these attitudes are revealed in the 1842 letter, discussed in chapter 2, which Dickens sent to the *Morning Chronicle*. He stresses that all who work in mines are endangered, women and men; their lives are "fraught with danger, toil, and hardship." But women are especially debased, and deterred from their truer calling. They work "by the side of naked men—(daughters often do this beside their own fathers)"; they are "harnessed to carts in a most revolting and disgusting fashion, by iron chains." Their labor must invariably "blot out from that sex all form and stamp, and character of womanhood"; it must "divest them of all knowledge of home, and all chance of womanly influence in the humble sphere of a poor peasant's hearth"; it makes them "but so many weaker men."

Dombey and Son—written when women in Britain still lacked the right to vote—does not in fact strike a blow for the complete emancipation of women; its portrait of the devoted Florence Dombey is certainly conventional, and entirely predictable for a Dickens novel. Still, one also senses his sympathy for the plight of one woman, Edith Dombey, and also—by extension—for those many women of his time and place who, in their way, were just as constrained and exploited as those forced to work in coal mines. These women, like Edith, were reared simply to end up as fit mates for well-heeled Dombeys. Edith herself is no shrinking violet: no shy kitten eager to be stroked. She is "wilful." She is angry because she has spent her life being steered about—and sold, which dooms her to a certain form of servitude. Like Estella in *Great Expectations*, Edith has been robbed of her childhood by a warped and dominating woman—her mother, the grotesque Mrs. Skewton. "What childhood did you ever leave to me?" Edith accusingly asks her mother at one point; "I was a woman—artful, designing, mercenary, laying snares for men—before I knew myself, or you, or even understood the base and wretched aim of every new display I learnt." "I am a woman," she later tells James Carker—another pursuer—"who, from her very childhood, has been shamed and steeled. I have been offered and rejected, put up and appraised, until my very soul has sickened. I have not had an accomplishment or grace that might have been a resource to me, but it has been paraded and vended to enhance my value, as if the common crier had called it through the streets."

Dombey enjoyed unchallenged supremacy during his first marriage: he is not, obviously, another of Dickens's henpecked husbands. But *Dombey and Son* does not extol his marital methods. Dombey, the novel makes clear, is what no husband—or reasonably attentive person— should ever, in any relationship, be. "Towards his first wife," one learns, "Mr. Dombey, in his cold and lofty arrogance, had borne himself like the removed Being he almost conceived himself to be. He had been 'Mr. Dombey' with her when she first saw him, and was 'Mr. Dombey' when she died. He had asserted his greatness during their whole married life, and she had meekly recognised it. He had kept his distant seat on the top of his throne, and she her humble station on its lowest step." Edith, he assumed, would follow suit. Like Merdle, the crooked financier in *Little Dorrit*, Dorrit bought a wife as one buys any envy-inducing object. (The ample bosom of Merdle's wife, one learns, "was not a bosom to repose upon, but it was a capital bosom to hang jewels upon. Mr. Merdle wanted something to hang jewels upon, and he bought it for that purpose.") Dombey assumed "that the proud character of his second wife would have added greatly to his own, merging into it and exalting his greatness. He had pictured himself haughtier than ever, with Edith's haughtiness subservient to his."

But Edith goes her own way. She befriends Florence, and often shows Dombey "her haughty glance of calm inflexible disdain." Dombey, in turn, resolves to "show her that he was supreme." He wants Edith to be proud, but "she must be proud for, not against him." It is "her cold supreme indifference—his own unquestioned attribute usurped—[that] stung him more than any other kind of treatment could have done; and he determined to bend her to his magnificent and stately will."

Dombey had turned up for his wedding in an oddly dandified state, sporting "fawn-colored pantaloons, and lilac waistcoat"; even his hair was—according to whispers—curled. But, once wed, he quickly reverts to his grim, grey, autocratic state. And for Dombey and wife the state of marriage becomes a state of war. As the novel proceeds, Dickens tries his hand at domestic drama, sometimes subduing his more melodramatic impulses as he seeks to convey more realistically the daily torture of an untenable marriage. Thus in chapter 40, the two are found in a moment of tense conversation. Edith looks "fixedly" at the husband who would keep her enchained; she turns "a bracelet round and round upon her arm; not winding it about with a light, womanly touch, but pressing and dragging it over the smooth skin, until the white limb showed a bar of red." It is a deft touch brilliantly placed: the "bar" suggesting a barrier as well as a prison cell, and showing particularly well Dickens's ability not only to see details, but to use them in a way that underscores subtly his central themes.

In his depiction of Carker, Dickens's use of symbolism is more overt and no less effective. Carker, who works for Dombey—and eventually leads him to financial ruin—is a shrewd, manipulating, acutely conscious man whose slick surface conceals a dark array of selfish designs. Like many of Dickens's most vivid creations, Carker is a bit of an actor who, in his way, sees the world as a stage. In one scene, he is, in the morning, preparing his costume and mask. He is "fully and trimly dressed," in "imitation of the great man he served." He rehearses his smile, for Carker's teeth are his most striking trait, and represent his sharklike stealth—his urge to devour all that he craves. Dickens points frequently to Carker's smile, and to those teeth (which are apparently fake), calling him "the man of teeth" and then wittily showing him, moments later, strolling about the meadows and lanes, "airing his teeth" as he thinks about Edith Dombey—the woman he aims to claim as his own. Elsewhere

Dickens makes Carker cat-like, stressing feline imagery; in fact, in one scene, Carker is "feline from sole to crown," as he "basked" in a "strip of summer light and warmth": with "hair and whiskers deficient in color at all times, but feebler than common in the rich sunshine, and more like the coat of a sandy tortoise-shell cat; with long nails, nicely pared and sharpened." Here, he is "Mr. Carker the Manager, sly of manner, sharp of tooth, soft of foot, watchful of eye, oily of tongue, cruel of heart, nice of habit," who "sat with a dainty steadfastness and patience at his work, as if he were waiting at a mouse's hole." Thus again, as often in Dickens, the comic and the sinister are splendidly combined—as they are when, in chapter 31, we watch Carker "with his white teeth glistening," as he "approaches Edith, more as if he meant to bite her, than to taste the sweets that linger on her lips."

It is Carker—with his villainy and teeth—who brings life to *Dombey and Son*, a book that, whatever its many virtues and good intentions, is rather difficult to read with mounting zest. Its central plot, in which a wealthy but obtuse man learns the hard way the real meaning of life, has long since become a literary—and certainly a cinematic—cliché. Indeed, *Dombey* is in some respects *Chuzzlewit* redux: another account of dull selfishness run amok. But then who, these days, reads Dickens for the plot? Who *ever* read Dickens for the plot? In Dickens the plot is the necessary platform for his cast of vividly memorable characters to perform upon: one needs a story of some sort as an excuse to enjoy the Dickens cabaret. And to his credit, in *Dombey and Son*, Dickens supplies several secondary characters who perform to perfection, among them Mrs. Skewton, as grotesque but convincing a hypocrite as one finds anywhere in Dickens's fiction—and, of course, in life. We find Mrs. Skewton at one point insisting that "Nature intended me for an Arcadian. I am thrown away in society. Cows are my passion. What I have ever sighed for, has been to retreat to a Swiss farm, and to live entirely surrounded by cows—and china." "What I want," she continues, "is Heart." She wants "frankness, confidence, less conventionality, and freer play of soul. We are so dreadfully artificial." But Mrs. Skewton, a woman of seventy, is—as Edith certainly knows—obsessed with status and society, and continues to dress in a manner "which would have been youthful for twenty-seven." Later we find Edith's mother, the victim of a "paralytic stroke," insisting that "rose-colored curtains" be hung in her room in order that her complexion might look more flattering when the doctors come around. Still she dons her "finery." She is bed-ridden, but "arrayed in full dress, with the diamonds, short-sleeves, rouge, curls, teeth, and other juvenility all complete." Dickens throughout his career showed a rather morbid fascination with decline, decay, decrepitude: a fascination that is quite clear in his depiction of Mrs. Skewton, who combats time in a manner that is quite grand in its way—but also comic and, finally, futile. "Paralysis was not to be deceived," the narrator of *Dombey* observes, "[it] had known her for the object of its errand," and had "struck" the vain woman "at her glass, where she lay like a horrible doll that had tumbled down."

Again, there is often this edge in Dickens, this tendency to balance out the sentimental with the absurd, the grotesque, the surreal: for every Little Nell there is a Quilp; for every Florence Dombey there is a Mrs. Skewton, or a Major Bagstock—another arresting presence in *Dombey and Son*. Bagstock is pompous and gassy, the sort of sorry, self-important ass (there are so many in Dickens) who prefers to refer to himself in the third person, as "Old Joe" or "Old J. Bagstock." Bagstock prides himself in being a "friend" to Mr. Dombey, whom he "puffs" frequently; indeed, "there never was a man who stood by a friend more staunchly than the Major, when in puffing him, he puffed himself." The bloated Major is also described as "an over-fed Mephistopheles," as being "blue-faced" and "over-ripe"; once we find him "giving vent, every now and then, to one of his horse's coughs, not so much of necessity as in a spontaneous explosion of importance," and walking along with "his legs majestically wide apart, and his great head wagging from side to side, as if he were remonstrating within himself on being such a captivating object." Mrs. Skewton, then, is "a doll." Bagstock is "an object." Dickens often suggests that men and women dehumanize themselves when they become little more than a pattern of eccentricities, a collection of unappealing quirks. And one frequently finds in Dickens's work, throughout his career, this way of scrutinizing human life in a cold and bitter way. It is this Dickens—the creator of Mrs. Gamp and Mrs. Skewton; of the Messrs. Vuffin and Bagstock—who has more in common with, say, H. L. Mencken or even Luis Buñuel than with many of his successful artistic contemporaries. It is this Dickens who, as Neil Sinyard has noted, has always had much in common with film-makers, including some at work today. Sinyard isolates "five key

Dickensian ingredients"—including not only "a spirit of out-
rageousness and a willingness to offend delicate sensibilities in
pursuit of its own truth," but also "a flair for baroque or for
caricature," a "sense of social rage and didacticism, a conviction that
society was rotten at the root," a "vision that was bizarre and
surreal," but that "also stood in some way as emblematic of the
Condition of England," and "a gift for poetic symbolism and
imagery," an "ability to invest the material world with all kinds of
mysterious overtones." Sinyard thus sees Dickensian elements in, for
example, Neil Jordan's *Mona Lisa* (1986) and Stephen Poliakoff's
Hidden City (1987), as well as in Stephen Frears's *My Beautiful
Laundrette* (1985), based on Hanif Kureishi's account of "a hero"
who, like Dickens's own Pip in *Great Expectations*, "is determined
to rise out of his own situation and background and whose passage
is eased by criminal money."

Still, tackling *Dombey and Son* will make some readers feel as if
they have been shut up in a close, dark room overstuffed with heavy
dark furniture: the Gothic House of Dombey seems at times like the
House of Wax, a set prepared for Vincent Price. It is described as
"sombre"; it has the reputation "as a haunted house"; its grounds
have been landscaped, it seems, by E. A Poe & Associates. Around
this "dismal" place we find only "two giant trees, with blackened
trunks and branches" that "rattled rather than rustled, their leaves
were so smoke-dried." In many ways, this is Dickens's most
"Victorian" novel, offering exclamatory, overwrought passages
and—in many places—a maudlin, solemn tone. There are descriptive
lines and passages that can only strike contemporary readers as
needless and corny; there are some lamentable intrusions into the
flow of the plot. One can only wince when, for example, the
narrator halts the action to tell Dombey to pay some heed to his
lovely daughter. More precisely, he *shouts* in Dombey's ear:
"Awake, unkind father! Awake now, sullen man! The time is flitting
by; the hour is coming with an angry tread. Awake!" Too, the
dialogue is often more operatic than realistic: Edith, for example, is
inclined to speechify, flattening Carker at last with these words:
"What should I say of honour or chastity to you! . . . What meaning
would it have to you; what meaning would it have from me! But if
I tell you that the lightest touch of your hand makes my blood cold
with antipathy; that from the hour when I first saw, and hated you,
to now, when my instinctive repugnance is enhanced by every

minute's knowledge of you I have since had, you have been a
loathsome creature to me which has not its like on earth." Carker,
incidentally, in this stagy scene is described in a manner that recalls
Nickleby: "The foam was on his lips; the wet stood on his
forehead." If Edith "would have faltered once, for only one half
moment, he would have pinioned her." But Edith stands "as firm as
a rock," like Britannia herself one thinks, "and her searching eyes
never left him." Such scenes suggest that *Dombey and Son*—and not
David Copperfield—would have made the better vehicle for the
shameless David O. Selznick, whose 1935 film production of the
latter was one long and virtually unwatchable exercise in raw
melodrama and sentimental goo.

In *David Copperfield*, and in the best of his subsequent novels,
Dickens's narrative voice is more subdued; he is somewhat more
willing to allow his readers to discern for themselves his points and
ironies. But in *Dombey*, particularly when Dickens has a Big Point
to make, the effect is more soporific than moving: one recognizes
rather uneasily that he has written in those weeping violins because
he realizes that a large part of his audience likes to keep things
simple and bluntly emotional—likes to see a vivid face-off between
virtue and vice. He recognizes too that a large segment of that
audience quite enjoys a good sermon, especially if it is delivered in
the sort of ornate language reserved for the pulpit and far from the
street. In at least one point in the novel, Dickens seems himself to
be rather tired of the message; he is, one suspects, hoping to keep
both himself and the congregation awake by waving his arms about
and pumping up the volume. "Alas!" he booms in chapter 47, "are
there so few things in the world about us, most unnatural, and yet
most natural in being so!" He continues, pointing again to the gross
inequities in health and wealth that, in much of Victorian London,
would be hard to miss—describing them in language that seems so
curiously artificial when compared, for example, to Nicholas's
meditations on poverty and social inequality near the close of
Nicholas Nickleby. Thunders Dickens:

Hear the magistrate or judge admonish the unnatural outcasts of society;
unnatural in brutal habits, unnatural in want of decency, unnatural in losing
and confounding all distinctions between good and evil; unnatural in
ignorance, in vice, in recklessness, in contumacy, in mind, in looks, in
everything. But follow the good clergyman or doctor who, with his life
imperiled at every breath he draws, goes down into their dens, lying within

echoes of our carriage wheels and daily tread upon the pavement stones. Look round upon the world of odious sights—millions of immortal creatures have no other world on earth—at the lightest mention of which humanity revolts, and dainty delicacy living in the next street, stops her ears, and lisps, "I don't believe it!" Breathe the polluted air, foul with every impurity that is poisonous to health and life; and have every sense, conferred upon our race for its delight and happiness, offended, sickened and disgusted, and made a channel by which misery and death alone can enter. Vainly attempt to think any simple plant, or flower, or wholesome weed, that, set in this foetid bed, could have its natural growth, or put its little leaves forth to the sun as GOD designed it. And then, calling up some ghastly child, with stunted form and wicked face, hold forth on its unnatural sinfulness, and lament its being, so early, far away from Heaven—but think a little of its having been conceived, and born, and bred, in Hell!

In his *Dickens* (1934), Maurois refers to "Dickensian dummies": figures "made of wood and mounted on wheels." "A character of Dickens is all of one piece," writes Maurois, "entirely good or entirely bad." This statement is too sweeping; but it has the ring of truth—at least when applied to Dickens's earlier fictions, including *Dombey* itself. But with *David Copperfield*, his eighth novel, one clearly sees a change. For the first time, Dickens writes a novel in the first person. This relaxes his prose, giving it the fluid, conversational quality that *Dombey and Son* tends to lack. Perhaps as a result, the characters in *Copperfield* become more real, more complex and contradictory: more like the people we know. *Copperfield* is, after *A Christmas Carol*, Dickens's best-known title, an unusually inviting work nearly universal in its appeal. As A. N. Wilson notes in his biography, *Tolstoy* (1988), Dickens was enormously popular in Russia throughout the nineteenth century; for his part, the author of *War and Peace* not only ranked Dickens as his favorite author, but *David Copperfield* his favorite book; it became, Wilson writes, "a model" for Tolstoy's own "auto-biographical reflections," including those contained in his *Childhood*. As Wilson rightly notes, "one of the extraordinary things about Dickens as a writer is the strength with which he kidnaps every reader's inner life. To some extent, those who are no more than readers of *David Copperfield* feel that David's childhood memories have been their own." Thus, David the boy is, for most readers, an unusually attractive figure, a soul mate of sorts. We see childhood again through David's eyes. We smell and feel it. Those

early chapters of *David Copperfield*, which so brilliantly and keenly
bring all of the senses into play, put us quite squarely in David's
childhood world: his memories become our own. We remember
Peggotty's work-box "with a sliding lid, with a view of St.
Paul's Cathedral (with a pink dome) painted on the top"; we remember
Murdstone's face, and "the dotted indication of the strong black
beard he shaved close every day," with its resemblance to "the wax-
work that had traveled into our neighbourhood some half a year
before"; we remember the "squeaking and scuffling of the old grey
rats down in the cellars" of Murdstone's waterside warehouse—a
place that, for Dickens himself, recalled Warren's blacking factory
in Hungerford Stairs.

But the adult David? The very teller of the tale? That, for many,
is another story. For Angus Wilson, David becomes insufferable as
his "smug, genteel, conformist quality" comes increasingly to the
fore. Wilson suggests that, by marrying Agnes Wickfield, David will
get exactly what he deserves: "A successful novelist guided by her
'deep wisdom,' would surely become a smug, insensitive,
comfortable old best seller of the worst kind." Wilson calls
Agnes—whose name is reverentially evoked in the novel's final
paragraph—"the first of a group of heroines who mark the least
pleasing, most frumpy, and smug vision of woman that [Dickens]
produced." For George Orwell, Agnes is "the real legless angel of
Victorian romance"—and, as Michael Slater suggests, yet another
Dickensian incarnation of the ever-good Mary Hogarth.

And yet you can love this book without also falling in love with
Agnes, or even caring much for David himself. Although one could
never tell from viewing Selznick's film (directed by George Cukor),
David Copperfield owes its superb readability—as well as its
longevity and its continuing relevancy—to the fact that its key
characters, including David himself, are conveyed with a sense of
psychological subtlety that is not evident, at least in long stretches,
in Dickens's earlier fiction. In *David Copperfield*, Dickens shows
not only a continuing awareness of the ironies and vicissitudes of
life, but of the many intricacies and inconsistencies of human
character. Of course *Copperfield* has its melodramatic moments; it
too includes characters who stand bluntly for evil and for good.
Clara Peggotty, David's nurse, has no vice. The black-clad
Murdstones show no Dickensian virtues. The novel has a happy
ending—or rather, happy endings. Wilkins Micawber is, for

example, finally transformed from a hopeless sponger to a pillar of social responsibility in Australia, where—the novel suggests—many who wash out in Britain can get a fresh start. (Dickens as a journalist supported the idea of widescale emigration as a means of easing some of Britain's social ills; in his private life, he helped several struggling souls start over elsewhere, including some of his children, who—unlike Micawber—did not find success in foreign lands.)

Certainly, the moral messages of *Copperfield* are plainly stated. Betsey Trotwood, David's eccentric aunt—and an odd fairy godmother of sorts—is one of its exemplars. Be "a firm fellow with a will of your own," she reminds David. And "never be mean in anything; never be false; never be cruel. Avoid those three vices," she urges, "and I can always be hopeful of you." Kindness, honesty, compassion: these are the virtues embodied by Clara Peggotty, and the members of her Yarmouth family. They are the virtues Dickens's novels repeatedly endorse. But *David Copperfield* also shows—sometimes comically, sometimes sadly—that while men and women frequently aspire to such goodness, they are, being human, inclined to make dreadful mistakes that damage others as well as themselves; that, moreover, one is because of what one was. In *Copperfield*, as in his later novels, Dickens reveals a strong and consistent interest in showing how factors of environment and personal history play a huge, if often overlooked, role in the shaping of character.

David throughout the novel is called many names, underscoring the fact that he is, during much of its action, something of a blank slate to be marked by those he meets along the way. To his charming and childlike mother, he is "Davy"—the same name Edward Murdstone calls him when the two first meet. But after making Clara Copperfield his wife, Murdstone demands that her son be called "Master Murdstone," signaling of course an abiding desire to own, shape, control. "Davy" is later called "Daisy" by James Steerforth, the older boy with the "genial manner" and "handsome looks" that Copperfield comes to idolize—and so idealize. In his own way, Steerforth also wants to dominate the rather passive David, telling him "I feel as if you were my property." Murdstone's own name is wonderfully apt, suggesting not only murder and *merde*, but also weight, heaviness, firmness (a key concept in *David Copperfield*), and thus a crushing oppression. Steerforth's name is

more plainly ironic. This figure who can direct and influence—i.e.,
steer—so many, including the romantic and impressionable "Little
Em'ly," is himself quite without direction on the sea of life, and
ends up dead beneath the waves.

Murdstone's sister, the ghastly Jane, also finds "a choice pleasure
in exhibiting what she called her self-command, and her
firmness"—a trait that, as many Dickens novels show, can be easily
perverted, abused. The Murdstones are not studies in subtlety. Early
in the novel, Dickens surrounds Jane Murdstone, as he does Sally
Brass in *The Old Curiosity Shop*, with images and words that
emphasize her mental rigidness and emotional inflexibility—in a
word, her inhumanity. She owns "a hard steel purse" that "hung
upon her arm by a heavy chain." When David first sees her, she is
hauling her belongings about in boxes that are "uncompromising"
and "hard" and "black." Later, we find her speaking in "an iron
whisper." For Dickens, the Murdstones stand for all that he loathed
in organized creeds that stressed sin and obedience over mercy,
forgiveness, and love. "The gloomy taint that was in the Murdstone
blood, darkened the Murdstone religion," David recalls, "which was
austere and wrathful," and came out of the notion—always absurd
to a liberal Protestant like Dickens—that children are inherently evil,
"a swarm of little vipers." Murdstone himself has a "shallow black
eye." "I want a better word to express an eye," David explains, "that
has no depth in it to be looked into—which, when it is abstracted
seems, from some peculiarity of light, to be disfigured, for a
moment at a time, by a cast." (With Dickens, one should always
watch the eyes. The eyes of Blandois, the demonic villain in *Little
Dorrit*, similarly have "no depth or charge"; a "clockmaker could
have made a better pair.") In sum, like his sister, Murdstone
is—beneath his imposing shell—eerily hollow. The man proclaims
the faith, but he lacks a soul.

Like Dickens's most vile characters, the Murdstones are devoid
of empathy: a useful trait for those taking up torture as a trade. And
the Murdstones *are* torturers, turning the "home" they occupy into
a microcosm of the tyrannical state, subjecting both David and his
mother to both physical and psychological abuse. Dickens's
description in chapter 4 of the Murdstones working as a pair to put
Clara Copperfield in her place is chillingly effective. Here Dickens
reminds us, as he did in *Dombey*, of just how viciously the politics
of power can be played within the domestic sphere. At the start of

the sequence, David's mother tries to assert herself, reminding the Murdstones that, perhaps, she should be permitted some say in the running of the household and the rearing of her son. But as Dickens shows, almost wholly through dialogue, the Murdstones have the measure of Clara's vulnerabilities: "My mother was the victim always," as David elsewhere notes. By the end of this compelling sequence, Clara Murdstone is apologizing for her "defects" and begging her jailers for forgiveness, imploring, "Pray let us be friends. I couldn't live under coldness or unkindness." The remark proves prophetic: like Little Paul Dombey, Clara dies of a life-dooming lack of love. David recalls his mother's death—and the death, soon thereafter, of her second son. He thinks: "The mother who lay in the grave, was the mother of my infancy; the little creature in her arms"—his half brother—was, in effect, "myself, as I had once been, hushed forever on her bosom."

But the novel shows that David remains something of an infant; he is prone to various delusions and misconceptions as he makes his way through adolescence and into early adulthood. On this rite of passage he is guided not only by his Aunt Betsey, but by another brilliantly rendered oddball, Micawber, who is less a father figure than a peer. Micawber is not only eccentric, but utterly self-absorbed. He is apparently oblivious to many things—including the fact that David is several decades his junior. Micawber is unable to function smoothly in a social system that demands both consistency and conformity: an inability that is detrimental to a man who has no independent means of support. Micawber owes everybody. And he owes much, as critics have long recognized, to Dickens's own father. Like John Dickens, Micawber spends much of his time fleeing from the sort of fires that chronic indebtedness can spark. He is similarly theatrical and florid in his style of talk. One sees something of Micawber in, for example, this letter written by John Dickens in 1824 and reprinted by Michael Allen in *Charles Dickens's Childhood*. Not surprisingly, the subject is money. Again John Dickens is in a pinch, moving and maneuvering his assets, robbing Peter to pay Paul:

My dear Sir, Circumstances compel me to seek your friendly aid as on a former occasion by accepting in lieu of *present payment* an order as above. I flatter myself you will take some pleasure in forwarding my views in this respect with the Committee when I assure you that I shall consider it a most signal act of friendship. A circumstance of great moment to me will be decided in the ensuing term which I confidently hope will place me in comparative affluence, and by which I shall be enabled to redeem the order before the period of Christmas Day. At any rate it will meet with the same attention as before, and I shall have the pleasure of expressing to you my sincere obligations.

Through Micawber, Dickens is perhaps gaining revenge on the man who brought him so much childhood misery. Micawber makes John Dickens look both comical and grotesque—not, obviously, the sort of tribute a father might wish from his son. But Dickens also likes Wilkins Micawber. Readers of *David Copperfield* sense this, and like him too. In some ways, Micawber is the most appealing character in all of Dickens—as likable as Pickwick, but more richly drawn. A splendid blend of arrogance, vulnerability, and self-delusion, Micawber wears "a brown surtout and black tights"; he carries "a jaunty sort of stick, with a pair of rusty tassels to it": his whole life is one long, exuberant, tragicomic, one-man show. Clearly, Micawber's elaborate, euphemistic use of language reveals his constant need to befuddle and becloud: to evade reality or, perhaps more precisely, to define it on his own terms. But of course Micawber's speech—like Vincent Crummles's—also suggests nothing more sinister than an endless pleasure in language: in the sound and very feel of words. Micawber has lines that still make readers laugh out loud. He adds life to an already-lively book whenever he appears: think of Micawber, for example, as he stands with his curious family near the ship that will take them to Australia (and to that great success that Mrs. Micawber has long forecast for her luckless mate).

"On the voyage, I shall endeavor [Micawber tells David] occasionally to spin them [his fellow passengers] a yarn; and the melody of my son Wilkins will, I trust, be acceptable at the galley fire. When Mrs. Micawber has her sea-legs on—an expression in which I hope there is no conventional impropriety—she will give them, I dare say, 'Little Tafflin' [a popular comic song of the day]. Porpoises and dolphins, I believe, will be frequently observed athwart our bows, and, either on the starboard or the larboard quarter, objects of interest will be continually descried. In short," said Mr. Micawber, with his old genteel air, "the probability is, all will be found so exciting, alow and aloft, that when the lookout, stationed in the main-top, cries Land-oh! we shall be very considerably astonished!"

Emotionally, Micawber is all over the place. And these abrupt shifts of mood—not to mention his compulsive need to spend more money than he has—are perhaps symptomatic of what we might today call manic-depressive behavior. When he is down, Micawber's grip loosens and he sees life in morbid and apocalyptic terms. The "bolt is impending" he tells David in one letter written at a time of acute financial distress, "and the tree must fall." Elsewhere he sees himself doomed "to walk the earth as a vagabond. The worm will settle my business in double quick time." But when he is up, Micawber is a joy to behold, and thoroughly delightful company. And indeed it is not his success in Australia that, in the end, "redeems" him; rather, it is this rare ability to find, like Pickwick, a keen delight in the very basic pleasures of life. In chapter 11, Micawber is described as "a thoroughly good-natured man, and as active a creature about everything but his own affairs as ever existed, and never so happy as when he was busy about something that could never be of any profit to him." In chapter 17—on the same night he will foresee his doom, proclaiming "the die is cast—all is over"—we find Micawber "uncommonly convivial" and "thoroughly jovial" as he enjoys "a beautiful little dinner" and the "hot punch" his wife prepares. Micawber "made his face shine with the punch," David relates, "so that it looked as if it had been varnished all over." Elsewhere Micawber concocts his own legendary bowl of punch: an act that appeals to his sensual side and makes his spirits soar. "I never saw a man," David recalls, "so thoroughly enjoy himself amid the fragrance of lemon-peel and sugar, the odour of burning rum, the steam of boiling water, as Mr. Micawber did that afternoon. It was wonderful to see his face shining at us out of a thin cloud of these delicate fumes, as he stirred, and mixed, and tasted, and looked as if he were making, instead of punch, a fortune for his family down to the latest posterity."

Like Micawber, Betsey Trotwood is made vivid by her eccentricities. When she first appears in chapter 1, she is described as a "strange lady" with a "rigidity of figure." Soon she is sparking fear in David's pregnant and recently widowed mother. Trotwood mocks Clara's late husband, making clear her disdain for Peggotty's family name, and predicting—or more precisely *asserting*—that "David" will be born a girl. Later we see her obsessively protecting her property, and trying to chase away the Murdstones who have unexpectedly appeared. (Jane Murdstone, fittingly, sits atop an ass.) "I won't be trespassed upon," Betsey asserts. "I won't allow it." But she has allowed into her home an odd, half-mad child-man she calls "Mr. Dick" and whose "advice" she holds dear.

But Betsey Trotwood is more than an amusing cartoon. She is no Sally Brass; she was created by a novelist interested in showing, as never before, that the human personality is often contradictory, and full of surprising possibilities; that, moreover, people are shaped—and often bent—by odd circumstances beyond their control. Betsey, we later learn, almost offhandedly, has been married to a "fine-looking man" who also, however, is "an adventurer, a gambler and cheat." Understandably referring to herself in the distancing third person, Aunt Betsey concedes that she "believed in that man most entirely," and that he "repaid her by breaking her fortune, and nearly breaking her heart." He beat her as well, apparently; for, as she tells David, "he had been so cruel to me, that I might have effected a separation on easy terms for myself; but I did not." She remains "an incurable fool" on this subject, still providing her estranged husband with "more money than I can afford." Given her history, Aunt Betsey's preference for girl infants—not to mention her preoccupation with trespassers—becomes understandable. And so does her decision to find companionship with the devoted and harmless "Mr. Dick"—who is also, in his way, "an incurable fool." Known legally as Richard Babley, the gentle Mr. Dick—florid, gray-haired, and infantile—would surely not have fared well in the rough world: Aunt Betsey has saved him from all sorts of horrors by giving him shelter. And Dick responds to her kindness with a generosity of his own. In his limited way, Mr. Dick is a good man, as *David Copperfield* makes clear: he is open, gracious, friendly—and acutely sensitive to Aunt Betsey's moods. Dickens, as George Gissing reminds us, "was fond of characters hovering between eccentricity and madness." Indeed, he "very often associates kindness of disposition with lack of brains," notes Gissing—a point further illustrated in *Copperfield* through the figure of David's nurse, Clara Peggotty. (Norman Page notes that "the curious and striking detail of the two women in David's early life having the same Christian name has" not surprisingly "been commented on: it is as if Dickens were polarizing his feelings about women—separating the feminine idea into housekeeper and sex-object—as, later in the novel, he does with Agnes and Dora.") Peggotty, for her part, is not only unschooled, but similarly childlike in her approach to the world. ("Now let me hear some more about the Crorkindills," she urges the young David as, early on, he reads to her from a book about crocodiles.)

Aunt Betsey is not quick to encourage David's wooing of Dora Spenlow; Dora's father also foresees problems with the match, calling it "youthful folly." David calls himself "earnest"—a word Dickens often used, without irony, as his correspondence suggests. ("Be earnest—earnest—in life's reality," Dickens urged a correspondent in 1851, "and do not let your life, which has a purpose in it—every life upon the earth has—fly by while you are brooding over mysteries.") But David is also ambitious, and his desire for Dora, linked with his decision to enter the legal field, might well stem from his desire—however unconscious—to forge his way into the more prestigious quarters of society. Mr. Spenlow, a lawyer, certainly *appears* prosperous with his gold watch chain and his spacious house.

But of course David's intense—and illogical—passion for the girl is also understandable on a much more basic level. Love, we know, is often all-consuming, rarely lending itself to rational analysis. Dickens's convincing depiction of David's passion for Dora clearly stems, in part, from his memories of those days when he was drunk on Maria Beadnell—as Dickens himself admitted, and as Slater, for one, in *Dickens and Women* (1983) more fully shows. As the novel unfolds, and as his absurdly immature little marriage drags on, David catches up with the readers of *David Copperfield*. Dora, he realizes, is flighty and utterly undeveloped—an alluring but tedious young woman who was no more ready for marriage than he was himself. But early on, in the first wave of love, she "was more than human to me. She was a Fairy, a Sylph. I don't know what she was—anything that no one ever saw, and everything that everybody ever wanted. I was swallowed up in an abyss of love in an instant." The idea of Dora was, he later recalls, "my refuge in disappointment and distress." "I don't think I had any definite idea where Dora came from or in what degree she was related to a higher order of beings; but I am quite sure I should have scouted the notion of her being simply human, like any other young lady, with indignation and contempt."

"I was steeped in Dora," David admits. "I was not merely over head and ears in love with her, but I was saturated through and through. Enough love might have been wrung out of me, metaphorically speaking, to drown anybody in; and yet there would have remained enough within me, and all over me, to pervade my entire existence."

Again, *David Copperfield* is very much about the fact of illusion and irony in human life; about the regrettable but inevitable fact that human beings often fall short of perfection; and that, alas, we all make mistakes. Betsey Trotwood has certain Pickwickian virtues: she is kindhearted, generous, and indomitable. But she is also crankily domineering. Wilkins Micawber is decent, generous, gracious—and so self-absorbed and stupid at times that he strolls straight into an alliance with the disgusting Uriah Heep. David tries to cultivate "habits of punctuality, order, and diligence"; "whatever I have tried to do in life," he explains, "I have tried to with all my heart to do well." But David blunders. He deludes himself. He is driven by factors and forces that—particularly in his youth—he could not begin to understand. In David's decision to marry Dora Spenlow, one perhaps also sees, besides simple sexual desire, something of the same compulsion to shape and control that drives the monstrous Murdstone. Murdstone gets his doting and rather dopey child-wife—and so does David. We know little of Murdstone's past. But David, we know, has, like countless others before and since, connected himself for better or worse to what is familiar: he marries a woman with his mother's most notable traits. Dora too is pretty, insecure, shallow: her lack of experience and decisiveness similarly dooms her to be the "victim" always.

David also romanticizes Steerforth—so much so that he is utterly obtuse to the latter's faults. Steerforth is selfish. And he can be amazingly cruel, as his treatment of Mr. Mell, the pathetic assistant master, clearly reveals. But David, being "blind"—to use Betsey's word—discerns only kindness, geniality, charm. "Ah, Steerforth!" he proclaims after introducing his smooth friend to the extended Peggotty clan. "It's well for you to joke about the poor! You may skirmish with Miss Dartle, or try to hide your sympathies in jest from me, but I know better. When I see how perfectly you understand them, how exquisitely you can enter into happiness like this plain fisherman's, or humour a love like my old nurse's, I know that there is not a joy or sorrow, not an emotion, of such people, that can be indifferent to you. And I admire and love you for it, Steerforth, twenty times the more!" David is partially right.

Steerforth is undoubtedly appealing in his aloof way; he can be gracious, with his "easy, spirited good-humour," his "natural gift of adapting himself to whomsoever he pleased." Nor can he be dismissed easily as a ruthless, incorrigible cad.

In fact, as Jenni Calder suggests, Steerforth would not have been wholly out of place among English undergraduates of his day. Calder, in her *Women and Marriage in Victorian Fiction*, quotes from an American visitor who went to Cambridge in the 1840s and was, apparently, stunned. "A large proportion of Englishmen," he now discovered, "even when they do not act upon the idea themselves," were ready to assent to the "proposition" that "shop-girls, work-women, domestic servants, and all females in similar positions, were expressly designed for the amusement of gentlemen, and generally serve that purpose." "Here is Steerforth," writes Calder: "not so much the impulsive, Byronic male, which is how he is usually interpreted, but an average English undergraduate."

Steerforth, moreover, has also been marked deeply by events and persons in his past. Left without a father, his mother has "spoiled" him. Indeed, Dickens in his fiction was forever warning of the dangers of rearing children too indulgently, an idea that would of course find much support among large numbers of his readers. In a rather heavy-handed passage, Steerforth himself suggests that "it would have been well for me (and for more than me) if I had had a steadfast and judicious father!"—a statement also applicable to many characters in Dickens's novels, including David himself. "His face," David now notes, "was always full of expression, but I never saw it express such a dark kind of earnestness as when he said these words."

David Selznick's Hollywood version of *David Copperfield* offers a simplified Little Em'ly; at first, she appears as little more than a human bonbon, complete with Shirley Temple curls. (As a boy, David, ever the romantic, idealized her as well: "I am sure my fancy raised up something round that blue-eyed mite of a child, which etherealised, and made a very angel of her. If, any sunny forenoon, she had spread a little pair of wings, and flown away before my eyes, I don't think I should have regarded it as much more than I had reason to expect.") But the novel suggests more strongly that—as with most people—there is rather more to Little Em'ly than meets the eye. Certainly, no alert reader of *David Copperfield* can close the work without considering the possibility that, like "Pet"

Meagles in *Little Dorrit*, she might have been better suited for adulthood if she hadn't been loved quite so possessively as a child. Mr. Peggotty is obviously meant to stand as one of the book's most appealing figures, displaying all of the virtues—compassion, patience, forgiveness, generosity—that Dickens, in both his fiction and his journalism, repeatedly hails. But in many ways *David Copperfield* reminds us that love is often immature and rooted in illusion; that it can be misguided, misconceived, misdirected; that it does not always lead to ceaseless bliss, contentment, and security. For the people we love can be complicated—and mysterious, as this book repeatedly shows. Little Em'ly, everyone's beloved little pet, has deep down all sorts of hopes and dreams of her own.

Again, one cannot easily build a case for Dickens as a "feminist" writer—at least in the more contemporary sense of that word. Like many notable men of his era—one thinks particularly of John Ruskin—Dickens believed, or at least wanted to believe, that women, or at least most of them, were somehow morally superior to men; were less innately brutish; and more "naturally" inclined to be compassionate, patient, and kind. (Dickens did of course conceive the likes of Jane Murdstone and Mrs. Gamp; still, as Bernard Shaw put it, he was unwilling to concede that "there is no such species in creation as 'Woman, lovely woman,' the woman being simply the female of the human species, and that to have one conception of humanity for the woman and another for the man, or one law for the woman and another for the man, or . . . for the matter of that, a skirt for the woman and a pair of breeches for the man, is as unnatural, and in the long run unworkable, as one law for the mare and another for the horse.") Certainly, those scenes that show Little Em'ly writhing with guilt in the wake of her flight with Steerforth would seem to support the supposition that, once again, Dickens simply lacked the stomach to challenge the prevailing values and assumptions of his largely middle class audience. When "Little Em'ly loses her purity," observes A. N. Wilson, "all readers are meant to agree that it would be better if the waters could close above her head."

And yet, as Kate Flint aptly notes in passing, *Copperfield* does offer "a suggestion that Steerforth, for example, exploits less controllable forces in Em'ly than a desire to better her social position." Certainly, those who know Dickens's later works are aware that he becomes ever more obsessed with themes of confinement and chance; in this context, Little Em'ly does herself resemble a prisoner of sorts. Obviously, she loves her guardian and her Yarmouth home. But, she has long aspired, however vaguely, for something else—something more. And aspiring for something more is something Dickens, driven since his own youth, could easily understand. Marrying Ham would bring Em'ly unending devotion from a good, if simple, man. But it would also end forever her hope of seeing the wider world. Thus, before she flees with Steerforth, before she becomes guiltracked and ashamed, Dickens shows Little Em'ly terribly conflicted. The language is melodramatic—but the tone, the emotion, is convincing. Em'ly knows that she should steer clear of Steerforth. But she also knows he represents her last chance for escape. Reared by good people, Em'ly wants to be a good and considerate person. But of course for girls living around Norfolk in the first decades of the nineteenth century, there were relatively few ways in which that goodness could be displayed—few ways in which the common human yearning for novelty and adventure could be assuaged. She never quite says as much, but Little Em'ly does not want to wind up like Mrs. Gummidge, "lone and lorn," her grim face turned always toward an uncrossable sea. "I want to be a better girl than I am," Little E. asserts in chapter 22, clearly aiming to convince herself that she wants what she is supposed to want. "I want to feel a hundred times more thankful than I do. I want to feel more, what a blessed thing it is to be the wife of a good man, and to lead a peaceful life. Oh me, oh me! Oh my heart, my heart!"

In Uriah Heep, Dickens invents one of his most perfectly detestable characters: a sleazy, scheming weasel who will never come close to possessing those gifts and charms that Steerforth has to burn. Heep has reptilian eyes, a "bony" physique and skeletonlike hands; he has the nervous habit of rubbing his palms together "as if to squeeze them dry and warm, besides often wiping them, in a stealthy way, on his pocket-handkerchief." The man jerks and writhes about, snakelike; he lusts for the angelic Agnes Wickfield, even "smacking his lips" at the idea of having her, "a ripe pear" he has long plotted to pluck. Worse, Heep is unctuous and fawning, chronically self-abasing, forever calling attention to his supposed humility. We hate Heep because we have all known Heeps: he is the smarmy hypocrite, the classic passive-aggressive type whose mask of forced *bonhomie* conceals a sensibility that is at once power-mad and insecure, forever plotting to gain an advantage or to secure revenge; to destroy all foes—real and imagined—who would stand in his way.

And it is because we find Heep so familiar and recognizable that we also find him so compelling—and appalling. He is a monster, but he is not—like earlier Dickens villains—a "demon" who has strayed into the novel from the pages of a fairy tale. It would be going too far to suggest that Dickens shows sympathy for this vile figure who, after all, also plots to defraud the father of Agnes Wickfield, David's true love. And yet, as he would more frequently in his later works, Dickens is careful to highlight the psychological subtext that informs this strange and vividly drawn character that readers love to loathe. Well into *David Copperfield*, we learn that Heep—unlike Quilp—has not in effect come from nowhere, or from some murky swamp, like the Creature from the Black Lagoon. Heep has a past. He had parents. He had an upbringing of sorts, reared like his father at "a foundation school for boys." Heep's mother, he reveals, "was likewise brought up at a public, sort of charitable establishment." Dickens was not, as Arnold Kettle notes, "in a crude sense, a social determinist; he does not imply that the social 'background' of a character is inescapable." Still, in these "humble" surroundings, Heep's level of social expectation was, obviously, kept low; his sense of self was shaped—or more precisely, twisted—around the notion that he could survive and perhaps even rise in a cutthroat, class-ridden world only if he behaved like a worm, slinking along, playing the game, showing no more pride than would befit one of his lowly station.

"They taught us all a deal of umbleness," he tells David in chapter 39. "Not much else I know of, from morning to night. We was umble to this person, and umble to that; and to pull off our caps here, and to make bows there; and always to know our place, and abase ourselves before our betters! And we had such a lot of betters! Father got the monitor-medal by being umble. So did I. Father got made a sexton by being umble.' . . . 'Be umble, Uriah,' says father to me, 'and you'll get on. It was what was always being dinned into you and me at school; it's what goes down best. Be umble,' says father, 'and you'll do!'" For David—and for the readers of *Copperfield*—this comes as a revelation. "It was the first time it had ever occurred to me," David recalls, "that this detestable cant of false humility might have originated out of the Heep family. I had seen the harvest, but had never thought of the seed."

Bleak House, Dickens's ninth novel, has often been called his masterpiece. It is in many ways his most ambitious work, employing two narrative voices, one of which belongs to a young woman, Esther Summerson—a rather bold gesture given the fact that critics had, almost from the start, found fault with his treatment of female characters. ("In my youth it was commonly said that Dickens could not draw women," is how Shaw put it—only "ridiculous idealizations of their sex.") Indeed, *Bleak House* shows Dickens again aspiring to a kind of artfulness and aesthetic cohesion not always obvious in his earliest works; here, most notably, he uses the Court of Chancery not only as a means of mocking, yet again, what he viewed as Britain's corrupt and Byzantine legal system, but as a symbol of all he found stagnant and corrupt about British society. The opening paragraphs of the book, perhaps the most famous in English fiction, have been widely analyzed, for they show Dickens using language in an especially careful and creative way, constructing a sort of overture that sets forth the themes he would build on as the novel proceeds. *Bleak House* is a novel about apathy, obfuscation, and deceit; and here, in these opening pages, Dickens describes London as dark and grimy and hard to traverse. London's streets he cakes with mud, tons of mud, "as if the waters had but newly retired from the face of the earth, and it would not be wonderful to meet a Megalosaurus"—of all things—"forty feet long or so, waddling like an elephantine lizard up Holborn Hill." He brings on the thick, pervasive fog for which London was famous: fog "everywhere. Fog up the river, where it flows among green . . . and meadows; fog down the river, where it rolls defiled among tiers of shipping, and the waterside pollutions of a great (and dirty) city." He then points his camera toward the legal district, specifically Temple Bar, where we find the High Court of Chancery, the home of suits and countersuits, and where, appropriately, "the dense fog is densest, and the muddy streets are muddiest."

As Michael Goldberg notes in *Dickens and Carlyle* (1972), this imagery of obfuscation and congestion can be traced back, like much in Dickens, to the contemporary writer he most admired. In "The Present Time," Carlyle's first *Latter-Day Pamphlet*, we can find references to the "universal Stygian quagmire of British industrial life," as Goldberg points out; from this "wretched inhabitants have 'oozed-in upon London' creating problems that loomed like 'enormous Megatherions, as ugly as were ever born of mud.' At the very center of this confusion Carlyle visualizes a 'Government tumbling and drifting on the whirlpools and mud-deluges' in precisely the way that Dickens associates mud, mire, and fog with the 'groping and floundering condition' of Chancery with its Lord High Chancellor enthroned at the 'very heart of the fog.'" These opening pages of *Bleak House*, Goldberg writes, "lightly touch on all the Carlylean themes" that the novel itself "explores in richly intricate detail." "The Megalosaurus at home in the London mud," for example,

suggests a society which, for all its apparent progress, had not made the evolutionary adaptations necessary to survival. The foot passengers in an "infection" of ill-temper anticipate the equalizing contagion that rages through all social classes in the novel. The mud accumulating on the pavement at the rate of "compound interest" points forward to the Smallweeds, the goblin usurers and the general theme of Mammonism. The description of the fog obscuring everything but lying most impenetrably in the region of Chancery, "that leaden old obstruction," prefigures symbolically the sense projected by the whole novel of the way institutions balk human life.

Those who attack the vast mountain of secondary material that now surrounds this richly layered novel will also learn, among other things, that legal reform was a rather hot topic in Britain when the novel appeared in the 1850s; that the vividly drawn figure of Harold Skimpole, a self-absorbed sponger of the highest order, is based largely on the poet-essayist Leigh Hunt, and was called "Leonard Horner" in earlier drafts; that Hunt—an old friend—was not delighted with the portrait; that, through Skimpole, Dickens underscores the book's larger attack on parasitical individuals and institutions; that he also ridicules, through Mrs. Jellyby, not the practice of philanthropy *per se*, but those unable to grasp the simple principle that it ought to start at home. Critics have also noted that Dickens derived the character of Inspector Bucket from one Inspector Charles Frederick Field, a prominent London cop of Dickens's acquaintance; that by creating Bucket—a "pre Sherlock sleuth" as Vladimir Nabokov calls him—Dickens not only reveals once more his lively interest in crime and the mechanics of its detection, but also contributes much to the genre of the urban mystery novel that begins to develop in the nineteenth century and remains so vastly popular today. Readers of Dickens criticism will also learn that in his portrait of Jo, the young street sweeper who dies of smallpox, the author of *Oliver Twist* shows his continuing interest in documenting the lives of poor, uneducated children lost in the system and forced to survive on the streets.

Indeed, in certain passages, particularly in "Tom-all-Alone's," where he depicts the sad life of Jo, Dickens strongly evokes memories of *Twist* as he employs what one critic has called "a rhetoric of direct attack that often unnerves the modern reader, but rarely leaves him unmoved." Here, in one of the book's most powerful passages, Dickens again pushes his readers to consider what, in the end, being human means. "It must be a strange state to be like Jo!" he writes, deliberately placing his readers in the place of this "poor wretch" who daily must "shuffle through" London's streets, unschooled and illiterate, puzzled by the rites of respectable society and awed by "those mysterious symbols, so abundant over the shops, and the corner of the streets, and on the doors, and in the windows!" Jo is "hustled, and jostled," and always told to move on; he learns he has "no business here, or there, or anywhere"; he assumes thus that he is "scarcely human," and has little or no connection to those "superior beings" whose appearance he shares. Dickens stresses that, in fact, dogs in Britain are treated better than the likes of Jo. Dickens now brings in a dog—"a drover's dog, waiting for his owner outside a butcher's shop"—who, with Jo, listens to the music of a passing band, but who—unlike the boy—has been "educated, improved, developed" to herd sheep and thus play a useful role in society. But of course, Dickens comments—again sounding the note of social apocalypse that he strikes frequently in his fiction from *Oliver Twist* on—"Turn that dog's descendants wild, like Jo, and in a very few years they will so degenerate that they will lose even their bark—but not their bite."

Being human, then, requires more than being human. It requires education, and the cultural reinforcement of appropriate values and ideals—without which none of us can hope to live much better than beasts. It also requires compassion, empathy, fellow-feeling—values that Skimpole, for one, so disgustingly lacks. Dickens dislikes Skimpole because Skimpole is, among other things, a fraud. He is a simpleton, a child-man; but, unlike Mr. Dick, he is not also the victim of mental impairment. Rather like Flora Finching, Skimpole has simply chosen not to mature. Worse: his simplicity and innocence is utterly faked, a ruse designed to evade all forms of social responsibility. "I ask only to be free," he pleads at one point. "The butterflies are free. Mankind will surely not deny to Harold Skimpole what it concedes to the butterflies!" Skimpole is not only lazy, but thoroughly self-absorbed, and thus thoroughly unable to identify with anyone else's suffering—always for Dickens the one unforgivable sin. In this regard, Skimpole is little better than the monstrous Quilp. In one scene, as Esther recalls, we find Skimpole, "on his back," extolling the virtues of "enterprise and effort" and proclaiming himself "truly cosmopolitan." But, as for a child, the world exists simply for Skimpole's amusement. "I lie in a shady place like this," he muses, "and think of adventurous spirits going to the North Pole, or penetrating to the heart of the Torrid Zone, with admiration. Mercenary creatures ask, 'What is the use of a man's going to the North Pole? What good does it do?' I can't say; but, for anything I *can* say, he may go for the purpose—though he don't know it—of employing my thoughts as I lie here." "Take an extreme case," Skimpole continues. "Take the case of the Slaves on American plantations. I dare say they are worked hard, I dare say they don't altogether like it. I dare say theirs is an unpleasant experience on the whole; but, they people the landscape for me, they give it a poetry for me, and perhaps that is one of the pleasanter objects of their existence."

As we have seen, Dickens often uses animal imagery when depicting characters whose lives are defined largely by brutal pursuit of selfish ends; similarly, in *Bleak House*—particularly through the Smallweeds—Dickens shows how this ceaseless scrapping after money must inevitably coarsen, cheapen, and demean. The Smallweeds are a superbly horrid bunch, the descendants of a "horny-skinned, two-legged, money getting species of spider, who spun webs to catch unwary flies, and retired into holes until they were entrapped. The name of this old pagan's God was Compound Interest. He lived for it, married it, died of it." The Smallweeds themselves, in their ruthless pursuit of profit, have "discarded all amusements, discountenanced all story-books, fairy tales, fictions and fables, and banished all levities whatsoever." In other words, having squashed their imaginative capacities—and those more wonder-provoking things that make us human—the Smallweeds have come to carry on like so many apes. The Smallweeds and their offspring "have been observed to bear a likeness to old monkeys with something depressing on their minds." The elder of the clan "drinks and smokes in a monkeyish way"; moments later we see him tossed back comically into a chair, "like a broken puppet." Given their upbringing, Smallweed's descendants are—like the schoolchildren in *Hard Times*—doomed never to know the innocent pleasures of childhood, and so to continue on in their brutish, soul-killing, and mechanical way. Judy Smallweed "never owned a doll, never heard of Cinderella, never played at any game"; she has no notion of a "youthful laugh." Her twin brother "couldn't wind up a top for his life. He knows no more of Jack the Giant Killer, or of Sinbad the Sailor, than he knows of the people in the stars."

Throughout much of *Bleak House* Dickens looks at his characters from a distance, and with a cold eye. The novel's tone does not make us think of Oliver Goldsmith or Pierce Egan or Henry Fielding. It is sharply bitter at times, suggesting utter disgust and reminding us that if one side of Dickens was sentimental, the other was perhaps rather cynical—or simply realistic, recognizing that the capacity for brute cruelty and rank stupidity among human beings is astonishingly great indeed. Thus we are told, for example, that Mr. Tulkington—the slick but shady lawyer who pries into Lady Dedlock's past—lives "in a large house, formerly a house of state," that is "let off in sets of chambers now; and in those shrunken fragments of its greatness, lawyers lie like maggots in nuts." And again we think of the bitter comedy of Samuel Beckett, perhaps, or more exactly Wyndham Lewis: twentieth-century writers prone to depict people as puppets, machines, automatons, compelled to act out an unending display of obsessions and quirks. Dickens describes one of the novel's more contemptible figures, Mr. Chadband, as a "large yellow man, with a fat smile, and a general appearance of having a good deal of train oil in his system." He "moves softly and cumbrously, not unlike a bear who has been taught to walk upright." Like many pious hypocrites in Dickens's novels, Chadband is ill at ease with the very fact of his body, and is "very much embarrassed about the arms, as if they were inconvenient to him, and he wanted to grovel; is very much in a perspiration about the head; and never speaks without first putting up his great hand, as delivering a token to his hearers that he is going to edify them."

Elsewhere, Dickens describes a sweltering London summer that seems a portrait in miniature of human absurdity, futility, and discontent; he notes "young clerks" who are "madly in love" and itching for "bliss" with their "beloved object." But he also alludes to "all the middle-aged clerks," those ardent wooers of not too long ago, who now "think their families too large." Meanwhile, at the Inns of Court, he calls in more dogs; these are "unowned dogs" who "pant about staircases and other dry places, seeking water" and giving "short howls of aggravation." Out in the street, "all the blind men's dogs," we are told, "draw their masters against pumps, or trip them over buckets"—an action that seems to stem as much from motiveless canine malignity as from some passing disorientation in the heat. *Bleak House* also features the infamous figure of Krook, who deals "in cat-skins among other general matters" and is grandly known as "the Lord Chancellor." Krook comes to an appropriately sordid end by disintegrating rather suddenly, the victim of "spontaneous combustion." The world of *Bleak House* is, in many ways, odd.

Again, as Jenni Calder has put it, Dickens's "inclinations towards the grotesque, the dramatic, and the exaggerated do not lend themselves to the depiction of an ordinary world. The whole tendency of his fiction questions whether normality exists." But as Calder rightly points out, Dickens does seem uneasy emphasizing these macabre and morbid tendencies in his fiction—at least for long. He was, she argues, "forced to employ certain conventions of normality, conventions sustained by a traditional Christian point of view, because the alternative is to accept an anarchic and destructive world." Dickens, Calder observes, "relishes the anarchy, the grotesqueries, he has a passion for the freakish in character and incident, but is he perhaps afraid of their implications? He must always balance these extremes with a version of solid normality, and most often solid normality means a domestic marriage, a limited, serving role for the woman and a kindly, protective role for the man."

This interpretation seems particularly applicable to *Bleak House*. Here, one narrative voice—Dickens's voice—is more clearly cold and ironical than the other, which belongs to Esther Summerson, the "orphan" who comes to Bleak House under the protection of the kindly John Jarndyce. Esther, who serves as housekeeper at Bleak House, has all the Dickensian virtues. She is industrious and self-sacrificing; she insists at one point that she hopes only to go "on my lowly way along the path of duty." Although afflicted with—and left scarred by—the smallpox that Jo, dying, brings to Bleak House, Esther does not become bitter; more importantly, she remains uninfected by the money urge that contaminates so many in the novel, including Richard Carstone, whose young life is fatally poisoned by his obsession with bringing the interminable case of *Jarndyce v. Jarndyce* to a profitable close. ("The one great principle of the English law," *Bleak House* tells us, "is, to make business for itself. There is no other principle distinctly, certainly, and consistently maintained through all its narrow turnings. Viewed by this light it becomes a coherent scheme, and not the monstrous maze the laity are apt to think it. Let them but once clearly perceive that its grand principle is to make business for itself at their expense, and surely they will cease to grumble.") At the novel's close, Esther is entirely content, nestled in a settled domestic world, married to a man, Doctor Allan Woodcourt, who devotes his life to healing people, including the poor, and who also understands that wealth and happiness are not inevitably the same. "We are not rich in the bank," Esther explains in the novel's closing paragraphs, "but we have always prospered, and we have quite enough."

Like David, Esther has had her critics; for some, she seems rather too primly dutiful and too self-satisfied, despite her initial disclaimer that she is "not clever." For too many, she is The Perfect Dickens Girl. And this person, writes Shaw, is "simply the perfect domestic convenience. Great as was his advance in sight and comprehension both before and after *Bleak House*, the jingling of Esther Summerson's housekeeping keys fulfilled his conception of feminine music to the last." Shaw called Esther "a maddening prig, though we are forced to admit that such paragons exist and are perhaps worthy of the reverent admiration with which Dickens regarded them." W. J. Harvey argues that Esther does in fact "fail" when functioning as narrator: she fails, in a "slight" way because "the exigencies" of the narrative compel Dickens "to reveal Esther's goodness in a coy and repellent manner; she is, for instance, continually imputing to others qualities which the author transparently wishes us to transfer to her. Esther's goodness is acceptable when she is least conscious of its effects radiating out to impinge on others. Similarly, her narrative is most acceptable when she is pushed from the centre of the stage by the typical inhabitants of the Dickens world. Happily this is usually so."

Bleak House strongly implies that Esther has also been shaped profoundly by her past. She has not been encouraged to be bold, confident, and proud. An "illegitimate" child, she was not allowed

to celebrate her birthday as a girl, instead compassionately informed
by her pious "godmother"—one of a long series of puritanical
neurotics to show up in Dickens's work—that "it would have been
far better, little Esther, that you had no birthday; that you had never
been born!" Esther's godmother stresses that "submission, self-
denial, diligent work, are the preparations of a life begun with such
a shadow on it." Understandably Esther, during her childhood,
confides in no one but her doll. "I would try," she tells the doll, "as
hard as ever I could, to repair the fault I had been born with (of
which I confessedly felt guilty and yet innocent), and would strive
as I grew up to be industrious, contented, and kind-hearted, and to
do some good to some one, and win some love to myself if I
could." Here then, the roots—the "seeds"—of Esther's personality
are revealed. And thus does the end of the novel circle back to its
early chapters. Esther has done her duty: she has been devoted,
patient, kind. And finally she gets her reward—a fact that
understandably triggers her pride, and leaves her a bit surprised.
"The people even praise Me as the doctor's wife. The people even
like Me as I go about, and make so much of me that I am quite
abashed."

Esther Summerson has Dickens's keen and retentive eye—for
detail and atmosphere, for the small signs that can reveal much
about character and personality. Indeed, sometimes she has his
voice. In chapter 14 she zeroes in on the idiocies of Mr.
Turveydrop, another of the novel's big spongers, employing comic
exaggeration and repetition in a way that recalls parts of *Martin
Chuzzlewit* or *Dombey and Son*, with its own model of falseness,
Mrs. Skewton. Turveydrop, Esther notes, was "a fat old gentleman
with a false complexion, false teeth, false whiskers, and a wig." He
was "pinched in, and swelled out, and got up, and stepped down";
he "had a cane, he had an eye-glass, he had a snuff-box, he had
rings, he had wristbands, he had everything but any touch of nature;
he was not like youth, he was not like age, he was not like anything
in the world but a model of Deportment." In the next chapter,
Esther's resemblance to her creator becomes even more obvious.
She points with comic sharpness to Mr. Quale—a disciple of the
absurdly self-righteous Mrs. Jellyby—who is very excited: "He
seemed to project those two shining knobs of temples of his into
everything that went on, and to brush his hair farther and farther
back, until the very roots were almost ready to fly out of his head

in inappeasable philanthropy." One day, Esther remembers, Mr.
Quale shows up for a visit accompanied by the redoubtable Mr.
Gusher. Esther describes Gusher as "a flabby gentleman with a
moist surface, and eyes so much too small for his moon of a face
that they seemed to have been made for somebody else." "A flabby
gentleman with a moist surface": that line has Dickens's prints all
over it. One recalls David Copperfield visiting Mr. Micawber in "a
little inn," where he "occupied a little room." "I think it was over
the kitchen," David notes, "because a warm greasy smell appeared
to through the chinks in the floor, and there was a flabby
perspiration on the walls." (Sylvère Monod once suggested that *little*
is "the most characteristic word in the whole Dickensian
vocabulary." But *firm* one sometimes thinks, must run a close
second—with *flabby* not far behind.)

Bucket, too, is carefully drawn from several angles and comes to
life. He is in fact one of the novel's most appealing figures,
combining shrewdness and simplicity in a manner much imitated by
later novelists inventing good-guy detectives and companionable
cops. In *Bleak House*, Bucket leads an investigation into the murder
of the lawyer Tulkington, bringing him into contact with many of
the novel's central figures. It also leads him finally to Mademoiselle
Hortense, Lady Dedlock's maid. Hortense, like many of Dickens's
characters, was inspired by a figure from life—one much in the
news. In manner and dress she owes much to the stylish and
mysterious Maria Manning, who was executed in 1849 for the
murder of her lover and who faced her death with defiance and
calm. Bucket's model, Inspector Field, was involved in the Manning
case, and was similarly respected by his peers. "He was really very
kind and gentle," Esther recalls as the dark plot thickens, and
Buckett pursues his inquiries. "I felt a confidence in his sagacity
which reassured me." "Everybody," she observes, seemed to know
Buckett, and to "defer" to him, no doubt because of his confident
but unpretentious air.

Dickens is careful to establish Bucket's simplicity as much as his
sagacity; like his many fictional descendants, Bucket is an ordinary
man doing an extraordinary job: a man of the lower-middle class
who deals daily, and calmly, with issues of good and evil, life and
death. Bucket in the morning has, "as a foundation to work upon,"
his eggs, tea, mutton chops, toast, and marmalade. Over the years
he's put down a bob or two on the horses—and, given his street

sense, knows when it helps to flatter, and when to bribe. In chapter 53, Dickens shows Bucket shrewdly pulling information out of a footman, "Mercury," in part by alluding to his own humble roots. "My father was first a page," Bucket relates, "then a footman, then a butler, then a steward, then an innkeeper. Lived universally respected, and died lamented. Said with his last breath that he considered service the most honourable part of his career, and so it was." Dickens, it is clear, identifies with Bucket far more than with most of the characters in the novel; like Bucket, his career followed a path that allowed him to move among—but never be quite part of—the upper-classes. And in *Bleak House* it is Bucket, as well as Esther, who gets the true measure of Skimpole. "'Whenever a person says to you that they are as innocent as can be regarding money,'" Bucket tells Esther, "'look well after your own money, for they are dead certain to collar it, if they can. Whenever a person proclaims to you In worldly matters I'm a child,' you consider that that person is only a-crying off from being accountable, and that you've got that person's number, and it's Number One.'"

There is nothing hard about *Hard Times*. It is Dickens's most bluntly propagandistic novel: as subtle as a billboard—or as *A Christmas Carol*. "It reads like a fable," writes Peter Ackroyd, "in a style which is very close to Victorian translations of fairy-stories of the same period." It is topical too. Labor unrest was not rare in Britain's industrial cities; there were food or "bread" riots too, notably in Liverpool, about a year after *Hard Times* appeared. The nation was becoming less rural, more industrialized. And many social critics were insisting that current industrial practice was exploiting—as well as maiming, and often literally destroying— many men, women, and children. Ruskin was one. In *The Stones of Venice* (1853), as elsewhere, he warns of the tendency to treat the industrial worker as if he were "an animated tool." "We have much studied and much perfected, of late," Ruskin writes, here sounding quite like Engels and Marx, "the great civilized invention of the division of labor; only we give it a false name. It is not, truly speaking, the labor that is divided, but the men—divided into mere segments of men—broken into small fragments and crumbs of life," who in the daily grind of their work lives can display little of their innate abilities and potential skills. Ruskin points to those engaged in the manufacture of glass beads—"utterly unnecessary" products that do not derive from the sort of "healthy and ennobling labour" he knew was essential for fulfillment of the mind and enrichment of the soul; they know nothing of the sort of "work-pleasure" that William Morris, Ruskin's disciple, later described. The beads "are formed by first drawing out the glass into rods; these rods are chopped up into fragments of the size of beads by the human hand, and the fragments are then rounded in the furnace. The men who chop up the rods sit at their work all day, their hands vibrating with a perpetual and exquisitely timed palsy, and the beads dropping beneath their vibration like hail. Neither they, nor the men who draw out the rods, or fuse the fragments, have the smallest occasion for the use of any human faculty; and every young lady, therefore, who buys glass beads is engaged in the slave trade." In "all our manufacturing cities," Ruskin writes, "we manufacture everything there except men; we blanch cotton, and strengthen steel, and refine sugar, and shape pottery; but to brighten, to strengthen, to refine, or to form a single living spirit, never enters into our estimate of advantages."

Carlyle raised similar concerns, repeatedly. In *Signs of the Times* (1829), he pointed not only to the great increase in mechanical devices, but to the various ways in which mechanical devices were altering, however subtly, the ways in which human beings view themselves and their place in the world. "Were we required to characterize this age of ours by any single epithet, we should," Carlyle wrote, "be tempted to call it, not an Heroical, Devotional, Philosophical, or Moral Age, but, above all others, the Mechanical Age. It is the Age of Machinery, in every outward and inward sense of that word; the age which, with its whole undivided might, forwards, teaches and practices the great art of adapting means to ends." The world thus gains in power, efficiency, productivity. But of course, as Carlyle would continue to note, there is more to human life and potential than power, efficiency, and productivity. The great danger of living in "the domain of Mechanism" is that men begin to think and act like machines, and so extol only the most utilitarian values. Man, Carlyle writes, has a "Dynamical nature" as well as a "Mechanical nature." From the latter arises "the mysterious springs of Love, and Fear, and Wonder, of Enthusiasm, Poetry, Religion, all which have a truly vital and *infinite* character"—and which are humankind's greatest, most ennobling endeavors. The Christian religion, Carlyle notes, sharply aware of his audience, "which, under every theory of it, in the believing or unbelieving mind, must be regarded as the crowning glory, or rather the life and soul, of our whole modern culture," did not "arise and spread" because of the "institutions, and establishments and well-arranged systems of mechanism." It arose "in the mystic deeps of man's soul." "Man's highest attainment was accomplished Dynamically, not Mechanically"; in fact, "we will venture to say, that no high attainment, not even any far-extending movement among men, was ever accomplished otherwise." Writes Carlyle: "If we read History with any degree of thoughtfulness, we shall find that the checks and balances of Profit and Loss have never been the grand agents with men; that they have never been roused into deep, thorough, all-pervading efforts by any computable prospect of Profit and Loss, for any visible, finite object; but always for some invisible and infinite one."

Dickens "inscribed" *Hard Times* to Carlyle. Michael Goldberg persuasively suggests that the novel "expresses his widespread dependence on Carlyle's teaching to an extreme extent." Set in dreary industrial Coketown, the novel attacks "statistical methods"—as did Carlyle in "Chartism" (1839). It attacks "ultra-rationalist methods in education"—as Carlyle did in *Sartor Resartus*. Even its characters, Goldberg suggests, "might be considered personifications of Carlylean criticism." Thomas Gradgrind, one of Coketown's most influential citizens, "embodies all that Carlyle denounces in the 'mechanists,' and his relationship with Bounderby, a Victorian 'captain of Industry,' reveals how easily Utilitarian ideas consort in practice with Philistinism." Bitzer, once a pupil at the factorylike school Gradgrind supports, "exemplifies the moral results of 'getting-on' in the world, which is reminiscent of Carlyle's attacks on the self-interest principle of laissez-faire economists, while Harthouse"—another politician—"strolls out of the pages of Carlyle's 'gospel of dilettantism.'"

Hard Times was published weekly in *Household Words* with the aim of boosting that publication's sagging sales. It offers no leisurely beginning, no artful descriptions woven in at the start to hint of forthcoming themes. Instead there is the figure of Gradgrind barking, in a bare "monotonous vault of a schoolroom," his "square forefinger" all but wagging in the reader's face. "Now, what I want is, Facts. Teach these boys and girls nothing but Facts. Facts alone are wanted in life. Plant nothing else, and root out everything else. You can only form the minds of reasoning animals upon Facts:

nothing else will ever be of any service to them. This is the principle on which I bring up my own children, and this is the principle on which I bring up these children. Stick to Facts, sir!" In fact, Gradgrind's children, like the pupils at his school, are shielded from anything suggesting the speculative or the silly, or the pleasures of creative play. "No little Gradgrind," the novel's narrator notes, "had ever associated a cow in a field with that famous cow with the crumpled horn who tossed the dog who worried the cat who killed the rat who ate the malt, or with that yet more famous cow who swallowed Tom Thumb: it had never heard of those celebrities." Gradgrind's children, Louisa and Tom, "had only been introduced to a cow as a graminivorous ruminating quadruped with several stomachs."

This is not a formula for happy and successful human living. In *David Copperfield*, Dickens revealed how the "seeds" of Uriah Heep's ghastly character were planted in his dreadful childhood. In *Hard Times*, particularly in its second section, "Reaping," he shows how Gradgrind's grossly limited view of the world has brought misery to many, including Louisa, who—at her father's behest—reluctantly marries a powerful and vulgar banker, Josiah Bounderby, whose name of course smacks strongly of the melodramatic stage. In chapter 12, Louisa finally faces her father, telling him that she regrets—indeed "curses"—her upbringing, her "destiny." "How could you give me life," she asks him, "and take from me all the inappreciable things that raise it from the state of conscious death?" "Where," she demands—using words that Estella will similarly throw at her maker, Miss Havisham, in *Great Expectations*—"are the graces of my soul? Where are the sentiments of my heart? What have you done, O father"—she strikes herself "with both her hands upon her bosom"—"what have you done, with the garden that should have bloomed once, in this great wilderness here!"

Dickens, in *Little Dorrit*, would evoke the phrase "Nobody's Fault" in a bluntly ironic way, hoping to make his readers think hard about the popular and lazy notion that, in social systems, things are as they are because—well—that's the way they are; things simply happen as they do. Certainly Coketown, *Hard Times* makes clear, is no accident, but the product of attitudes and ideas held by powerful men like Gradgrind, who is so emotionally thick, so rigid, so devoid of imaginative powers, that he finds time to worry about what the locals might be perusing down at the local library. "It was a disheartening circumstance," he realizes, "but a melancholy fact, that even these readers"—these workers, like Stephen Blackpool, cut off from the world of nature and kept so busy with their mindless tasks—"persisted in wondering. They wondered about human nature, human passions, human hopes and fears, the struggles, triumphs and defeats, the cares and joys and sorrows, the lives and deaths, of common men and women! They sometimes, after fifteen hours work, sat down to read mere fables about men and women, more or less like themselves, and about children, more or less like their own. They took Defoe to their bosoms, instead of Euclid, and seemed on the whole more comforted by Goldsmith than by Cocker"—the mathematician whose book on arithmetic was so widely used, for more than a century, that the phrase "according to Cocker" became synonymous with accuracy and hard, indisputable *fact*. Gradgrind's Coketown is not a place where intuition or imagination or even silliness—all crucial to human life—can begin to bud, much less grow. It is "a triumph of fact," a place conceived and run by men with no idea of beauty and absolutely no use for spiritual refreshment or play; men for whom the "bottom line"—to use a more contemporary phrase—governs all. It is a town "of machinery and tall chimneys." It has "a black canal in it, and a river with ill-smelling dye." It has streets "all very like one another, and many small streets still more like one another, inhabited by people equally like one another, who all went in and out at the same hours, with the same sound upon the same pavements, to do the same work, and to whom every day was the same as yesterday and tomorrow, and every year the counterpart of the last and the next." Everything in Coketown "was severely workful." Everything is severely functional, monotonous: "The jail might have been the infirmary, the infirmary might have been the jail, the town-hall might have been either, or both. . . . " "Fact, fact, fact," the narrator observes, "everywhere in the material aspects of the town; fact, fact, fact, everywhere in the immaterial."

Such descriptions are of course recognizable by anyone who has any acquaintance with the world's industrial regions, be they in Britain or the United States. *Hard Times* makes us think—as few Victorian novels can—that this *is* the world our values and attitudes have made, and is still making, as D. H. Lawrence, a collier's son, so thoroughly realized. "Now though perhaps nobody knew it," wrote Lawrence in "Nottingham and the Mining Countryside" (1930), "it was ugliness which really betrayed the spirit of man, in the nineteenth century. The great crime which the moneyed classes and promoters of industry committed in the palmy Victorian days was the condemning of the workers to ugliness, ugliness, ugliness: meanness and formless and ugly surroundings, ugly ideals, ugly religion, ugly hope, ugly love, ugly clothes, ugly furniture, ugly houses, ugly relationships between workers and employers. The human soul needs actual beauty even more than bread."

There is little beauty in the life of Stephen Blackpool, a power-loom operator who for Dickens represents the typical industrial laborer of his day: a man utterly without power and money and for whom, thus, life is not likely to grow better and more meaningful with time. Stephen is trapped in a loveless marriage to a woman much given to drink, but is blocked by the law from marrying the woman he loves. (Although the wealthy Bounderby walks easily away from his own union to the unhappy Louisa Gradgrind.) Blackpool—his very name suggesting darkness, hopelessness, drowning—is accused of a crime he did not commit. He loses his job for failing to support a worker's strike. He tumbles down a mine-shaft and, after much suffering, dies.

Hard Times illustrates particularly well Dickens's belief, expressed in a letter of 1854, that "one of fiction's highest uses," must be to "interest and affect the general mind in behalf of anything that is clearly wrong—to stimulate and rouse the public soul to a compassionate or indignant feeling that it *must not be*." Still, in *Hard Times,* Dickens does not urge the nation's workers to storm the barricades. The novel describes economic disparity and social suffering as explicitly as any of Dickens's works. It sets forth to show how bleak and depressing life is for so many—thanks to the Gradgrinds and Bounderbys of the world. But it obviously puts no great faith in the world's workers, or in the fledgling labor movement of the day. "There is a point" writes Peter Ackroyd, "when the narrative looks likely to become a saga of union and management, and one in which Dickens would repeat his often stated belief that the workers suffered just as much under bad union representatives as they ever did under bad employers." Dickens, as novel after novel shows, "supported the rights of working people to a proper education, as well as proper sanitation and housing"; he could certainly register "imaginative sympathy with the individual victim"—like Blackpool. But then, as Ackroyd notes, such sympathy almost always turned to hostility or anger "if those victims organised together and in any way threatened the *status quo*." Dickens "was not generally opposed to the claims or methods of the more advanced industrialists of his period; he reserved his animus for the remnants of the aristocracy"—Sir Mulberry, say—"and for the government bureaucracy"—the Court of Chancery, the Circumlocution Office—"which seemed to be impeding 'Progress' at every turn." And progress, as *Household Words* itself rightly predicted, would come from improved education and better sanitation—as well as the proper application of new scientific discoveries and old religious truths. By the close of *Hard Times*, Gradgrind finally gets the message. He does not turn into Pickwick exactly—but at the close of his life he will become, we learn, "a white-haired decrepit man, bending his hitherto inflexible theories to appointed circumstances; making his facts and figures subservient to Faith, Hope, and Charity; and no longer trying to grind that Heavenly trio in his dusty mills."

With *Hard Times*, Dickens was again attacking dogmatism and puritanism as much as ruthless capitalism. It also targets those religious and civic leaders who, over the decades, had deemed it essential to license theaters or ban drinking or prohibit Sunday shopping—even Sunday strolling. Dickens sanely understood that such laws simply add to the misery and discontent of people who otherwise did little else but sleep and work in a grim struggle to survive. In this respect, this rather late Dickens novel resembles *Nicholas Nickleby* with its suggestion that, in a hard and largely heartless world, the imagination, broadly defined, must play a central role; to deny it is to insure problems for the individual, and for society as a whole. The world requires paternal benevolence, Dickens often implies. But it also needs the sort of fanciful and healing escape that kind, colorful souls like Vincent Crummles or Sleary, in *Hard Times*, can provide. Sleary, who runs a circus, suffers from asthma and speaks with a lisp; he is not a "gentleman"; he has "a flabby surface, and a muddled head which was never sober and never drunk." But he and his performers represent the book's central values: they have not yet been crushed and confined within the Bounderby-Gradgrind system. "They were not very tidy in their private dresses, they were not at all orderly in their domestic arrangements, and the combined literature of the whole company would have produced but a poor letter on any subject." And yet, "there was a remarkable gentleness and childishness about these people, a special inaptitude for any kind of sharp practice, and an untiring readiness to help and pity one another, deserving, often of as much respect, and always of as much generous construction, as the everyday virtues of any class of people in the world." As we have seen, "childishness"—at least when it implies gentleness, innocent goodness, a sense of wonder, and playful curiosity—is one of the great Dickensian virtues. Sissy Jupe understands this too: At the close of *Hard Times* she appears as the mother of "happy children," for Sissy is herself "learned in childish lore; thinking no innocent and pretty fancy ever to be despised; trying hard to know her humbler fellow-creatures, and to beautify their lives of machinery and reality with those imaginative graces and delights, without which the heart of infancy will wither up, the sturdiest physical manhood will be morally stark death."

Hard Times is then a representative Dickensian fiction, arguing that work does not require the shutting of theaters or parks or the banning of Sunday fairs; it does not need more apostles of discipline and productivity. What it *does* need are more people like Sissy Jupe. The narrator makes this point rather ominously in chapter 6, when he directly addresses "Utilitarian economists, skeletons of schoolmasters, Commissioners of Fact, genteel and used-up infidels, gabblers of many little dog's-eared creeds, the poor you will always have with you. Cultivate in them, while there is yet time, the utmost graces of the fancies and affections to adorn their lives so much in need of ornament; or, in the day of your triumph, when romance is utterly driven out of their souls, and they and a bare existence stand face to face, Reality will take a wolfish turn, and make an end of you!"

"The people," in other words, as Sleary himself puts it, "muth be amuthed."

4

Money and Mystery

Little Dorrit, Great Expectations, Our Mutual Friend
The Mystery of Edwin Drood

One should not go to *Little Dorrit* looking only for laughs. An early reviewer complained that "we admit that Mr. Dickens has a mission, but it is to make the world grim, not to recreate and rehabilitate society." Nor should one expect a tightly tailored plot. The novelist John Wain correctly calls *Little Dorrit* "one of the greatest novels of the nineteenth century." But as Wain notes, it is also Dickens's "most stationary novel; its impact is even less dependent on 'plot' than is customary throughout Dickens's work; its development is by means of outward radiation, rather than linear progression. As everyone who has read it attentively has seen, it is built up on two metaphors, the prison and the family."

Little Dorrit "is, in essence, a plotless novel," writes Wain. For "all the scurry of event on its surface," [*Little Dorrit*] "never for a moment suggests genuine movement. It is an intricate labyrinth, designed so that the reader, on whatever path he sets out, will always be brought back to the point where one or the other of the two principal metaphors is confronting him." It is also, Wain writes, Dickens's "most tragic novel. It deals tragically both with society and with personal relationships; and it is engineered so as to convey, ineffaceably, that the two are inextricably linked." *Little Dorrit* stems from Dickens's belief that "when a society becomes oppressive, human relationships within that society become warped." Wain—like other critics—notes that in *Little Dorrit*, Dickens depicts nineteenth-century England as a place "where genuine happiness is impossible. It is a prison, in which all the convicts are members of one family. Alternatively, it is a family which organizes its life after the fashion of a prison." Thus in *Little Dorrit*, we find, among other wounded and imprisoned figures, Amy Dorrit, the novel's title character, "who has put all her energies into relieving the sufferings of her weak and selfish father, and as a result is left in a permanently disabled psychological state in which the relationship of a father and daughter is the only one she can think of as real." We find too, in Arthur Clennam, "a man whose emotional life has been stifled by the harshly repressive behaviour of his mother, so that for years he has been in the habit of thinking a normal marriage is something he can no longer hope for."

Themes of repression and imprisonment are also played out among the novel's secondary characters, including the Meagles, who are "systematically ruining their daughter's chances for happiness by smothering her in kindness and protecting her from life to such an extent that she ["Pet" Meagles] will arrive at womanhood with no more knowledge of herself than to marry a cad who will make her miserable. The cad himself, Henry Gowan, is expressly shown as the product of another distorted family relationship"—one which has social snobbery at its core.

Wain points perceptively to this theme of imprisonment that pervades *Little Dorrit*, as well as to its interest in exposing the corrosive effects of snobbery and social climbing. Given its tone and its topics, many readers will find that *Little Dorrit* has a more "contemporary" quality than Dickens's other works; some, perhaps, will think of Jean-Paul Sartre's *No Exit*, with its closing injunction that "Hell is other people." For these readers, the Circumlocution Office is a particularly apt institution to be evoked so vividly in the novel's early chapters. It is a vast, pointless place, where Arthur Clennam can find no help and no clarity; it can represent any ill-run and nonproductive bureau or institution. Through his depiction of the Circumlocution Office, Dickens sustains his attack on the sort of governmental indifference and lassitude that he had long found at work in Britain, and that is of course at the heart of both *Oliver Twist* and *Bleak House*. The letters Dickens wrote as he worked on *Little Dorrit* vividly reveal a continuing sense of angry frustration at the practice of politics on every level of British society. In one, sent to the actor William Macready, Dickens admits that in *Little Dorrit* he was "blowing off a little of indignant steam which would otherwise blow me up." "I have lost hope even in the ballot," he told Macready, a longtime friend. "We appear to me to have proved the failure of representative institutions without an educated and advanced people to support them." Dickens continues:

What with teaching people to "keep their stations," what with bringing up the soul and body of the land to be a good child, or to go to the beer-shop, to go a-poaching and go to the devil; what with having no such thing as a middle class (for though we are perpetually bragging of it as our safety, it is nothing but a fringe on the mantle of the upper); what with flunkyism, toadyism, letting the most contemptible lords come in for all manner of places, reading The Court Circular for the New Testament, I do reluctantly believe that the English people are habitually consenting parties to the miserable imbecility into which we have fallen, *and never will help themselves out of it*. Who is to do it, if anybody is, God knows. But at present we are on the down-hill road to being conquered, and the people WILL be content to bear it, sing "Rule Britannia," and WILL NOT be saved.

In chapter 10, when Clennam shows up at the Circumlocution Office, wanting to "know" the facts behind William Dorrit's imprisonment, he enters a great maze of incompetence and indifference that brings him at last to "Barnacle Junior"—the member of a parasitic family for whom this governmental bureau has become a sort of family preserve, or dynasty. Of Barnacle Junior, Clennam—exasperated—demands: "I want to know."

"Look here. Upon my soul you mustn't come into the place saying you want to know, you know," remonstrated Barnacle Junior, turning about and putting up the eye-glass.

"I want to know," said Arthur Clennam, who had made up his mind to persistence in one short form of words, "the precise nature of the claim of the Crown against a prisoner for debt, named Dorrit."

"I say. Look here. You really are going it at a great pace, you know. Egad, you haven't got an appointment," said Barnacle Junior, as if the thing were growing serious.

"I want to know," said Arthur, and repeated his case.

Barnacle Junior stared at him until his eye-glass fell out, and then put it in and stared at him until it fell out again. "You have no right to come to this sort of move," he then observed with the greatest weakness. "Look here. What do you mean? You told me you didn't know whether it was public business or not."

"I have now ascertained that it is public business," returned the suitor, "and I want to know"—and then repeated his monotonous inquiry.

Its effect upon young Barnacle was to make him repeat in a defenceless way, "Look here! Upon my SOUL you mustn't come into the place saying you want to know, you know!"

As such a scene suggests, the Circumlocution Office allows Dickens ample room for comedy. He is even funnier when, in the same chapter, he describes a pair of indifferent bureaucrats who simply ignore Clennam's presence in order to chat leisurely about an "inestimable" hunting dog. One of them is "polishing a gun-barrel on his pocket-handkerchief, while the other was spreading marmalade on bread with a paper-knife."

In a larger sense, the Circumlocution Office is also meant to remind us of what happens to the quality of civic life when social institutions grow too large and impersonal; when people in an urbanized, fragmented, anonymous world find themselves looking far afield for solutions to their most basic concerns; when they come to believe that certain inequities and injustices are simply too vast or complex to solve, and must then get far worse before ever getting any better. London, Dickens once told a reporter, is "a city where 99 percent are strangers to everybody," a place where "people would as soon read the Directory as stop and observe every new face they encountered." The office stands, arguably, for human life itself in the modern, industrial age. Life in *Little Dorrit* is nothing more than endless anticipation and muddling about: it all comes to nothing in the end.

But this is too grim. *Little Dorrit* is not entirely "tragic," not entirely an exercise in morbid brooding. Barbara Hardy has rightly noted that the world of *Little Dorrit* is "less tense, grim, and enclosed" than the world of *Bleak House*; the Tite Barnacles are, she suggests, "flimsy and silly"—and, for better or worse, figures of "Dickensian fun." "It would be hard to imagine Flora Finching and her Aunt, for instance, in *Bleak House*," notes Hardy. But it is not at all difficult to think of (say) Preston Sturges or even Neil Simon as one reads the absurd dialogue quoted above. Moreover Clennam is depicted early in the novel as a man who has managed to come to grips with his life's disappointments: he is well-steered by those Christian virtues that Dickens always saw as essential to life—by the sort of mental firmness that Dickens himself sought always to maintain, not always with ease. Clennam sometimes broods in his black moods; but he is also inclined "to judge not, and in humility to be merciful, and to have hope and charity." This then "saved him" from a "whimpering weakness"—from pondering too excessively his relatively small place in the grand scheme of things. "A disappointed mind he had, but a mind too firm and healthy for such unwholesome air. Leaving himself in the dark, it could rise into the light, seeing it shine on others and hailing it."

Indeed, as Dennis Walder suggests, *Little Dorrit* can also be read as "a sustained attempt by Dickens to show that one can free oneself from the imprisoning forces associated with a narrow Old Testament faith of stern self-denial and wrathful vengeance by means of the broadly redemptive, loving spirit of the New." In *Little Dorrit* that spirit of morbidity and vengefulness is amply displayed by Arthur's adoptive mother. In some ways she foreshadows Miss Havisham, an even more looming presence in *Great Expectations*. Mrs. Clennam stays put in her darkened room, self-confined, attending only to her "business duties" and sometimes praying "that her enemies (she made them by her tone and manner expressly hers) might be put to the edge of the sword, consumed by fire, smitten by plagues and leprosy, that their bones might be ground to dust, and that they might be utterly exterminated." Mrs. Clennam hauled Arthur to church when he was a child—to interminable services that stressed sin and "Perdition." The bitter, fearful, and life-denying spirit of Mrs. Clennam was—as Dickens's novels repeatedly suggest—a constant threat to human communities, and much too evident in the England of his day. This mix of puritan fervor with the gospel of endless work had combined to make a place that was a prison for too many of Britain's citizens—particularly on Sundays. Dickens begins chapter 3 of *Little Dorrit* by describing "a Sunday evening in London, gloomy, close, and stale." What follows recalls the books *Bleak House* and *Hard Times*:

Maddening church bells of all degrees of dissonance, sharp and flat, cracked and clear, fast and slow, made the brick-and-mortar echoes hideous. Melancholy streets, in a penitential garb of soot, steeped the souls of people who were condemned to look at them out of windows, in dire despondency. In every thoroughfare, up almost every alley, and down almost every turning, some doleful bell was throbbing, jerking, tolling, as if the Plague were in the city and the dead-carts were going round. Everything was bolted and barred that could possibly furnish relief to an overworked people. No pictures, no unfamiliar sounds, no rare plants or flowers, no natural or artificial wonders of the ancient world—all *taboo* with that enlightened strictness, that the ugly South Sea gods in the British Museum might have supposed themselves at home again. Nothing to breathe but streets, streets, streets. Nothing to change the brooding mind, or raise it up. Nothing for the toiler to do, but to compare the monotony of the seventh day with the monotony of his six days, think what a weary life he led, and make the best of it—or the worst, according to the probabilities.

Clennam himself "was a dreamer" of sorts. He "was a man who had, deep-rooted in his nature, a belief in all the gentle and good things his life had been without." He has, then, "a warm and sympathetic heart"—and this, the novel suggests, finally brings him happiness in life through his marriage with Amy Dorrit. The novel's quiet but rather hopeful ending, Jenni Calder contends, demonstrates again that—for Dickens—"part of the struggle of humanity was to protect itself from this violent world." Dickens was "preoccupied with this idea of protection, which played an essential part in his version of ideal marriage." He "felt not only that marriage should be a refuge," writes Calder. "But that it was the only refuge, and if one did not find this in one's own marriage one found it by being the accessory to the marriage of others"—a role John Jarndyce, for example, assumes in *Bleak House*. In the final paragraph of *Little Dorrit*, Clennam and Amy are "married with the sun shining on them through the painted figure of Our Saviour on the window." They leave the church, next door to the Marshalsea, "alone." After pausing in the pretty sunshine "on the steps of the portico," they "went down"—down, Dickens writes, "into a modest life of usefulness and happiness." They are "inseparable and blessed," passing by "the noisy and the eager, and the arrogant and the forward and the vain," who—around them, in an image that recalls the closing lines of Matthew Arnold's "Dover Beach"—"fretted and chafed, and made their usual uproar." "It seems to me," writes Calder, "that nowhere in Dickens is it so positively indicated that the reward of the doll's house for the hero and heroine represents, not a victory over the real world, but a withdrawal from it"—further proof, then, of Dickens's personal and political despair.

Many, surely, have seen in the close of *Little Dorrit* a simple description of marriage's main goal. Of course for most people, across centuries and across continents, marriage has always been—whatever else—a form of sheltering and mutual support in the face of life's hardships and absurdities. Barbara Hardy adds that the similar conclusion of *Bleak House*—where "the good housekeeper and the good doctor" are rewarded with each other—again reveals Dickens's fondness for "the conventional happy ending," indicating as well that he "found it possible to feel boundless hope in the human heart, none in societies and institutions." It's a point that also applies not only of *Little Dorrit*, but to *Pickwick Papers*, *Oliver Twist*, and *Nicholas Nickleby*.

Little Dorrit is then, in several respects, less dispiriting than *Bleak House*. It is more overtly funny, more frequently hopeful—and it offers a rather wider range of characters who are both convincing and sympathetic. There is, for example, Young John Chivery, who loves Amy Dorrit, and who, when he was nineteen, had "inscribed in chalk on that part of the wall which fronted her lodgings, on the occasion of her birthday, 'Welcome sweet nursling of the Fairies!'" But the best of these is surely Pancks, the rent collector who has "a scubby little black chin" and "coaly" hands, and hair that sticks out from his head "like forks or hairpins." Pancks himself has been exploited, as the novel reveals. He calls himself "a Grubber," his life having been devoted to little more than "fag and grind, fag and grind"—just what one could expect from a man on the fringe trying to survive. "I haven't been agreeable to myself," Pancks comes to admit, "and I haven't been likely to be agreeable to anybody else." But in a novel filled with slick, shallow, and preposterous imposters, the blunt Pancks also shows an instinct for decency and justice; through him, Dickens underlines his frequent theme that, often, it is not what is on the surface that counts. Pancks's gruff vitality also provides an effective counterpoint to Clennam's more morose broodings: Pancks laughs heartily when Clennam describes himself as "growing old." And "there was something so indubitably genuine in the wonderful laugh, and series of snorts and puffs, engendered in Mr Pancks's astonishment at, and utter rejection of, the idea, that his being quite in earnest could not be questioned."

Even more important to the novel, however, is Amy's father—and *her* imprisoner—William Dorrit, who is not only one of the most brilliantly realized characters in Dickens, but in all of English fiction. Even more than Wilkins Micawber, Dorrit is a tossed salad of contradictions—by turns proud and self-pitying, vain and insecure, full of hope and full of despair. A bit larger than life, Micawber can, even in his moroseness, spark laughter. But Dorrit is more clearly part of the modern tradition of literary comedy or, perhaps more precisely, tragicomedy: watching him one thinks of Luigi Pirandello, say, or of the Ekdal family in Henrik Ibsen's *The Wild Duck*—of any number of modern dramatists concerned with the thin line between fantasy and reality, with role-playing in human life. Dickens in one sentence in chapter 6 captures the central contradiction of Dorrit's character. He is, on the one hand, a "shabby old debtor with the soft manner and the white hair." In this guise he is no different from many other men who come and go at the Marshalsea, where "a generation might be calculated as about three months." But Dorrit is separate from—has separated *himself* from—the larger population. He has lived on and on at the place, through countless "generations," for more than twenty years. And thus, "his words were remembered and repeated; and tradition afterwards handed down from generation to generation . . . that the shabby old debtor with the soft manner and the white hair, was the Father of the Marshalsea." The Father of the Marshalsea: "he grew to be proud of the title. If any imposter had arisen to claim it, he would have shed tears in resentment of the attempt to deprive him of his rights."

Dorrit is a vulnerable soul, easily wounded. He is also "vain" as his fellow inmates and his own family know. He is a failure in society who—in his small world—maintains a regal manner, greeting the prison's new residents with a grave and "punctilious" air—"a kind of bowed-down beneficence." Still, the Father is also a beggar, cadging bits of coin from other inmates and visitors at the prison; these he receives "as tributes, from admirers, to a public character." The word *character* is crucial: Dorrit, like Micawber and many of Dickens's other characters, has taken on a role—the lead role—in a continuing play of his own creation. For Dorrit, the real world is depressing and flat; it is far better when the world's a stage.

Unlike Pancks, or his own daughter Amy, Dorrit is not then "indubitably genuine." Dickens portrays Dorrit with wonderful vividness, giving him a sort of nervous stutter: "ha" he says between words, and "hum." Dorrit clears his throat a lot, often bringing his fingers, trembling, to his lips. The scenes in which we watch Dorrit wheedling affection and praise from his daughter show the cracks in his confident facade, and are especially effective. Most memorable is the scene in chapter 19 in which Dorrit—now rich, out of prison, and on his grand tour of Italy—rises from the long table at Mrs. Merdle's posh dinner party to proclaim himself once more the "Father of the Marshalsea." Here in Rome, amidst the *nouveaux riches*, in a group that includes "the usual French Count and the usual Italian Marchese," Dorrit, looking "indefinably shrunken and old," begins to hallucinate, and the boundaries between fantasy and reality completely collapse. He's back at the Marshalsea with Bob the turnkey, the father of Young John and a man, we know, of "true politeness" and "native delicacy." Once more Dorrit announces that, despite his woes, he manages to "uphold a Tone here—a Tone." Mrs. Merdle is mortified; the guests flee, but of course Amy tends lovingly her dying father, bringing him back home to bed where "from that hour his poor maimed spirit, only remembering the place where it had broken its wings, canceled the dream through which it had groped, and knew of nothing beyond the Marshalsea. When he heard footsteps in the street, he took them for the old dreary tread in the yards. When the hour came for locking up, he supposed all strangers to be excluded for the night. When the time for opening came again, he was so anxious to see Bob, that they were fain to patch up a narrative how that Bob—many a year dead then, gentle turnkey—had taken cold, but hoped to be out to-morrow, or the next day, or the next at furthest." There are times in *Little Dorrit* when Dorrit—brilliantly played by Alec Guinness in Christine Edzard's film version of the novel—sparks nothing but contempt. In this scene, however, one feels everything *but* contempt for this "poor maimed spirit" unable—before and after his imprisonment—to function with consistent success in a larger social system run by ruthlessness and greed.

In *Little Dorrit* one finds several characters who are, no less than Mrs. Skewton, frozen in time: Dorrit himself; Clennam's mother; and of course Flora Finching, Arthur's former flame, who "left herself at eighteen years of age." In one scene, Flora persists in putting herself and Arthur "in their old places, and going through all the old performances—now, when the scene was dusty, when the scenery was faded, when the youthful actors were dead, when the orchestra was empty, when the lights were out." We cannot stop time, this novel repeatedly notes. And we certainly cannot escape the past, or the environments that have shaped us—one of Dickens's main themes from *A Christmas Carol* to *Bleak House* to *Little Dorrit* to *Great Expectations*. Certainly, it is a fact that Amy Dorrit must often face: "It was but the other day," she explains at one point, "that my sister told me I had become so used to the prison that I had its tone and character." Later, after Dorrit's release, she detects again in her father's "whole bearing towards her," that "well-known shadow of the Marshalsea wall. It took a new shape, but it was the old sad shadow. She began with sorrowful unwillingness to acknowledge to herself that she was not strong enough to keep off the fear that no space in the life of man could overcome that quarter of a century behind the prison bars. She had no blame to bestow upon him, therefore: nothing to reproach him with, no emotions in her faithful heart but great compassion and unbounded tenderness."

Amy is admirable because she does not give in to the "society mania" that infects her sister Fanny—and so many other characters in the book. Amy's patience with her father is, from the start, unending: Dorrit, we learn in chapter 15, is rarely "simply loving." Often he is "sententious and didactic," displaying the same impulse for unending selfishness and self-pity that Dickens would always condemn—perhaps most famously through the figure of Miss Havisham in *Great Expectations*. "I have done what I could to retain you a position here," Dorrit, the manipulative debtor, reminds his devoted daughter. "I may have succeeded; I may not. You may know it; you may not. I give no opinion. I have endured everything here but humiliation. That I have been spared—until this day." Here Dorrit, as was his custom, moves his pocket-handkerchief to his face and assumes the role of the brave but broken man, forced at times to wipe the tears from his eyes. It works, as always; Little Dorrit "clasped her hands in quite an agony of distress." For Little Dorrit, we learn elsewhere, "accepted him as he was—when had she not accepted him as he was!—and made the most and best of him."

For some critics, Little Dorrit is little more than Little Nell, had she lived, about ten years on. Dickens's preoccupation with patient and loving young women is undeniable—and very probably proof of his need to revive, over and over, Mary Hogarth, the kind and gentle girl who in a kinder world would not have died at seventeen. On the whole Amy Dorrit is, perhaps, too good be true, showing infinite kindness to her simpleminded companion Maggy, who—like old Dorrit himself—"was very susceptible to personal slights, and very ingenious in inventing them." (And who was beaten in child-hood, we learn in passing, by a gin-drinking grandmother who used "broom-handles and pokers.") Still, Amy Dorrit is not some celestial being. Sometimes she is "a little lonely and a little low"; she knows a "feeling of depression." Barbara Hardy notes too that she has "a certain grotesqueness—a stuntedness and sexlessness— which helps both to stylize her character as an image of virtue and to make her a more natural prison-child." And she is not, one thinks, *that* rare. For of course the world abounds with people who, against all reason, remain devoted to flawed parents, husbands, and wives.

Amy, like Esther Summerson—like virtually all of Dickens's most admirable characters—has no interest in money or social status; she does not give in to the "society mania" that infects her sister Fanny and so many other characters in the book, like the superbly stupid Mrs. General, who "had no opinions. Her way of forming a mind was to prevent it from forming opinions. She had a little circular set of mental grooves or rails on which she started little trains of other people's opinions, which never overtook one another, and never got anywhere." Amy Dorrit tells Arthur Clennam in a letter that she hopes "you will never think of me as the daughter of a rich person; that you will never think of me as dressing any better, or living any better, than when you first knew me. That you will remember me only as the little shabby girl you protected with so much tenderness, from whose threadbare dress you have kept away the rain, and whose wet feet you have dried at your fire." She is thus the direct opposite of Mrs. Merdle, the wife of the famous—and soon to be infamous—financier. Mrs. Merdle has "unfeeling eyes," Dickens tells us, and "dark unfeeling handsome hair, and a broad unfeeling handsome bosom." Like Tite Barnacle (who "wound and wound folds of white cravat round his neck, as he wound and wound folds of tape and paper round the neck of the country"), Mrs. Merdle is tightly bound; she has "an unfeeling handsome chin that looked as if, for certain, it had never been, in familiar parlance, 'chucked' by the hand of a man, it was the chin curbed up so tight and close by that laced bridle." For Mrs. Merdle, wealth is everything. Appearance is all. Like the pathetic Dorrit, she is also obsessed with displaying a certain "tone," and so in chapter 33 lectures her husband on his manner, his preoccupied air: "There is," she tells him, "a positive vulgarity in carrying your business affairs about with you as you do."

"I don't expect you," said Mrs. Merdle, reposing easily among her cushions, "to captivate people. I don't expect you to take any trouble upon yourself, or to try to be fascinating. I simply request you to care about nothing—or seem to care about nothing—as everybody else does."

"Do I ever say I care about anything?" asked Mr. Merdle.

"Say? No! Nobody would attend to you if you did. But you show it."

"Show what? What do I show?" demanded Mr. Merdle hurriedly.

"I have already told you. You show that you carry your business cares and projects about, instead of leaving them in the City, or wherever else they belong to," said Mrs. Merdle. "Or seeming to. Seeming would be quite enough: I ask no more. Whereas you couldn't be more occupied with your day's calculations and combinations than you habitually show yourself to be, if you were a carpenter."

"A carpenter!" repeated Mr. Merdle, checking something like a groan. "I shouldn't so much mind being a carpenter, Mrs. Merdle."

As Merdle reminds his wife: "You supply manner, and I supply money." That Merdle *has* money seems never in doubt. Where it comes from, however, is another question. And it's one that Merdle's worshipers would have done well to ask. For Merdle is also playing a part. Everyone assumes that "Mr. Merdle was immensely rich." He was "a man of prodigious enterprise; a Midas without the ears, who turned all he touched to gold." Merdle "was in Parliament, of course. He was in the City, necessarily. He was Chairman of this, Trustee of that, President of the other." He has, in short, the reputation of wealth—the image of success. And that's more than enough for many to sing his praises and seek his advice, his supposed "Midas" touch. "The weightiest of men had said to projectors, 'Now what name have you got? Have you got Merdle?' And, the reply being in the negative, had said, 'Then I won't look at you.'"

Merdle is bland because, in this case, Dickens is less interested in the villain than in the adulation he provokes. Merdle has no clear talents. He has no apparent virtues. He has only this remarkable reputation for having and getting cash. ("Nobody knew with the least precision what Mr. Merdle's business was," the narrator explains, "except that it was to coin money.") He, *Little Dorrit* laments, is what passes as a hero in a crass and materialistic age. Merdle is, writes Dennis Walder, "a Dombey beyond redemption, a hollow man created by his time: 'The name of Merdle is the name of the age,' the newly wealthy William Dorrit informs his entourage, Mrs. General bowing her head 'as if she were doing homage to some graven image.' Dickens alludes to Christian ideas in judging

Mr. Merdle: he is the rich man, 'who had in a manner revised the New Testament, and already entered into the kingdom of Heaven'; when he goes up the stairs in his house, 'people were already posted on the lower stairs, that his shadow might fall upon them when he came down.'"

Dickens knew the type. Fraudulent and fallen financiers were common enough in his day, particularly in the 1840s, when speculation in Britain's railroads was particularly rampant and often reckless. The year 1847 saw a major commercial crisis triggered by bad railroad investments. George Hudson, the celebrated but unscrupulous "railway king" fell in 1849, generating much publicity. (A similar crisis occurred in 1857, when many financial firms and banks folded in the wake of poor railroad investments in the United States.) Dickens apparently modeled Merdle, in part, on one John Sadleir, MP, who in 1856 killed himself when the bank he was running suddenly collapsed and his shady dealings were about to be disclosed.

In *Little Dorrit*, after Merdle's suicide with a pen-knife in a public bath, Dickens steps forward and, not mincing words, suggests again that Merdle is a false Messiah whose values and beliefs will inevitably lead to some bleak and gloomy end:

[Merdle,] the uncouth object of such wide-spread adulation, the sitter at great men's feasts, the roc's egg of great ladies' assemblies, the subduer of exclusiveness, the leveler of pride, the patron of patrons, the bargain-driver with a Minister for Lordships of the Circumlocution Office, the recipient of more acknowledgment within ten or fifteen years, at most, than had been bestowed in England upon all public benefactors, and upon all the leaders of all the Arts and Sciences, with all their works to testify for them, during two centuries at least—he, the shining wonder, the new constellation to be followed by the wise men bringing gifts, until it stopped over a certain carrion at the bottom of a bath and disappeared—was simply the greatest Forger and the greatest Thief that ever cheated the gallows.

Structurally, *Little Dorrit* and *Great Expectations* are very different books. Bernard Shaw called the latter "a most compactly perfect book." *Great Expectations*, writes John Irving, offers "the most wonderful and most perfectly worked-out plot for a novel in the English language." But *Great Expectations* also deals with many of the themes and concerns found in *Little Dorrit* and in Dickens's earlier books. It is also very much about money, status, and fatherhood. It is about appearance and reality—about the comforts and pains that self-delusion bring.

Moreover, one finds in both a clear autobiographical core. Through William Dorrit, Dickens again offers a partial portrait of his father. Through Clennam, as many critics have suggested, Dickens is voicing those feelings of longing and regret that dogged him with growing intensity during the final decades of his life. In *Great Expectations*, through the figure of Pip, Dickens again focuses on a character who—like Dorrit—finds himself suddenly with a great deal of money and so gains a second chance for a great social rise. But Pip, like Dorrit, is not fully satisfied. Pip, like Scrooge—like so many of Dickens's characters—is also haunted by the past.

Those who haunt Pip, however, are not spirits but figures of blood and bone. One, Estella, is the subject of Pip's lifelong passion. But she remains distant, as cold in her way as the marmoreal Paul Dombey. Estella was created by a great novelist with an abundantly rich imagination; she does not then require a real-life analogue in order to be memorable or convincing. Still, understandably, some critics and biographers have again found in Estella shades of the young Maria Beadnell; others suggest her more direct inspiration was Ellen Ternan. These writers note that Dickens was not as close to Ternan as he might have desired: emotionally, she kept him at bay. Given the more restrictive social codes that prevailed in Dickens's day, and given Dickens's own desire to observe them—at least in public—such a relationship was doomed from the start to remain furtive and tenuous.

Pip's obsession with Estella certainly allows Dickens to explore, as he did in *Copperfield*, the often misguided and disorienting nature of love and sexual longing—and its power, at once exhilarating and frightening, to consume all in its path. (In this context, Miss Havisham's death by fire is bleakly appropriate.) Pip tells Estella of his passion in one of the novel's most melodramatic passages; his language recalls David Copperfield during his period of infatuation with the problematic Dora. "You are part of my existence," Pip tells Estella, "part of myself."

You have been in every line I have ever read, since I first came here, the rough common boy whose poor heart you wounded even then. You have been in every prospect I have ever seen since—on the river, on the sails of the ships, on the marshes, in the clouds, in the light, in the darkness, in the wind, in the woods, in the sea, in the streets. You have been the embodiment of every graceful fancy that my mind has ever become acquainted with. The stones of which the strongest London buildings are made are not more real, or more impossible to be replaced by your hands, than your presence and influence have been to me, there and everywhere, and will be. Estella, to the last hour of my life, you cannot choose but remain a part of my character, part of the little good in me, part of the evil.

By falling for Estella, Pip is also, ironically, dancing madly to Miss Havisham's tune. Like the young Copperfield, he must become a more astute reader of character—a more clever interpreter of human action and motivation. For too long Pip sails along under the assumption that this weird and embittered women, with her "witch-like eagerness," aimed not only to make him a "gentleman," but was preparing Estella to be "the prize" that was "reserved for me." Miss Havisham—like Betsey Trotwood—has been scarred by a bad experience in love. Aunt Betsey, however, has carried on in her quirky way, treating Mr. Dick, we know, with kindness and charity. But Miss Havisham has turned inward; she too is frozen neurotically in time, and schooling Estella in a black and bitter way. Estella—as Pip's friend Herbert Pocket puts it—is "hard and haughty and capricious to the last degree, and has been brought up by Miss Havisham to wreak revenge on all the male sex." And Pip, being ambitious, gullible, and self-absorbed, makes the perfect target. One night, in a scene particularly rich with irony, he tosses sleepless in his bed, his head full of Estella, as "Miss Havisham's words, 'Love her, love her, love her!'" resound in his ears. "I adapted them for my own repetition, and said to my pillow, 'I love her, I love her, I love her!' hundreds of times. Then a burst of gratitude came upon me that she should be destined for me, once the blacksmith's boy."

Miss Havisham is, like Heep, both a victim and a victimizer; like William Dorrit, she prompts pity as well as disgust—disgust because she is another of Dickens's abusers of power: a tormenter of the young. Miss Havisham has, in her way, pampered Estella; but she has effectively jailed her too, shielding the girl from healthy and healing influences. As a result, Estella has "no heart," as she reminds Pip at one point. "I have no softness there, no sympathy—sentiment—nonsense." This was Havisham's aim. "I am what you have made me," an anguished Estella tells her guardian in chapter 38. "Take all the praise, take all the blame; take all the success, take all the failure."

In melodrama, the scoundrel must often confront the full awfulness of his vice and his crimes. In *Great Expectations*, Miss Havisham—like Ralph Nickleby—finally sees the error of her ways. ("That all humankind, even hardened criminals, had hearts that could be moved, innate moral responses that could be tapped, by the message of Christian love" was, as Kaplan notes in *Sacred Tears*, a basic operating principle among Dickens's contemporaries—and was often portrayed in the literature of the day.) Miss Havisham wrings her hands in chapter 49; she crushes her hair, cries out repeatedly, "What have I done!" Pip now spells out the nature of this wretched woman's sin. It was bad enough for this woman to transform an "impressionable child" into a vessel for her own "wild resentment" and "wounded pride." But it was worse to shield herself—and Estella—from the world; for, in "shutting out the light of day, she had shut out infinitely more." In other words, Miss Havisham would have done well, early on, to spend a few nights over the punch bowl with the Micawbers. She should have romped about with Pickwick in the meadows and country lanes. She might have become more selfless, and cultivated the habit of doing some good in the world. Instead, Miss Havisham's life becomes one unending torch song, one long, grotesque rendition of "The Man Who Got Away." Over and over she replays that day, many decades before, when Compeyson left her a jilted bride. Miss Havisham had "secluded herself from a thousand natural and healing influences"; her mind, "brooding solitary, had grown diseased, as all minds do and must and will that reverse the appointed order of their Maker." "In Dickens's world," as Angus Wilson has pointed out, the "good forces are always energetic and outward-looking," and "never more so than at the end of his life."

Indeed, these lines in *Great Expectations* recall similar points made by Dickens in a letter of 1850 to a correspondent in Denmark, Emily Gotschalk, who was apparently wont to stew, gloomily and alone, over books. Dickens (who of course was no stranger to gloomy states) tells Gotschalk that "the state of mind which you describe is not a wholesome one," and "not a natural one." But "the remedy for it," he adds, "is easy, and we all have it at hand—action, usefulness—and the determination to be of service, even in little things, to those about you, and to be doing something." "In every human existence," Dickens instructs, "however quiet or monotonous, there is range enough for active sympathy and cheerful usefulness. It is through such means I humbly believe that God must be approached, and hope and peace of mind be won. The world is not a dream, but a reality, of which we are the chief part, and in which we must be up and doing something. A morbid occupation, as your mind with books—even good books—and sad meditation is not its purpose."

Pip, for his part, comes to pity Miss Havisham. "Could I look upon her without compassion," he asks, "seeing her punishment in the ruin she was, in her profound unfitness for this earth on which she was placed, in the vanity of sorrow which had become a master mania, like the vanity of penitence, the vanity of remorse, the vanity of unworthiness, and other monstrous vanities that have been curses in this world?"

Pip's actions also show that he is himself quite capable of compassion, sympathy, and forgiveness. Eventually he helps his friend Herbert Pocket, as well as Magwitch, the self-proclaimed "father" he initially scorns. Pip also comes to recognize more fully that his brother-in-law, Joe Gargery, an illiterate blacksmith, possesses an innate goodness and dignity that is, even among "gentlemen," rare. Like Clara Peggotty and her brother Daniel—like Ham and Amy Dorrit—Joe, "a mild, good-natured, sweet-tempered, easy-going, foolish, dear fellow," is anything but vain. "I am most awful dull," he readily admits. Serenely, he accepts his lot in life. He has seen cruelty at close range (his own father routinely beat his mother), and he has thus resolved to be kind. As the novel shows, Pip has learned much from Joe, who is in some ways his surrogate father. But it is a lesson he loses for a long stretch of time. *Great Expectations*, like *David Copperfield*, is very much about the search for identity; about the consequences of choice; about the complex ways in which our experiences and our environment combine to make us who we are. Pip's own sense of identity is, throughout most of the novel, not as well formed as Joe Gargery's. Pip has "expectations": he wants to rise. He views Estella as a "prize." He comes to regard Joe with condescension—even contempt. Of course, *Great Expectations* is, like *Copperfield*, structured in a way that allows Pip to look back with some wisdom and regret at his more obtuse and callow self. He alludes in chapter 29 to "those wretched hankerings after money and gentility that had disturbed my boyhood," and to "those ill-regulated aspirations that had first made me ashamed of home and Joe."

For those familiar with Dickens's early life, the phrase "Those hankerings after money and gentility that had disturbed my boyhood" is especially resonant. One thinks: here is Dickens, nearly forty years on, still sending a message to his father, whose "hankerings" after money and social status were no less obsessive or "disturbing" than Pip's, and who—it is now clear—haunts in some way nearly every novel that Dickens ever wrote. Pip, like John Dickens, proves himself very good at spending money he doesn't have, a practice that affects Herbert Pocket as well as himself. "My lavish habits," he concedes, led Pocket's "easy nature into expenses he could not afford, corrupted the simplicity of his life, and disturbed his peace with anxieties and regrets." Corrupt and disturb; breed anxiety, regret: this, in Dickens's world, is what money tends to do.

But one also sees shades of John Dickens in Abel Magwitch, the rough, resilient ex-con turned sheep farmer who, after vanishing for years, suddenly returns and proves to be Pip's mysterious benefactor, the real source of his sudden wealth and social elevation. "Look'ee here, Pip," Magwitch points out in chapter 39. "I'm your second father. You're my son—more to me nor any son." John Dickens was not, one assumes, *this* crude; he was reared in a "respectable" home, found a good clerical job with the government, and—like Micawber—cultivated a certain genteel air. Surely he was not in the habit of loudly shoveling down his supper in an "uncouth, noisy, and greedy" way and then proudly announcing that "I'm a heavy grubber." Still, given his thriftless habits, John Dickens was long a source of social embarrassment to his son. He was, too, a rather vulgar social climber who managed to gain a level of social success that, at least for a time, surpassed the "expectations" of his class: the son of servants, he kept servants of his own. But then John Dickens became, in his own way, a criminal, and did time at the Marshalsea. Charles's success was, of course, tougher to get, but proved more enduring. It could be measured in all sorts of ways: big houses, trips to the Continent, a membership at the Athenaeum— London's most exclusive club. But there was his father, this rather clownish figure in the background, blowing his salary, bringing distress, a living symbol of the past that Dickens could never quite shake.

In other ways, Magwitch parallels Miss Havisham. "I've made a gentleman on you!" he tells Pip soon after his reappearance from Australia. "It's me wot has done it! . . . I worked hard that you should be above work." Magwitch insists that Pip should not "feel a obligation. Not a bit." He is returning a favor, he explains; for Pip had—albeit under duress—helped Magwitch years before, in the novel's opening chapter. Still, Magwitch does gloat that his own "master mania"—to use Pip's term—has paid off. By working hard and saving his earnings he was able to "make a gentleman" out of this blacksmith's boy. Magwitch then, like Havisham, has sought to dictate the fate of another person—a more vulnerable person through whom he could vicariously live. As Pip recalls:

"Look'ee here!" [Magwitch] went on, taking my watch out of my pocket, and turning towards him a ring on my finger, while I recoiled from his touch as if he had been a snake, "a gold 'un and a beauty—*that's* a gentleman's, I hope! Look at your linen—fine and beautiful! Look at your clothes—better ain't to be got! And your books too," turning his eyes round the room, "mounting up, on their shelves, by hundreds! And you read 'em, don't you? I see you'd been a-reading of 'em when I come in. Ha, ha, ha! You shall read 'em to me, dear boy! And if they're in languages wot I don't understand, I shall be just as proud as if I did."

But Magwitch is also one of Dickens's recurring prisoners. He is, in effect, what the Artful Dodger was destined to become, having been "in jail and out of jail, in jail and out of jail, in jail and out of jail," for most of his life. Although he is obviously "out" again when he turns up on Pip's doorstep, he is perfectly prepared to chain himself to Pip—much to the latter's profound unease. He calls Pip "my gentleman."

"Once more he took me by both hands," Pip recalls, "and surveyed me with an air of admiring proprietorship." And, initially at least, he plans to stay close by in order to keep an eye on his investment—never mind that, by doing so, he is risking among other things the prospect of "death by the rope, in the open street not fur from this." He will survive by changing his costume and thus his identity; "there's disguising wigs can be bought for money," he reminds Pip, "and there's hair powder, and spectacles, and black clothes—shorts and what not. Others has done it safe afore, and what others has done afore, others can do agen." Of course, Pip himself has "done it afore"—gone from blacksmith's boy to young gentleman with the help of the right cuts of cloth. Later, however, Pip discovers that making over Magwitch presents a particular challenge; "there was something in him that made it hopeless to attempt to disguise him. The more I dressed him, and the better I dressed him, the more he looked like the slouching fugitive on the marshes"—the fleeing convict he helped years before, in chapter 1. Thus Magwitch, like Joe Gargery, is now fixed in his identity. And like William Dorrit—like Heep for that matter—he finally cannot conceal the sad facts of his past. "I believed," Pip recalls, "that he dragged one of his legs as if there were still a weight of iron on it, and that from head to foot there was convict in the very grain of the man."

In all his ways of sitting and standing, and eating and drinking—of brooding about, in a high-shouldered reluctant style—of taking out his great horn-handled jack-knife and wiping it on his legs and cutting his food—of lifting light glasses and cups to his lips as if they were clumsy pannikins—of chopping a wedge off his bread, and soaking up with it the last fragments of gravy round and round his plate, as if to make the most of an allowance, and then drying his fingers on it, and then swallowing it—in these ways and a thousand other small nameless instances arising every minute in the day, there was prisoner, felon, bondsman, plain as plain could be.

Great Expectations suggests, among other things, that wealth is almost always tainted—always linked in some way with criminality (remember the Chuzzlewits, the Merdles, etc.). It certainly mocks the notion that wealth can be gained without work—*somebody's* work—defying Pip's immature sense that, in the normal scheme of things, it is quite possible to wake up one morning and find oneself moving smoothly among the idle rich. Of course, it also mocks the idle rich, particularly in the shape of Drummle, the cruel lout who is "next heir but one to a baronetcy" and who, with the help of his wealth, makes Estella his bride. Again, *Great Expectations* cannot be read primarily as a direct assault on the British social system; Joe, the novel's moral core, certainly nurses no class resentment, and apparently regards class distinctions as one inevitable part of the natural order of things. "Pip, dear old chap," he says, "life is made of ever so many partings welded together, as I may say, and one man's a blacksmith, and one's a coppersmith. Diwisions among such must come, and must be met as they come." Still, Pip is at his most absurd, and least likable, when he assumes an aristocratic air—in chapter 27, for example, when he treats Joe in an inexcusably patronizing way. Here Pip, ensconced in his new London digs, learns in a letter from the kindhearted Biddy that Joe plans to pop in for a visit, "for the love of poor old days." "I was bound to him by so many ties," Pip admits, lightly underlining one of the novel's key themes. Still, Pip views Joe's arrival with "considerable disturbance, some mortification, and a keen sense of incongruity." "If I could have kept him away by paying money, I certainly would have paid money"—and so we see that already Pip, like Dombey, has become well aware of the magic of cash.

But the blacksmith arrives. And what follows is, in its way, one of the best passages in all of Dickens, a superb example of this or any novelist's art. Dickens knew Gargery well. He knew him inside and out—as he knew all of his most convincing characters, not only because they were all in some way a part of himself, but because he took great pains to see them vividly in his mind's eye. Mary Dickens would recall the rare morning she was allowed to rest in her father's study and so quietly watched him at work—watched as he "wrote busily and rapidly at his desk" and then "suddenly jumped from his chair and rushed to a mirror which hung near, and in which I could see the reflection of some extraordinary facial contortions which he was making. He returned rapidly to his desk, wrote furiously for a few moments, and then went again to the mirror. The facial pantomime was resumed, and then turning toward, but evidently not seeing, me, he began talking rapidly in a low voice." Here then, as Peter Ackroyd puts it, we see "the father looking at his daughter but not seeing her, muttering to himself, acting out scenes in the mirror, alert and alive only to the world of his imagination, peopling his study with other men and women and children, hearing other voices."

So Dickens, who knows Gargery—who *sees* him nervously entering Pip's fine new abode—does not send him bolting straight up to Pip's apartment, booming Pip's name. Instead he shows the man, dressed to the nines, uncertainly ascending the stairs. More precisely, he describes Joe's climb through Pip's ears: "I knew it was Joe by his clumsy manner of coming upstairs—his state boots being always too big for him—and by the time it took him to read the names on the other floors in the course of his climb. When at last he stopped outside our door"—Pip is now living with Pocket—

"I could hear his finger tracing over the painted letters of my name, and I afterwards distinctly heard him breathing in at the keyhole. Finally he gave a single rap." That Pip should wait for Joe in his confusion to mount the stairs reveals well his new sense of social propriety, as well as his dread of facing this life-size reminder of all that he left behind. Then: "I thought he never would have done wiping his feet, and that I must have gone out to lift him off the mat, but at last he came in." Thus, within a few sentences, Dickens captures much about Joe's character, showing his nervous self-consciousness, his lack of education, and his low social standing—his acute awareness that he is about to step into strange terrain. Inside, however, Joe responds with instinctive eagerness and spontaneity; he "caught both my hands," Pip relates, "and worked them straight up and down, as if I had been the last-patented pump."

But Joe, it becomes clear, soon recalls that—on this stage—he is completely without the proper gestures and lines. (Pip himself had to be taught them, one recalls, by the patient Herbert Pocket.) Joe continues to clutch his hat; he coughs "behind his hand as if he had time to catch the whooping-cough since he came." Joe doesn't stay long, aware that Pip, on this stage, in that costume, is not someone to whom he can easily relate. Significantly, Joe has just come from a play, where he has seen the absurd Wopsle—aka Waldengarver—attempt his first professional performance, presenting himself in a publicity release as "the celebrated provincial amateur of Roscian renown, whose unique performance in the highest tragic walk of our national bard has lately occasioned so great a sensation in local dramatic circles." Joe now realizes that, henceforth, he will present himself simply as Joe; thus the costume that Pip finds so absurd—"utterly preposterous as his cravat was, and as his collars were"—will have to go. "You and me is not two figures to be together in London; nor yet anywheres else but what is private, and beknown, and understood among friends. It ain't that I am proud, but that I want to be right, as you shall never see me no more in these clothes. I'm wrong in these clothes. I'm wrong out of the forge, the kitchen, or off th' meshes. You won't find half so much fault in me if, supposing as you should ever wish to see me, you come and put your head in at the forge window and see Joe the blacksmith there at the old anvil, in the old burnt apron, sticking to the old work."

Great Expectations, like *David Copperfield*, is an enormous pleasure to read; the first-person narrative voice enables Dickens to keep the prose flowing concretely, unaffectedly, and with artful precision. One could, of course, go anywhere in the novel to find an example of Dickens neatly combining clarity, elegance, rhythm, repetition. Consider, for example, this paragraph in chapter 57, when Pip, recovering from a long illness, realizes again the full extent of Joe's attentiveness and generosity.

After I had turned the worse point of my illness, I began to notice that while all its other features changed, this one consistent feature did not change. Whoever came about me, still settled down into Joe. I opened my eyes in the day, and, sitting on the window-seat, smoking his pipe in the shaded open window, still I saw Joe. I asked for a cooling drink, and the dear hand that gave it me was Joe's. I sank back on my pillow after drinking, and the face that looked so hopefully and tenderly upon me was the face of Joe.

John Irving has noted that Dickens "never wants a reader to be lost; but, at the same time, he never wants a reader to *skim*. It is rather hard going to skim Dickens; you will miss too much to make sense of anything. He made every sentence easy to read because he wanted you to read every sentence." But this last point—i.e., that Dickens made "every sentence easy to read"—does not apply as well to *Our Mutual Friend*. For whatever reason—exhaustion, distraction, or misdirection—Dickens's last novel, although brilliant in many ways, is often all but unreadable. Its related plots are particularly convoluted, and it is repeatedly slowed by wordiness and pretentious phrasing—by sentences that are often more flabby than firm. In chapter 4, for example, introducing "The R. Wilfer Family," he describes Mr. and Mrs. Wilfer entering, in their home, "a little basement room, half kitchen, half parlour, where a girl of about nineteen, with an exceedingly pretty figure and face, but with an impatient and petulant expression both in her face and in her shoulders (which in her sex and at her age are very expressive of discontent), sat playing draughts with a younger girl, who was the youngest of the House of Wilfer. Not to encumber this page by telling off the Wilfers in detail and casting them up in the gross, it is enough for the present that the rest were what is called 'out in the world,' in various ways, and that they were Many." Why the parenthetical comment, one wonders? Dickens is clearly foreshadowing here, telling us something about Bella Wilfer we ought to know—but an "impatient and petulant expression" would, in a person of any age, or either sex, indicate discontent.

In the next chapter, we find Mr. Wegg producing "a small pocket-handkerchief of a penitentially-scrubbing character, and took himself by the nose with a thoughtful aspect. Also, while he still grasped that feature, he directed several thoughtful looks down the street, after the retiring figure of Mr. Boffin. But, profound gravity sat enthroned on Wegg's countenance. . . . His gravity was unusual, portentous, and immeasurable, not because he perceived it necessary to forestall any doubt of himself in others. And herein he ranged with that very numerous class of imposters, who are quite as determined to keep up appearances to themselves, as to their neighbours." Admittedly, the portentous syntax here can be seen as pointing toward those calculating and duplicitous aspects of Wegg's character that will become more clear as the novel proceeds. Still, one can't help thinking that the phrase "of a penitentially-scrubbing character" is a bit much; that the second reference to "that feature" could be trimmed; that "face" would, perhaps, work just as well here as "countenance."

Our Mutual Friend is an ambitious work—and stands as absolute proof of Dickens's own indomitable will and willingness to tackle a major creative project while at the same time enduring the stresses of a failing marriage, bad health, and other family pains (his fourth child, Walter, who was deaf, died in India just before the novel began serialization). The Veneerings illustrate what is weak about the novel. They are "bran-new people in a bran-new house in a bran-new quarter of London." They bear a name that bluntly suggests falsity, shallowness, pretension. And they are not hugely compelling; in fact, they function as little more than Dickensian props, continuing in a rather obvious way his satire on empty materialism and middle-class complacency. But the book has its strengths. Bella Wilfer, noted above, is one of the more convincing of Dickens's young female characters; her essential goodness has not left her entirely immune from certain tendencies toward impatience and pride. (Harry Stone's invaluable edition of *Dickens's Working Notes for His Novels* reveals Dickens taking pains to ensure that Bella not seem entirely unsympathetic; "Says she is mercenary and why," Dickens notes. "*But indicate better qualities. Interest the reader in her.*") Bradley Headstone is easily one of

Dickens's best villains—the young schoolmaster in his "decent black coat and waistcoat, and decent white shirt, and decent formal black tie" who is "sullen" about his poor origins and who seethes with passion for Lizzie Hexam: a passion that prompts him to attempt a murder that leads, eventually, to his own demise.

Our Mutual Friend also features one of Dickens's most memorable images, or "symbols" if you will: those ever-present dustheaps that provide a source of wealth for certain of the novel's key characters. Boffin, a former servant, becomes known as the "Golden Dustman" after inheriting the estate of "Old Harmon," a "tremendous old rascal who made his money by dust"—or, in other words, rubbish, garbage, trash. This equation of money with waste occurs before in Dickens (Merdle's name obviously, like Murdstone's, hints of *merde*). Much of *Our Mutual Friend* is, as its title suggests, very much about true and false forms of friendships—a subject Dickens first explored in *The Old Curiosity Shop*. But it also seeks to show yet again that the pursuit of money almost always plays to the lowest of human traits. Boffin then becomes one of the novel's more sympathetic figures when he pretends to be a miser in order to highlight for Bela her own materialistic tendencies. "Wealth is seen as corrupting in *Our Mutual Friend*," writes Norman Page, "whether the angle of vision is comic (as in Wegg's cupidity), satirical (as with the Veneerings), or serious (as in Bella Wilfer's mercenary impulses)."

Our Mutual Friend has attracted many critics, and has certainly had its advocates. One, Jack Lindsay, in *Charles Dickens: A Biographical and Critical Study* (1950), called it "one of the greatest works of prose ever written, a work which finally vindicates Dickens's right to stand, as no other English writer can stand, at the side of Shakespeare." But Lindsay, one thinks, was caught up in the flush of the moment, writing about an intriguing and neglected Dickens novel at a time when, in academic and critical quarters, Dickens's reputation was just beginning to rise and even Lionel Trilling had begun boosting Dickens to the skies. John Lucas was closer to the mark when, twenty years later, in *The Melancholy Man*, he described *Our Mutual Friend* as "not so great a novel as either *Bleak House* or *Little Dorrit*," not because of "its obvious but trivial flaws"—its flashes of sentimentality, say—but because of the "tired perfunctoriness about much of its actual prose"; because it shows "a making-do with gestures towards the defining of characters rather than the inexhaustible energy that we customarily associate with Dickens. This is not necessarily a flaw, but it does entail a scaling-down of the imaginative energy we find in *Bleak House* and *Little Dorrit*. Inevitably, it limits the final achievement of *Our Mutual Friend*."

Initially, sales of *Our Mutual Friend* in its serial form had been exceptional, running around forty thousand copies—the result, in part, of a massive publicity campaign. Chapman and Hall, Dickens's publishers, had—as Norman Page notes—poured over a thousand pounds into publicizing the novel, mainly through handbills and posters, many on omnibuses. But sales sank steadily; by the time the final installment appeared, Dickens's publishers were running fewer than twenty thousand copies. The book got no boost from its reviews; Henry James, in his now famous verdict, called it "the poorest" product of a novelist who was in any event limited in his artistry. *Our Mutual Friend* was, complained the influential *Saturday Review*, a "very tedious performance." As Richard Altick notes in *The Presence of the Present* (1991), a brilliant chronicle and analysis of Victorian literature and culture, other readers and reviewers expressed the view that Dickens had become too predictable in his politically-charged art. One of these, Justin McCarthy, observed in 1864, just as *Our Mutual Friend* was beginning to appear, that "it is difficult to name any important subject which has arisen within the last quarter of a century on which [Dickens] has not written something." McCarthy believed, however, that

his criticism has generally come too late. The account of the Fleet Prison in "Pickwick" was published in the year in which the Act for the Amendment of the Insolvent Laws was passed. The Poor Laws had just been improved when "Oliver Twist" exposed the horrors of the workhouse system. The description of Mr. Bounderby and the hands of Coketown closely followed the last of a series of statutes regulating the management of factories. Jarndyce and Jarndyce might or might not have been true in the time of Lord Eldon, but it bears about as much relation to the present practice of the Court of Chancery as to that of the Star Chamber. It is all very well meant, but very ignorant.

What then of *The Mystery of Edwin Drood*? This work, begun four years after Dickens completed *Our Mutual Friend*, has also attracted a great deal of critical commentary in recent years—much of it bent on constructing the ending that Dickens could not provide. Before he died, six numbers of *Drood* had reached the racks, six more were scheduled to come. Sales of the serial were high, hitting fifty thousand copies. "It has very, very far outstripped every one of its predecessors," as Dickens in a letter would proudly proclaim.

Barbara Hardy rightly calls Dickens, even the later Dickens, "an author who wrote hand to mouth, even if with a sense of design"; often, that which finally made Dickens's inspiration flare was the cold fact of an approaching deadline. This being the case, the artistic success and the continuing appeal of *Drood* is even more impressive than its sales totals, and stands as wonderful proof not only of Dickens's indomitable will, but of his enormous creative powers. *Edwin Drood* is a remarkably good book with its *noir* atmosphere and tightly rising suspense, its impressive use of a wide range of characters including not only Neville and Helena Landless (among Dickens's most distinctive), but Hiram Grewgious and Septimus Crisparkle—who are, as Hardy writes, "interesting serious treatments of eccentrics who would in an earlier novel have been exaggeratedly comic."

Dickens had of course dealt frequently with crime and mystery before. But with *Drood* he was aiming more deliberately to construct the sort of "sensation fiction" that was then in vogue, and that included such particularly popular titles as Mary Braddon's *Lady Audley's Secret* (1862), and Collins's *Woman in White*. Of course, *Drood* is unmistakably Dickens's own; his voice rings clear through the gloom and the choking fog of this novel, which again reworks some of his favorite issues and themes. In *The Mystery of Edwin Drood*, Dickens looks again at the mystery of love and the power of sexual attraction; he shows his interest in costume and disguise, in the bits and pieces of experience and temperament that in the end add up to human identity. The novel moves well, and has moments of comic appeal—with scenes and characters that are superbly "Dickensian" in their construction and atmosphere. In chapter 11, for example, Dickens takes us to the chambers of Mr. Grewgious, at Staple Inn, Holborn. Mr. Grewgious is at the end of a long line of Dickens's lawyers; he lives amid account-books and strongboxes, all of them precisely arrayed ("the apprehension of dying suddenly, and leaving one fact or one figure with any incompleteness or obscurity to it, would have stretched Mr. Grewgious stone dead any day").

Mr. Grewgious keeps a clerk, Bazzard—another minor, wretched soul whose dim hope of vitality has presumably been squeezed out, year by year, by a cramped life of legal dealings and office routine. He is "a gloomy person," with "big dark eyes that wholly wanted lustre, and a dissatisfied doughy complexion, that seemed to ask to be sent to the baker's." Edwin Drood comes on this night to Mr. Grewgious's chambers, and the two converse in a scene that, in its minor but excellent way, reminds us of Dickens's great skill as a writer of dialogue—a skill sharpened by his acute sense of what needs to succeed in *one* scene so that a series of scenes will come to comprise a good play. Here, Mr. Grewgious stands before his fireplace and chats in a leisurely but lawyerly way with Edwin; watching them, hearing them, we appreciate once more the many ways in which Dickens's novels are, in Barbara Hardy's phrase, "like plays in action."

"I have lately been down yonder," said Mr. Grewgious . . . ; "and that was what I referred to, when I said I could tell you you are expected."

"Indeed, sir! Yes; I knew that Pussy was looking out for me."

"Do you keep a cat down there?" asked Mr. Grewgious.

Edwin colored a little, as he explained: "I call Rosa Pussy."

"Oh, really," said Mr. Grewgious, smoothing down his head; "that's very affable."

Edwin glanced at his face, uncertain whether or no he seriously objected to the appellation. But Edwin might as well have glanced at the face of a clock.

"Umps," said Mr. Grewgious, with a nod. But with such extraordinary compromise between an unqualified assent and a qualified dissent, that his visitor was much disconcerted.

"Did PRosa—" Edwin began, by way of recovering himself.

"PRosa?" repeated Mr. Grewgious.

"I was going to say Pussy, and changed my mind;—did she tell anything about the Landlesses?"

"No," said Mr. Grewgious. "What is the Landlesses? An estate? A villa? A farm?"

"A brother and a sister. The sister is at the Nuns' House, and has become a great friend of P—"

"PRosa's," Mr. Grewgious struck in, with a fixed face.

Now something else happens—the sort of thing that, one suspects, could only happen this successfully in a Dickens novel. Grewgious has asked Bazzard to fetch supper from a nearby hotel.

Bazzard duly returns, accompanied "by two waiters—an immoveable waiter, and a flying waiter; and the three brought in with them as much fog as gave a new roar to the fire." It is a paragraph of comic relief that bears many of the hallmarks of Dickens's style: it is funny, vivid, and very visual—the sort of thing that we might expect from the man who wrote *The Pickwick Papers* and who knew the pleasure of running about on stage, in a farce, wearing a comical wig. Again one thinks of Preston Sturges, or the Brothers Marx, as one also appreciates the subtle commentary on work and relationships of power:

The flying waiter, who had brought everything on his shoulders, laid the cloth with amazing rapidity and dexterity; while the immoveable waiter, who had brought nothing, found fault with him. The flying waiter then highly polished all the glasses he had brought, and the immoveable waiter looked through them. The flying waiter then flew across Holborn for the soup, and flew back again, and then took another flight for the made-dish, and flew back again, and then took another flight for the joint and poultry, and flew back again, and between whiles took supplementary flights for a great variety of articles, as it was discovered from time to time that the immoveable waiter had forgotten them all. But let the flying waiter cleave the air as he might, he was always reproached on his return by the immoveable waiter for bringing fog with him, and for being out of breath. At the conclusion of the repast, by which time the flying waiter was severely blown, the immoveable waiter gathered up the tablecloth under his arm with a grand air, and having sternly (not to say with indignation) looked on at the flying waiter while he set clean glasses round, directed a valedictory glance towards Mr. Grewgious, conveying: "Let it be clearly understood between us that the reward is mine, and that Nil is the claim of this slave," and pushed the flying waiter before him out of the room.

Constructing a "novel of sensation" enabled Dickens to give some play to his melodramatic impulses: to deal bluntly with villains and heroes, with questions of evil and good. But much of the unique and continuing appeal of *Drood* comes perhaps from the fact that, being both unfinished, and late, its Dickens villains cannot be easily distinguished from its Dickens heroes; that, moreover, a character like Jasper—the choirmaster who takes opium, lusts for Rosa, and very probably killed Drood—becomes particularly intriguing precisely because he is such an effective blend of conflicting drives. Moreover Jasper, Rosa's "music-master," has as Fred Kaplan writes, "a full armament of mesmeric weapons: the power of his music, eyes, hands, touch, voice, presence," all of them at work in a novel full of sexual overtones. Jasper, Rosa tells Helena Landless, has

made a slave of me with his looks. He has forced me to understand him, without his saying a word; and he has forced me to keep silence, without his uttering a threat. When I play, he never moves his eyes from my hands. When I sing, he never moves his eyes from my lips. When he corrects me, and strikes a note, or a chord, or plays a passage, he himself is in the sounds, whispering that he pursues me as a lover, and commanding me to keep his secret. I avoid his eyes, but he forces me to see them without looking at them. Even when a glaze comes over them (which is sometimes the case), and he seems to wander away into a frightful sort of dream in which he threatens most, he obliges me to know it, and to know that he is sitting close at my side, more terrible to me than ever.

In chapter 19, Drood is presumed dead and Jasper declares himself to Rosa; the scene is stagy, as it often is in Dickens when the talk turns to love. But it's effective too. Jasper, so cool, cracks:

"Reckon up nothing at this moment, angel, but the sacrifices that I lay at those dear feet, which I could fall down amongst the vilest ashes and kiss, and put upon my head as a poor savage might. There is my fidelity to my dear boy [Edwin] after death. Tread upon it!"
With an action of his hands, as though he cast down something precious.
"There is the inexpiable offence against my adoration of you. Spurn it!"
With a similar action.
"There are my labors in the cause of a just vengeance for six toiling months. Crush them!"
With another repetition of the action.
"There is my past and my present wasted life. There is the desolation of my heart and my soul. There is my peace; there is my despair. Stamp them into the dust, so that you take me, were it even mortally hating me!"
The frightful vehemence of the man, now reaching its full height, so additionally terrifies her as to break the spell that has held her to the spot. She swiftly moves towards the porch; but in an instant he is at her side, and speaking in her ear.
"Rosa, I am self-repressed again. I am walking calmly beside you to the house. I shall wait for some encouragement and hope. I shall not strike too soon. Give me a sign that you attend to me."
She slightly and constrainedly moves her hand.
"Not a word of this to any one, or it will bring down the blow, as certainly as night follows day. Another sign that you attend to me."

She moves her hand once more.

"I love you, love you, love you. If you were to cast me off now—but you will not—you would never be rid of me. No one should come between us. I would pursue you to the death."

So Dickens—who began his novel-writing career with a central figure who is kind and serene, hopeful and wholly content with life's pleasures and possibilities—now ends it by focusing on an obsessed, "self-repressed" man who talks of his "wasted life," of "the desolation of my heart and my soul."

It would hardly be fair to extract from the unfinished *Drood* one passage meant to represent its full vision, or that of its author at the close of his career. But perhaps some readers, remembering Pickwick, have been particularly struck by the paragraph at the start of chapter 11 where Dickens returns to Holborn—very close to where Oliver Twist walked and Mrs. Gamp lived. Here, he points to

a little nook composed of two irregular quadrangles, called Staple Inn. It is one of those nooks, the turning into which out of the clashing street, imparts to the relieved pedestrian the sensation of having put cotton in his ears, and velvet soles on his boots. It is one of those nooks where a few smoky sparrows twitter in smoky trees, as though they called to one another, "Let us play at country," and where a few feet of garden mould and a few yards of gravel enable them to do that refreshing violence to their tiny understandings.

Dickens himself was inordinately complex; in *Drood*, he is very probably admitting to these often conflicting desires and drives by focusing in large part on a tormented man with a double life. *Edwin Drood*, like the life of Charles Dickens, must remain something of a mystery.

But Dickens's novels are not particularly hard to understand. They deal with themes and situations fundamental to great literary works—and to great myths—that cross cultures and centuries. He writes about parenthood and passion. He writes about loss, regret, and redemption; about choice; about the miraculous persistence of goodness and the bitter reality of evil. His central characters are questers; they pursue their identities; they face tribulation; they look for home.

At times Dickens seems dated. He knew precisely what words and images and plots would move and amuse the people of his time who bought or borrowed or listened to his books, and of course all of those people are, in the literal sense, gone. Today, few perhaps think of sinking down for the night with *Dombey and Son* or *Barnaby Rudge*. But the fact that there remains a considerable audience for Dickens's major works is proof not only of his inimitable inventiveness, but of the universality of his themes. Dickens still speaks to our imaginations, to our unconscious longings and fears, and to our collective conscience. "What was Dickens all about?" writes Alan S. Watts. "What did he spend his life doing? What is the thread which runs through all his work?" "The Victorians, of course" Watts observes, "had no doubt about it." Dickens, he concludes:

was striking mighty blows for the poor. He was preaching the love of humanity. He was asking people to be kind and thoughtful towards one another. . . . With all his faults . . . these are the things that Dickens was trying to do and which in great measure he succeeded in doing. This was his achievement, and we, in our cynical age, should not overlook it.

Select Bibliography

Novels

There are many editions of Dickens's novels. The volumes in the Clarendon series are designed for scholarly readers and thus offer the most authoritative texts. The Norton Critical Editions, geared for classroom use, are more widely available, and are also generally recommended by Dickens scholars—as are the titles currently in the World's Classics series of Dickens's novels published by the Oxford University Press. At this time, the Penguin series of Dickens's works is more complete, and will also more than meet the needs of most readers.

The Pickwick Papers (1837)
Oliver Twist (1838)
Nicholas Nickleby (1839)
The Old Curiosity Shop (1841)
Barnaby Rudge (1841)
Martin Chuzzlewit (1844)
Dombey and Son (1848)
David Copperfield (1850)
Bleak House (1853)
Hard Times (1854)
Little Dorrit (1857)
A Tale of Two Cities (1859)
Our Mutual Friend (1865)
The Mystery of Edwin Drood (unfinished, *1870*)

Secondary Sources

Ackroyd, Peter. *Dickens.* New York: Harper Perennial, 1990.
_____. *Introduction to Dickens.* London: Sinclair-Stevenson, 1991.
Allen, Michael. *Charles Dickens's Childhood.* New York: St. Martin's Press, 1988.
Altick, Richard D. *The Presence of the Present: Topics of the Day in the Victorian Novel,* Columbus: Ohio State University Press, 1991.
Bentley, Eric. *A Century of Hero-Worship.* Boston: Beacon Press, 1957.
Bottum, Joseph. "The Gentlemen's True Name: *David Copperfield* and the Philosophy of Naming," in *Nineteenth Century Literature,* Spring 1995.
Brown, James M. *Dickens: Novelist in the Market-Place.* Totowa, NJ: Barnes & Noble, 1982.
Butt, John, and Kathleen Tillotson. *Dickens at Work.* New York: Oxford University Press, 1957.
Calder, Jenni. *Women and Marriage in Victorian Fiction.* New York: Oxford University Press, 1976.
Carlyle, Thomas. *The Works of Thomas Carlyle,* (13 vols). New York: Collier, 1897.
Carey, John. *The Violent Effigy: A Study of Dickens' Imagination.* London: Faber and Faber, 1973; second ed. 1991.
Chesterton, Gilbert Keith. *Appreciations and Criticisms of the Works of Charles Dickens.* New York: Dutton, 1911.
Cockshut, A. O. J. *The Imagination of Charles Dickens.* New York: New York University Press. 1962.
Collins, Philip. *Dickens and Crime.* New York: St. Martin, 1962.
_____. *Dickens and Education.* New York: St. Martin, 1963.

_____, ed. *Dickens: The Critical Heritage*. New York: Barnes and Noble, 1971.

Coolidge, Archibald C. *Charles Dickens as Serial Novelist*. Ames: Iowa State University Press, 1967.

Davies, Robertson. "The Devil's Burning Throne" and "Phantasmagoria and Dream Grotto," in *One Half of Robertson Davies*. New York: Viking, 1977.

Flint, Kate. *Dickens*. Brighton, Sussex: Harvester, 1986.

Ford, George. *Dickens and His Readers*. Princeton: Princeton University Press, 1955.

Forster, John. *The Life of Charles Dickens*. 3 vols. London: Chapman and Hall, 1872-74.

Garis, Robert. *The Dickens Theatre: A Reassessment of the Novels*. London: Oxford University Press, 1965.

Gissing, George. *Charles Dickens: A Critical Study*. New York: Dodd, Mead, 1898.

Glancy, Ruth. *A Tale of Two Cities: Dickens's Revolutionary Novel*. Boston: Twayne, 1991.

Goldberg, Michael. *Dickens and Carlyle*. Athens: University of Georgia Press, 1972.

Grant, Allan. *A Preface to Dickens*. London: Longman, 1984.

Gross, John, and Gabriel Pearson, eds. *Dickens and the Twentieth Century*. Toronto: University of Toronto Press, 1962.

Hardy, Barbara. *The Moral Art of Dickens*. New York: Oxford University Press, 1970.

_____. *Dickens: The Later Novels*. London: Longmans, Green & Co., 1968.

Harvey, W. J. "Chance and Design in *Bleak House*," in *Dickens and the Twentieth Century*.

Hibbert, Christopher. *The Making of Charles Dickens*. New York: Harper and Row, 1967.

House, Humphry. *The Dickens World*. London: Oxford University Press, 1941.

House, Madeleine, and others, eds. *The Letters of Charles Dickens*. Pilgrim Edition. New York: Oxford University Press, 1965-1994. (7 volumes published to date.)

Ingham, Patricia. *Dickens, Women, and Language*. New York & London: Harvester, 1992.

Irving, John. "The King of the Novel: An Introduction to *Great Expectations*," in *Great Expectations*. New York: Bantam Books, 1986.

Jackson, T. A. *Charles Dickens: The Progress of a Radical.* New York: International Publishers, 1938.

Johnson, Edgar. *Charles Dickens: His Tragedy and Triumph.* 2 vols. New York: Simon and Schuster, 1952.

Kaplan, Fred. *Dickens: A Biography.* New York: Morrow, 1988.

_____. *Dickens and Mesmerism: The Hidden Springs of Fiction.* Princeton: Princeton University Press, 1975.

_____. *Sacred Tears: Sentimentality in Victorian Literature.* Princeton: Princeton University Press, 1987.

Kaufman, Gerald. "The Many Faces of Shylock Exposed," *Financial Times* (London) Weekend. 2 April, 1994.

Kettle, Arnold. "Dickens and the Popular Tradition," in *Marxists on Literature*, David Craig, ed. Harmondsworth, Middlesex: Penguin, 1975.

_____. "Our Mutual Friend," in *Dickens and the Twentieth Century.*

Leavis, F. R. and Q. D. Leavis. *Dickens the Novelist.* London: Chatto and Windus, 1970.

Le Quesne, A. L. *Carlyle.* Oxford: Oxford University Press, 1982.

Lettis, Richard. *Dickens on Literature: A Continuing Study of His Aesthetic.* New York: AMS Press, 1990.

Lucas, John. *The Melancholy Man: A Study of Dickens's Novels.* London: Methuen, 1970.

Mackenzie, Norman, and Jeanne Mackenzie. *Dickens: A Life.* New York: Oxford University Press, 1979.

Magnet, Myron. *Dickens and the Social Order.* Philadelphia: University of Pennsylvania Press, 1985.

Marcus, Steven. *Dickens: From Pickwick to Dombey.* New York Basic Books, 1965.

Maurois, André. *Dickens.* New York: Frederick Ungar, 1967.

Miller, J. Hillis. *Charles Dickens: The World of His Novels.* Cambridge: Harvard University Press, 1958.

Monod, Sylvère. *Dickens the Novelist.* Norman: University of Oklahoma Press, 1968.

Moss, Sidney P. *Charles Dickens's Quarrel with America.* Troy, N.Y.: Whitson, 1984.

Nabokov, Vladimir. *Lectures on Literature.* New York: Harcourt Brace Jovanovich, 1980.

Nelson, Harland. *Charles Dickens.* Boston: Twayne, 1981.

Newman, S. J. "Decline and Fall Off? Towards an Appreciation of *Our Mutual Friend*," *The Dickensian* 85 (Summer 1989), 99-103.

Ober, William B. "Of Dickens and Diagnoses," *MD*, April 1992.

Orwell, George. *A Collection of Essays*. New York: Harcourt Brace Jovanovich, 1946.

Page, Norman. *A Dickens Companion*. New York: Schocken, 1984.

Paroissien, David, ed. *Selected Letters of Charles Dickens*. Boston: Twayne, 1985.

Philpotts, Trey. "The Real Marshalsea," *The Dickensian* 87 (Fall, 1991), 133-46.

Priestley, J. B. *Victoria's Heydey*. New York: Harper & Row, 1972.

Pritchett, V.S. *George Meredith and English Comedy*. New York: Random House, 1969.

Ruskin, John. *The Works of John Ruskin*, (39 vols, Cook and Wedderburn, eds.). London: George Allen, 1903-12.

Russell, Norman. *The Novelist and Mammon*. Oxford: Clarendon Press, 1986.

Sinyard, Neil. "Dickensian Visions in Modern British Film," *The Dickensian* 85 (Summer 1989), 99-103.

Slater, Michael. *Dickens and Women*. Stanford: University of Stanford Press, 1983.

Symons, Julian. *Charles Dickens*. London: Arthur Barker, 1951.

Tomalin, Claire. *The Invisible Woman: The Story of Nelly Ternan and Charles Dickens*. New York: Knopf, 1991.

Wagenknecht, Edward. *Dickens and the Scandalmongers*. Norman: University of Oklahoma Press, 1965.

Wain, John. "Little Dorrit," in *Dickens and the Twentieth Century*.

Walder, Dennis. *Dickens and Religion*. Boston: Allen & Unwin, 1981.

Watts, Alan S. *The Life and Times of Charles Dickens*. New York: Crescent Books, 1991.

Welsh, Alexander. *From Copyright to Copperfield: The Identity of Dickens*. Cambridge: Harvard University Press, 1987.

Wilson, Angus. *The World of Charles Dickens*. New York: Viking, 1970.

Wison, A. N. *Tolstoy*. New York: W. W. Norton & Company, 1988.

Wilson, Edmund. *The Wound and the Bow: Seven Studies in Literature*. Boston: Houghton Mifflin, 1941.

Index